Liberal Concierge
→ D'accord

SCHOOL OF ORIENTAL
University of London

Please return this book on or before the last date shown

Long loans and One Week loans may be renewed up to 10 times
Short loans & CDs cannot be renewed
Fines are charged on all overdue items

Online: http://lib.soas.ac.uk/patroninfo
Phone: 020-7898 4197 (answerphone)

2 1 FEB 2007

The Democracy Makers

The Democracy Makers

Human Rights and International Order

Nicolas Guilhot

COLUMBIA UNIVERSITY PRESS   NEW YORK

Columbia University Press
Publishers Since 1893
New York   Chichester, West Sussex
Copyright © 2005 Columbia University Press
All rights Reserved

Library of Congress Cataloging-in-Publication Data

Guilhot, Nicolas, 1970–
    The democracy makers : human rights and
international order / Nicolas Guilhot.
        p. cm.
    Includes bibliographical references and index.
    ISBN 0–231–13124–0 (cloth) —
    ISBN 0–231–50419–5 (electronic)
    1. Human rights. 2. Democracy. 3. Globalization.
4. Anti-globalization movement. I. Title.

JC571.G7855 2005
323 — dc22   2004061103

Columbia University Press books are printed on
permanent and durable acid-free paper
Printed in the United States of America

c   10   9   8   7   6   5   4   3   2   1

References to Internet Web Sites (URLs) were accurate
at the time of writing. Neither the author nor
Columbia University Press is responsible for Web sites
that may have expired or changed since the book was
prepared.

To Margot

Contents

Acknowledgments ix

Introduction: The Cosmopolitics of Democratization   1

1. From Cold Warriors to Human Rights Activists   29

2. The Field Of Democracy and Human Rights: Shaping a Professional Arena Around a New Liberal Consensus   69

3. From the Development Engineers to the Democracy Doctors: The Rise And Fall of Modernization Theory   101

4. Democratization Studies and the Construction of a New Orthodoxy   134

5. International Relations Theory and the Emancipatory Narrative of Human Rights Networks   166

6. Financing the Construction of "Market Democracies": The World Bank and the Global Supervision of "Good Governance"   188

Conclusion   222

Appendix   225
Notes   227
Bibliography   245
Index of Names   267
Index of Subjects   271

Acknowledgments

This book evolves out of a Ph.D. dissertation written at the European University Institute in Florence. I first wish to express my gratefulness to my supervisor, Philippe Schmitter, who gave me the invaluable freedom to develop my own approach to a field he knows better than anybody else, and without whose support this research would have been impossible. A number of persons have read and commented parts of my work. I would like to thank in particular Peter Wagner, Gianfranco Poggi and Claus Offe, who took time to discuss it with me. I am also indebted to Yves Dezalay, whose work has been a source of inspiration, and who provided many useful and critical comments at various stages. During my stay at the London School of Economics, I benefited from the challenging and insightful comments of Leslie Sklair. Many people have been very helpful in directing me toward the relevant interlocutors or the right material: I wish to thank the librarians of the National Endowment for Democracy, the World Bank archives, the Hoover Institution, the European University Institute and the London School of Economics for their assistance. At USAID, NED, various universities and foundations, several of the actors mentioned in this book have taken time to talk with me and answer my questions. Their input has been crucial. I am extremely grateful to Peter Dimock and Anne Routon at Columbia University Press for their trust and support. Leslie Bialler did a great job copyediting the book. Two anonymous reviewers made very useful comments on an earlier draft of this book.

I am also indebted to many friends and colleagues who made this work enjoyable throughout its various stages: Valérie Amiraux, Fredrik Bergström, Imco Brouwer, Geoff Cox, Bernard Gbikpi, Jürgen Grote, Malik Mazbouri, Pandelis Nastos, Sylvain Rivet. Patrizia Nanz and Alana Lentin deserve special thanks for bearing with me while I was in the writing stage of my thesis: although ultimately limited, their patience has been immense.

Finally, I want to express my gratitude to Giorgia and Margot for having delayed the completion of this book.

The Democracy Makers

Introduction

The Cosmopolitics of Democratization

Double agents are chameleons. Good doubles don't *act* their parts, they live them. . . . With doubles you assume a certain wastage of loyalty. The opposition is always more attractive to them than the home side. That's their nature. They're constant rebels.

—John le Carré, *Our Game* (New York: Ballantine Books, 1995), p. 62.

One has heard of double and triple agents who themselves in the end no longer exactly knew for whom they were really working and what they were seeking for themselves in this double and triple role playing. . . . On which side do our loyalties lie? Are we agents of the state and of institutions? Or agents of enlightenment? Or agents of monopoly capital? Or agents of our own vital interests that secretly cooperate in constantly changing double binds with the state, institutions, enlightenment, counterenlightenment, monopoly capital, socialism, etc., and, in so doing, we forget more and more what we our "selves" sought in the whole business?

—Peter Sloterdijk, *Critique of Cynical Reason* (London: Verso, 1988), pp. 113–14

With the end of the cold war, democracy and human rights seem to have become the organizing principles of a new international order, whose protracted birth might not be over yet.[1] It is from these superior principles that, increasingly, national and international jurisdictions are required to derive their legitimacy. Inherited from conflict-ridden centuries of state-building, sovereignty itself is being transformed; it can no longer exist unless erected upon these powerful normative foundations. Democracy and human rights are coming close to being the *Grundnorm* which sustains the very idea of law itself, in a fashion reminiscent of the cosmopolitical order Kelsen envisioned in the first decades of the twentieth century.

Against the notion of state sovereignty, Kelsen had asserted that, from a formal point of view, the concept of juridical equality of states implied that international law was a higher normative order than national laws. This primary juridical order, which bestowed validity upon the secondary orders constituted by national jurisdictions, not only was based upon the ethical idea of normativity but also the integrity of law implied its democratic nature (Kelsen 1960[1928]). The most distinguished jurists today are legitimate heirs to Kelsen and his cosmopolitical vision when they elevate democracy to nothing less than "a *requirement of international law*, applicable to all and implemented through global standards," in other words the only criteria making statehood legitimate (Franck 1992: 47). By becoming the principle expected to validate all forms of governance, it is argued, democracy is on its way to becoming a universal right, "a global entitlement . . . that increasingly will be promoted and protected by collective international processes" (Ibid.: 46). This book is about these "collective international processes" of promotion and protection of democracy. It explores the historical conditions of their institutionalization, the social history of the networks of practitioners and activists on which they have built, as well as the scientific history of the expertise on which they rely.

Such "processes" have become a growth industry extending far beyond the highly dramatic and visible cases of military restoration of the rule of law. Human rights activists, dissidents of all kinds, nongovernmental organizations (NGOs), networks based on political or ideological solidarity, or in some cases even churches have traditionally been channels for democratic reform movements. But a variety of other institutional and individual actors are increasingly investing their resources and their expertise in this expanding field: think tanks, philanthropic foundations, state administrations, international organizations such as the United Nations or the World Bank, private consulting firms, professional associations, activist lawyers and, last but not least, academic scholars. Concerned with the study of "transitions" to democracy these scholars are actively involved in what looks like the system-maintenance of a potentially global democratic polity. Their contributions range from exporting constitutional models, drafting legislation or building parliamentarian libraries to training pollsters, observing elections, promoting independent news reporting, teaching campaign management to political party officials, or enhancing the professionalism of nongovernmental activists.

The United States is the principal purveyor of such expertise. According to some estimates, $700 million are invested every year in this field

(Carothers 2000). The United States Agency for International Development (USAID), the branch of the State Department in charge of extending and managing foreign aid, provides most of these funds, notably through the Center for Democracy and Governance established in 1994. A real market, all the more competitive since it actually represents a tight and specialized niche, has developed around the profitable business of exporting democracy and the rule of law. In Washington, private consulting firms previously working in the area of development aid (Chemonics, Associates in Rural Development, or Management Systems International, to name but a few) are now successfully expanding into the areas of democracy, human rights, and good governance, as many fields in which they can hope to bid in major tenders organized by aid agencies or the World Bank and receive funds for managing specific projects. Independently, some organizations with a traditional interest in international affairs, or professional associations that could rely on strong international networks, have also contributed their expertise or their social clout to this new field. Other institutions have been created specifically in order to deal with technologies of democratization, such as the National Endowment for Democracy or the International Foundation for Electoral Systems. Over time, other countries have sought to create similar institutions and have thus contributed to consolidating this new field of international practices.

By investing their resources and their knowledge in international practices, these institutions and their agents have made a major contribution to the transformation of the nature, the form and the function of emancipatory activism. While still based upon ideals of individual and collective emancipation, struggles for rights, and social progress, this activism is nonetheless remote from the traditional forms and repertoires characteristic of democratic movements or grass-roots politics. Its practitioners are, increasingly, professionals. They act on the basis of technical specialization, not civic commitment. They fly to faraway places and deliver expertise; they build and cultivate international networks of contacts; they write good-looking annual reports. State institutions, international bureaucracies, and professional networks have colonized the turf of social movements. And as in any process of colonization, they have appropriated the local resources for themselves: the languages, the concepts, the strategies, the outlooks.

They are now speaking a language that, once upon a time, belonged exclusively to protesters, campaigners, dissenters, or committed citizens. And so, this professionalization of activism also corresponds to the *migration of socially progressive repertoires of collective action*, inherited form anti-imperialist campaigns, struggles for rights, emancipatory causes, *from social movements often opposing state institutions to the most dominant state institutions themselves.* By the same token, the very same institutions that were associated with the cold war and were then most often attacked in the name of human rights or democracy are today at the cutting edge of a new global democratic activism. The U.S. State Department, once the foe of the human rights movement, claims now to be supporting transnational issue networks in the field of human rights; the World Bank, attacked in the past for indirectly supporting authoritarian forms of modernization in developing countries, now purports to follow exclusively "bottom-up" methodologies and "grass-roots" approaches, and promotes political participation, the rule of law and "good governance." Market forces have not been lagging behind: faced with growing criticism, multinational corporations have developed ethical strategies meant to respond to this challenge. They sell not only commodities but also, increasingly, values, commitment, environmental awareness, or social responsibility. Here again, somewhat paradoxically, it is often the most challenged who invest the most in the new ethical trend: the World Business Council for Sustainable Development, for instance, comprises 150 multinational corporations ranging from Procter & Gamble to Gazprom, many of them companies known for their poor social or ecological record.

Conversely, NGOs have become crucial actors of globalization. They have moved from subordinate and antagonistic positions to dominant positions in the global networks of power. With a seat at every official policy table, virtually present in every corner of the globe, delivering expertise on a wide range of issues, NGOs are now run like multinational firms, by professionals whose career trajectories perfectly illustrate the new complementarity between NGOs and international organizations. Previously remote from each other, these institutional worlds are now getting closer as their boundaries are blurred and as a same personnel circulates between them or simultaneously occupies positions in both fields. By denouncing corruption practices, human rights abuses, electoral fraud, environmental depredation, or restrictions of individual freedom, NGOs contribute to the establishment and the enforcement of global standards. In the field of political and civil liberties or economic corruption, such standards already exist and are in part policed through the "rating" practices of Freedom House or Transparency International, two NGOs which rank countries according to their record in these fields and which have managed to achieve international credibility. Every year, the publication of their rankings makes it to the headlines of the most important newspapers.[2]

Civic Virtue and the Aristocratic Project of a "Global Civil Society"

All these new forms of international activism and moral entrepreneurship are firmly located within the global networks of power. Far from fulfilling some counter-hegemonic role, as it is often argued or wishfully thought, they actually represent a specific mode of exercising global power. The project of a "global civil society" which is at the center of most initiatives aiming at a cosmopolitan democracy (e.g. Held and Archibugi 1995; Kaldor 2003; Keane 2003) is also far from embodying the all-inclusive participatory forum hoped for by its proponents. The main reason is that creating and managing an NGO often requires the mobilization of material resources, social capital, linguistic and other international skills that are far from being evenly distributed across society and tend to be concentrated in its upper tiers.[3] In fact, the increased inclusion of NGOs in international forums or organizations and the resulting professionalization of their staffs only increases this tendency.

But there is also another reason for which this project plays a necessarily ambivalent role in the articulation of a system of "global governance." It has to do with the nature of their claims and, more generally, with the conceptual language in which they cast their action. Advocacy groups, NGOs, issue networks and the like operate within the repertoire of civic *virtue*, in the strictest sense of the word. In the classical political tradition, the republican language of virtue is opposed to the liberal and imperial language of rights (Pocock 1985). While the latter conceives of liberty as freedom from coercion (*libertas* as opposed to *imperium*), the former makes participation to power a condition for the exercise of liberty (*libertas* as participation in *imperium*). Civic virtue is precisely the active participation in the production of the common good. This form of dedicated citizenship is today enacted by NGOs on the global scene, in particular through their reliance on "participation" as a method for solving some of the world's most pressing problems such as hunger, indigenous rights, human rights abuses, the oppression of women, child labor, or other causes. The idea of global "forums," defined as institutionalized sites of participation, is also associated with this tradition. To the extent that it is not fixed *de jure* by some legal entitlement, such participation — which can take the concrete forms of lobbying, information campaigns, involvement in the policymaking process and other forms of action — becomes legitimate because of its *moral* nature: it takes place in the name of and for the sake of universal values or common goods. This form of political virtue is exactly the opposite of the pursuit of private interests through politics — which the classical political tradition equated with corruption. Indeed, as we shall see, most of the academic literature on NGOs stresses this moral dimension and ultimately posits their disinterestedness, as collective actors motivated by values and not by material interests.

Yet, this conception of civic virtue has always been the ideology of an aristocratic form of politics. For it is those who have raised themselves above material contingencies who can be trusted not to put their own interest before the common good and who represent the best guarantee against corruption. Civic virtue is best served by those whose already dominant social status is a guarantee that their motives are pure and disinterested. Virtuous government is the rule of the *honoratiores*, as Max Weber has taught us: it is those whose status and standing guarantees that they "live *for* politics, without living *from* politics" who emerge as the best defenders of political virtue (Weber 1978: 290).[4] For the same reason, republican thought in the eighteenth century considered property as the material guarantee of civic virtue. The language of virtue, as historian Pocock reminds us, is also the language of aristocratic rule.

This digression into conceptual history therefore provides useful indications for empirical analysis. It speaks for paying more attention to the sociological reality of NGOs and other moral actors, and to the function and the legitimating effects of the ideology of global citizenship and civic virtue which is associated with them. Virtue is guaranteed by status, wealth, and recognition. Virtue, in other words, presupposes economic and social capital. NGOs are the *honoratiores*, the *optimati*, that is, the aristocratic class of the present times. In the same fashion, the Neiers (Human Rights Watch), the Soroses (Open Society Network), the Eigens (Transparency International) are leading members of the republican aristocracy within the Empire.

Transparency International best exemplifies this ambivalent relation between NGOs and the concept of civic virtue. This organization has indeed established its reputation on the fight against corruption. It publishes every year a comprehensive list of countries ranked according to the levels of corruption found in public markets, state administrations, and the main sectors of international trade.[5] The story of Transparency International shows that the exposure and the denunciation of corruption needed to find an NGO channel in order to achieve credibility. The idea initially came from officials working in the African Bureau of the World Bank who realized that the issue of corruption could not be handled directly by the Bank

(Coeurdray 2003). As a result, some of them left the bank and created Transparency in 1989 as an instrument that could perform this task. At the same time, although it was formally an NGO, TI placed the fight against economic corruption within the orbit of international financial institutions. Its success rested on the capacity of its founders to mobilize powerful networks close to the World Bank itself, multinational consulting firms or business circles. TI also contributed to establish the legitimacy of these circles as moral entrepreneurs and to demonstrate their civic virtue. This closeness between these social strata, the elite of the financial professions, and the issue-area of corruption appears very clearly in TI's strategies. In its crusade against economic and political corruption, it therefore mobilized the instruments that were most familiar to its constituency and its founders: those of global financial regulation. For putting pressure upon individual countries, TI adopted the principle of evaluating and ranking countries, thus replicating in the field of civic virtue the instruments used by rating agencies such as Moody's or Standard & Poor's in the assessment of the financial standing of stocks or bonds.

This is not to say that NGOs are subservient to the needs or the interests of developed countries, that they are the Trojan horses of neoliberal globalization, or that they have been simply co-opted — although such strategies are sometimes deliberately pursued by foundations (Roelofs 2003). Many of them obviously engage critically with problematic aspects of globalization and sometimes successfully confront powerful organized interests. But, overall, NGOs as such have become key regulatory actors of globalization, on equal footing with financial institution or international organization. As a result of this success, their identity has been dissolved in a seamless web of "global governance" where they interact and sometimes overlap with government agencies, international organizations, and corporations. The NGO "format" has become a specific modality of the exercise of power. The very label "NGO" has become meaningless and political scientists are at pain attempting to classify the plethora of institutional forms cohabiting under this label, ranging from state-sponsored organizations and international networks of professionals to neighborhood associations.

Idealism and Professionalism

All these difficulties stem from the fact that while we acknowledge the deep transformation of the international scene and the constant shifting or disappearance of the symbolic boundaries that modernity has produced (morality / politics, national / international actors, etc.), we still analyze this novel reality with the categories of the old world order of nation-states and of its "science" of politics. In the era of Realpolitik, during the cold war, things were plain and straightforward: ethical principles such as human rights, humanitarian pledges, or claims to political accountability were typically used by individuals against the coercive power of states, while international politics was seen and theorized as a field of purely instrumental and strategic calculations by states, separate from any reference to moral or ethical values. By codifying such practices as "realism," international relations theorists conveniently turned the cynicism of Western and Eastern rulers into a science. But with idealism replacing realism as the main ideological cast of international affairs in the jubilatory atmosphere of the 1990s, things became more muddled and less clear-cut. Democracy and human rights, once weapons for the critique of power, have now become part of the arsenal of power itself. Historically developed as an absolute limit of politics, the doctrine of human rights has given birth to a politics of human rights — a notion that while familiar to us is paradoxical if not self-contradictory.[6] From an ongoing increase of autonomy and participation, democracy has become a commodity that can be exported. Promoting democratization or defending human rights are privileged channels for the exportation of political technologies, economic recipes, or juridical models. No longer providing the basis for the critique of power, they have become the main language of global power — a transformation that has gone unnoticed in the enthusiastic atmosphere of the last fin-de-siècle. Democracy and human rights have come to represent a new form of what sixteenth-century political theorist Giovanni Botero called the "Reason of State," that is, an instrumental rationality geared toward the consolidation of power. Or, to put it in the words of two proponents of a new way of looking at and practicing globalization, there is no longer an "outside" to the constitution of Empire (Hardt and Negri 2000).

I will highlight some social and historical aspects of this paradoxical transformation in this book. One way to look at this structural displacement of moral resources and activism is to focus on the history and the sociology of activist movements themselves. In part, this transformation matches a process of professionalization of activist movements. As Howard Becker noted in his classical study of deviance à propos moral entrepreneurs, the moral crusader needs at some point in his career the services of a professional (Becker 1963: 152). The need to build up expertise, to deal with complex scientific or legal arguments, to do public relations or have a media strategy, are indeed powerful factors of change for activist organizations: they pursue their goals more efficiently, of course, but such changes also affect their recruitment patterns, their outlook, and their relations with other institutions.

Because it increases specialization and focuses on one set of issues, professionalism tends to dissociate activism from broader, more encompassing projects of social transformation. Often, this trend toward greater professionalism also serves wider strategies and overlaps with a tendency to adopt positions more compatible with those of other professionals — lawyers, managers, officials, economists, etc. In other words, it usually overlaps with mainstreaming, or even with the construction of an orthodoxy. In the case of the environmental movement in the United States, for instance, it has been shown that its professionalization under the aegis of the "Gurus" of the Ford foundation (a committee of lawyers from the American Bar) was the prelude to its rapprochement with business and industry circles (Gottlieb 1993: 139). In the same way, the professionalization of the human rights movement has helped make it appealing to the legal elite and to move it closer to the very state institutions against which it was initially built (Dezalay and Garth 2002: 164).

The trend toward professionalization has most definitely transformed democracy and human rights organizations. This, however, should not conceal the ideological origins of the democratization industry. While the idealism of these initiatives seems very remote from the realism of power politics, they are still a product of the cold war, not its antithesis. From the outset, democratization programs were highly ambivalent. The fight for human rights after World War II was also to a large extent a fight against Communism. Likewise, the struggle for democracy was a weapon used selectively during the era of bipolar confrontation. Once again, it should be emphasized that this record does not necessarily qualify democracy promotion as a conspiratorial activity. Rather, it means that this field of international policies has developed as a bridge or as a common ground between progressive, internationalist areas of American politics on the one hand, and a cadre of cold war strategists on the other hand. The success of this agenda lies precisely in its ambivalence, that is, in its capacity to lend itself to different interpretations and to accommodate different strategies, whether those of genuinely concerned activists and dissidents, or those of State Department planners.

The Congress for Cultural Freedom, created in 1950 under the aegis of the CIA and consisting mostly of left-wing intellectuals, was an early example of these ambiguous democratic crusades. In her recent study of this organization, Frances Stonor Saunders observes that the political entrepreneurs behind this democratic crusade were "an assorted group of former radicals and leftist intellectuals" but that the "tradition of radical dissenter" they represented was "suspended in favor of supporting 'the American proposition'" (Stonor Saunders 1999: 2). The same phenomenon can be observed in the case of the National Endowment for Democracy, a more recent creation which I study at greater length in this book. Established in 1983 by a cadre of neoconservatives close to the Reagan administration, the NED drew its legitimacy from the enrollment both of academic factions of the human rights movement and of the social democratic left in its cold war project.

This particular position at the confluence of different political traditions allowed the organizations involved in the promotion of democracy to generate wide alliances and, therefore, to build hegemonic agendas. But rather than a mere "suspension" of former beliefs, as Saunders suggests, I instead argue that the individuals involved in these initiatives not only had the impression they were remaining somehow loyal to their principles but also managed to read progressive purposes into these hegemonic projects. Although in a confused and mystified way, the international promotion of democracy appeared to some as an acceptable continuation of revolutionary internationalism, to others, it was the natural outcome of their previous engagement in civil rights struggles or against imperialism. To others yet, it was a good and pragmatic strategy for exercising influence abroad. The strength of these organizations, therefore, while lying primarily in their capacity to capture and recycle this symbolic and political legacy, also lay in the organizational schemes and the working methods of various progressive and internationalist traditions, while putting them at the service of what Saunders called "the American proposition." For these reasons, it would be simplistic to speak of mere co-optation or to explain away the trajectory of these agents as a process of defection or conversion. Other models are required indeed.

Double Agents

In order to trace this transformation from realist power politics into idealist internationalism, I adopt a perspective centered on the individual actors. Indeed, when considering the new repertoires of international politics (activism as opposed to technocracy, critique of the state, centrality of "civil society," etc.) and their transformation from providing the language of op-position and dissent to being the language of hegemony, it is useful to under-stand these repertoires of action as skills or dispositions borne by individ-uals. Just as specific varieties of plants are diffused to remote areas by pollination, repertoires migrate to different institutional contexts along with the individuals who mobilize them in their professional practice. From this perspective, understanding why the World Bank today is promoting "good governance" or how a Reagan-era foundation is concerned with human rights is also about identifying the agents who have brought such concerns in these institutions and retracing their trajectories.

The history of promotion of democracy is in the first place the history of "democracy makers" who have managed to institutionalize their interna-tional skills or to sell their expertise successfully. In doing so, they have brought to major state agencies or international institutions a know-how originally acquired elsewhere, usually in socially progressive or reformist politics. They converted this critical knowledge into a dominant interna-tional expertise. In other words, today's exponents of new international or-thodoxies are often former heretics. The processes, and paradoxes, of their conversion are central to this book. I will examine the case of former Trots-kyists who joined the Reagan administration and pioneered the first inter-national democratization programs; critical academics trained in Latin American studies and strongly opposed to Jeane Kirkpatrick who endorsed an organization created by her closest entourage; fellow-travelers of the de-pendency school who ended up as the political economists of the World Bank in the 1990s.

The actors who contributed the most to constructing and expanding the field of promoting democracy are those who were able to play on different levels, to occupy pivotal positions at the junction of academe, national and international institutions, activist movements, and to mobilize the diversified resources of all these fields — knowledge, affiliations, networks, financial re-sources, etc. They were able to appear as both reformist and realist, to ac-commodate different agendas, and therefore to establish strong positions.

In order to characterize these actors, it is useful to think of them in some sense as "double agents." While more is involved, to make this somewhat ironic reference to characters in spy novels captures well the intrinsic am-bivalence involved. Yet, my intent is less to be provocative than to provoke thought. To speak of "double agents" is a way to take into account the mul-tiple affiliations of social actors, rather than to ascribe to them a unilateral role and to confine them within a limited area of social relations or a single institutional context. Indeed, most actors, and the more dominant ones in particular, occupy multiple positions in different areas of society (Boltanski 1973). In that sense, it is highly reductive — actually, it is epistemologically wrong — to assign them a unique property or a set of necessarily congruent characteristics. For instance, one can be at the same time a political science professor, an occasional consultant for the National Security Council, and the board member of an important international human rights NGO. Should we speak of a "state actor" or of a "non-state actor," to use two fashionable labels having currency in the academic literature on international relations and transnational networks? In 1988, the World Bank hired James Clark, former head of Oxfam's policy unit, in order to improve its relations with NGOs: is he a representative of the interests of international financial institutions, or of the NGO sector? Really, such clear-cut concepts are no longer operational (if they ever were) when it comes to providing a reliable sociological analysis of international processes. The same thing can be said about other related notions, such as "civil society actors" or "human rights activists": such notions cannot be taken as appropriate descriptions of social actors for they capture only specific *roles* negotiated in specific *contexts*. Therefore, using the notion of "double agents" (or multiplying the affiliations and speaking of "triple agents" or even multiple agents, as suggested ironically by Peter Sloterdijk in the epigraph of this introduction) is also intended as a reminder of the fact that social actors can act in different capacities according to the arenas in which they engage. This capacity to multiply affiliations and positions is indeed the very stuff of which networks are made. By the same token, this notion has also a critical intent: it shows that the symbolic boundaries between the national and the international, between the governmental and the nongovernmental, between the for-profit and the non-profit, the scientific and the activist, are actually constructs rather than facts, and that these artificial partitions are blurred by the behavior of agents who constantly shift between these "capacities" but have at the same time and for the same reason an interest in the maintenance of such boundaries.

By acting in different guises or capacities, social actors can indeed engage in several arenas and participate in different networks. These divisions and boundaries are maintained by the practitioners themselves but also, as we shall see, by scholars of political science or international relations who constantly produce and reproduce categories such as "non-state actor," "NGO representative," "local group," "grass-roots movement," etc., separating artificially ideal roles that are actually merged within dense social networks.

Notwithstanding the constant work of division and classification that they perform, the twilight world of global governance and market democracies is inhabited only by double agents.

By using this notion, my aim is not to deconstruct the categories of agency or to work toward some kind of post-modern dissolution of social identities. On the contrary, keeping in mind that actors cannot be confined to a single domain of social life is a sound methodological precaution that avoids reductive ascriptions and makes the researcher more receptive to empirical complexity. In particular, it takes some distance with a too superficial "constructivism" that has tended to define these new international actors exclusively in terms of their location within advocacy networks (e.g. Keck & Sikkink 1998) or "epistemic communities" (Haas 1992). It calls for taking into consideration other social properties — professional careers, class, position within professional or institutional hierarchies, resources used (economic, cultural, scientific, etc.) and access to resources — and for resituating the universalistic and moralistic agendas of these agents within well-defined social contexts.

Finally, there can be double agents only where there is conflict and contending agendas. This is crucial dimension to the analyses. The genesis of global prescriptions for democratization or human rights and the production of international norms in a variety of regulatory areas are conflictual processes. Goals, means, strategies, models, interlocutors, experts, grantees are constantly being contested. The meaning of concepts themselves is at stake in these struggles: for instance, the debate about human rights in the 1980s was entirely about deciding whether human rights were a universal norm that could be opposed to any form of government (as liberals would argue), or whether they did not exist outside of national political traditions and legal systems (as neoconservatives would say) — which then meant, in the latter case, that the defense of U.S. interests could not be contrary to human rights, and that exporting and imposing the rule of law and democracy was the only possible human rights policy. The opposition between different political and social agendas is the perfect ground for the emergence of a thick layer of intermediaries, mediators, arbiters, and go-betweens shuttling back and forth between contending groups, between dominant institutions and NGOs, between the national and the international, between the detached position of the academic and the involvement of the practitioner. These double agents tend to occupy the middle ground and to be in the best position to make hegemonic institutions more sensitive to emancipatory claims, while at the same time disciplining or moderating NGOs and activists. By doing so, they seem to further all agendas at once. In the 1980s, for instance, the most successful advocates of democratization programs included committed U.S. and Latin American political scientists who had been promoting both democratization and the limitation of democracy to the political sphere.

All this entails no judgment about the psychological motivations of actors. Talking of double agents does not imply that individuals follow cynical self-serving calculations. Cynicism is a model of individual rationality which is anthropologically dubious and epistemologically untenable. On the contrary, the individuals who appear in this book are often idealists, motivated by a real commitment to the causes they champion. What has changed is the place and the role of this idealism in the global context. What makes them "double" agents is the structural context in which they participate. It is not an issue of character. While the demands for a more ethical foreign policy and other forms of international democratic activism were once clearly critical elements, they have become today the building blocks of new world orders. The construction of "market democracies" across the world has been adopted as a crucial element of the U.S. security doctrine and also an instrument of economic liberalization, while the exportation of democracy has given birth to new forms of political, legal, and scientific imperialism. In this new context, democratic activism has obviously changed its signification, if not its sides.

Paradoxically, it is their very loyalty to democratic internationalism and their unchanged commitment to ideals — quite the reverse of conversion or defection — that turns activists into double agents. To a large extent, the "idealist turn" in international relations and the introduction of morality to the international scene are developments that, to their credit, generations of activists have contributed to bring about. But this change has deprived them of their old critical weapons, leaving them unarmed in front of global institutions that have recast their policies in the language of democratization and vested their hegemony under the cloak of emancipation. For sure, a hegemony built on the notion of democracy and human rights is, at least in my view, highly preferable to a hegemonic system regulated only by national interests and geopolitical calculations. Yet, having acknowledged this, one should also observe that effects of domination, power asymmetries, and coercion have not ceased altogether.

This book does not provide answers to these dilemmas. At most, its only ambition is to highlight them, in the hope that a proper understanding constitutes a first step toward the invention of new courses of action.

Understanding hegemony

I am well aware that this way of proceeding strays away from the kind of structuralism which, most of the time, forms the theoretical background of critical theories of international relations and American foreign policy, whether they are inspired by world-system theories (Wallerstein 1995) or use Gramscian concepts in order to formalize and understand international processes (Cox 1987; Gill 1993). The value of this literature should be acknowledged, for it aptly captures not only the asymmetries of power relations and the unequal distribution of resources, against the liberal-pluralistic representations of international arenas as spaces of bargaining between equals, but also the role of ideology and culture in legitimating and stabilizing these asymmetric relations. This approach has inspired the work of several authors on U.S. policies of "democratization" (in particular Robinson 1996; Gills, Rocamora and Wilson 1993). It was somehow natural that the topic has proven appealing to Gramscian theorists: as I argue in this book, in recent U.S. history, the promotion of democracy abroad has been mostly thought and designed as a *cultural* if not as an *ideological* policy. This cultural dimension is a straightforward invitation to analyze this policy in terms of "hegemony" and to extend some of Gramsci's concepts to the analysis of international relations. For hegemony, as Gramsci uses the term, must be universal in form: it should not appear as the expression of particularistic interests (Gramsci 1991).The moral appeal of democracy and human rights, therefore, makes them perfect instruments for organizing a broad national and international consensus to the policies that are thus pursued and to the existing world order. While they certainly offer valuable insights — I think in particular of the effort made to relate political developments to the transformation of the economy — these works ultimately rest on a conception of hegemony as a process of centrifugal or top-down diffusion of power, permeating civil society, culture, educational institutions and so forth, without ever encountering resistance. They move from the assumption of a seamless project of domination that runs from the highest echelons of the political structure down to its "organic" intellectuals and the public at large — an assumption that does not do justice to the complexity of historical situations nor to the different strategies that are constantly combined and recombined in these projects. In his study of U.S. democratization policy, William Robinson posits for instance "a class-conscious transnational elite based in the core of the world-system" (1996: 33) and organized under the hegemony of its fractions representing financial capital, from which the whole logic of democracy promotion as an instrument of this hegemony seems to flow. Undemocratic regimes tolerated or even supported in the past have become, in the era of globalization, "a fetter to the emergent patterns of international capital accumulation" (Ibid., 37) and are therefore transformed into market democracies by the local allies of this transnational class. "Democratization," in this respect, mechanically unfolds from the nature of the global economy and is a process of adjustment to the new requisites of capital, which requests open societies and states fully integrated in the international system. While there is no doubt, in my mind, that globalized financial capital is reshaping the forms of governance at different levels, from the corporation to the nation-state, there is a very strong functionalist streak in the way the argument is made. Political and social change tends to be reduced to the mechanical unfolding of a plan contained *in ovo* in the contemporary composition of capital and implemented in the most efficient way by the U.S. state apparatus. As a result, a theoretical premium is given to the capacity of the system to reproduce itself and to its overall coherence. The paradox is that these critical theories posit the immutability of precisely what they would like to change.[7] They also tend to ignore the very real conflicts that not only riddle the "hegemony" they describe but actually constantly shape and reconfigure it. While the "promotion of democracy" might well be the object of a new policy consensus, what this new paradigm should include is far from being consensual. It becomes the stake of struggles in which many different actors try to redefine their positions, their role and their importance. The existence of such conflicts must be taken into account in the analysis, for they are themselves a vector of hegemonic processes. As Yves Dezalay and Bryant Garth (2002) argue in their study of legal and economic prescriptions and their international circulation across the Americas, "leading global powers, including the United States, tend to export not just specific approaches or products, but also their internal fights and the strategies used to fight them." So-called "neo-Gramscian" studies of international relations tend to ignore the deep splits that travail even hegemonic "blocs" and constantly refashion their composition. Overstating the coherence and the stability of relations of domination, this approach is unable to account for the numerous reversals, changes, and strategic redeployments that clearly show that the perpetuation of power also entails its transformation and adaptation.

When they turn to the academic discourses about democracy, development or human rights, these works tend to reduce the scientific and cultural spheres to a passive appendix registering the impulses of central power or legitimating its policies: the same functionalism is at work here when these scholars posit "a close 'fit' in the post-World War II period between U.S. foreign policy and the mainstream academic community" (Robinson 1996: 42). While it is obvious that certain academic products (such as modernization theory and, later, democratization theory, both mentioned by Robinson and discussed here in chapters 3 and 4) have been used in order to legitimize certain aspects of foreign policy, the existence of this "fit" is posited as a premise rather than taken as the outcome of a whole process of social construction that has yet to be explained. In short, most of the descriptions of international processes found in these works are often deduced from the very strong theoretical premises characterizing this body of literature rather than the result of empirical work and substantiation. For if the creation of market democracies across the world is only a functional requisite of global capital, then the empirical modalities under which this project is articulated are of little theoretical significance. Indeed, what is lacking here is a more fine-tuned sociological analysis of the making of this new paradigm of international government.

By contrast, I consider that it is fundamental to inquire into the historical and social construction of these new processes of domination by focusing more closely on the actors, their institutional contexts, the social and the scientific resources they mobilize in the different arenas where foreign policy is made. For even as political economists remind us of the relation existing between "democracy promotion" as a new paradigm of world governance and the nature of global capitalism, it is useful to remind ourselves, following Marx, that capital is not some external and mysterious entity blowing in the back of actors, but a *social relation*. The reference to the structural economic context should not prevent us from attempting to write a historical sociology of this new field of international practices. If one of the chapters in this book includes an analysis of recent changes at the World Bank, it is precisely in order to show, in full agreement with the new political economy literature, that democratization is now part of a "policy of capital" but also that the institutionalization of this policy is a complex and conflictual process that cannot be understood without taking into account its multiple dimensions: the transformation of economics as a discipline, the international brokerage of knowledge and expertise, the definition of new development actors such as "civil society organizations," the delegitimation of foreign aid and the promotion of "good governance" and the rule of law, etc. It is also important to keep in mind that this new paradigm was successful because it converged with concomitant developments in other fields, and in particular because it could find elsewhere actors possessing an international know-how inherited from the Cold War and its ideological and cultural struggles, perfectly equipped to wage the new democratic campaigns.

Other works have been going further, towards a sheer denunciation of the moralistic universalism of democracy promotion as a new form of imperialism. Obviously, it is always possible to suggest that "democracy" and "human rights" are nothing else but a sham disguising the use of sheer power and hardly concealing vested interests. This cannot be always ruled out, as the U.S. occupation of Iraq has recently demonstrated. But such an assumption would miss the point, for it leaves out the question of why and how these concepts have become the central paradigm of world government, or at least of international politics. It would also overlook the fact that democratization programs and human rights policies are not simply empty catchwords; they actually have a content. They are usually the vehicles for exporting a variety of political technologies, legal models, normative discourses regarding the economy or the organization of civil society. One of the purposes of this book is to retrace the construction of this new space of politics where knowledge, techniques, networks, ideas, and ideologies are traded and circulated.

If this critical review of the new political economy literature may sound harsh, it is in part because I am driven to distinguish myself more strongly from works which are very close to this one in their general outlook and in their grasp of the topic. Actually, the present book has much more in common with the literature just mentioned than it has with studies of transnational "advocacy-" or "issue networks" which form the bulk of contemporary research on international democratic activism (e.g. Keck and Sikkink 1998). For if these works come closer to an empirical analysis of the production of global rules and norms, in particular because of their focus on norm entrepreneurs and their networks, they however tend to remain entirely captive of the viewpoint of the actors. In this perspective, the progressive adoption of democracy and human rights as principles of foreign policies is the result of successful campaigns waged by committed activists and NGOs against states and international organizations. The turning point is unanimously considered to have taken place in the 1980s, when an initially reluctant Reagan administration was forced, under the pressure of rights campaigners, to adopt human rights as a principle of its foreign policy. Although it is conceded that the use of human rights by the Republican administration was purely instrumental and entirely geared toward defeating the Soviet Union, it became eventually binding as the government had to show some consistency with its self-professed principles and, in particular, put up with the facts established by increasingly professional human rights organizations. As Human Rights Watch founder Aryeh Neier observes, "Reagan was eventually driven by its own rhetoric" (Neier 2003: 188).

As a pioneer and committed participant in these struggles, who personally contributed to build pressure for the adoption of human rights principles in U.S. foreign policy, Neier is legitimately entitled to hold such a view. But this participant's view has been imported within political science without the slightest methodological consideration and transformed into nothing less than a theory of human rights. The capacity of a legal rhetoric to become binding and to drive policies, the constraining "power of human rights," and more generally the "power of ideas," has indeed become the focus of recent works on the legalization and democratization of politics (e.g. Risse, Ropp and Sikkink 1999). Because some kind of causal force is attributed to the very *idea* of human rights promoted by advocacy networks, these analyses are based on epistemological *idealism*. In a quite Hegelian fashion, social actors become the instrument through which the idea of human rights realizes itself in history.

Rather than an empirical analysis of these advocacy networks, describing their dynamics, their resources, their position within the social structure and their own internal hierarchies, these works ultimately view these social realities as the embodiment of values, and reduce the role of social actors to that of giving flesh to an idea. This tendency is reinforced by what can be called the "heroic illusion" which permeates these theories of transnational networks: by reducing democracy or human rights to mere "ideas" that transnational non-state actors have successfully placed on international agendas or forced upon reluctant administrations, they not only reformulate the sophomoric distinction between morals and politics under the guise of a distinction between non-state and state actors, but also fail to see that "human rights" or "democracy" are not *ideas* but *mediums* through which conflicts are fought, *fields* within which different actors struggle to establish and impose their legitimacy and their expertise.

More importantly, one of the stakes of these conflicts is precisely the capacity to impose the relevant definition of "human rights" or "democracy." For defining such concepts is also a way of defining, implicitly but nonetheless effectively, who are the legitimate actors in these fields, who retains the relevant knowledge for furthering such causes, and what counts as an issue. Are human rights, strictly speaking, rights, that is, enforceable legal provisions? Or are they, on the contrary, a "positive international morality" that does not quite reach legal status, as some jurists (in particular Austin or Hart) have argued (Zolo 1995)? Are they limited to political and civil liberties or should they include social and economic rights? Are they above national interests? Is democracy promotion only a matter of promoting free and fair elections? Is a democratic system only a procedure for the peaceful resolution of political conflicts (Przeworski) or does it include some form of active participation of the citizens? These questions are not only academic, for they also determine who the legitimate participants in the "human rights advocacy networks" and the "democracy activists" should be. At the same time, they indicate that human rights and democracy are not straightforward concepts but "contested concepts" to use once more Connolly's ([1974] 1983) over-used expression.

Being contested is both the weakness and the strength of these concepts. It means, on the one hand, that beyond a consensual core of meaning their scope is ill-defined and their boundaries are not clear-cut. It is in these hazy areas that struggles to extend or to limit the rights falling under the "human rights" label take place, or the conflicts around what "democracy promotion" abroad should include. This is what undermines their pretense to universality, namely that their applicability is in part determined by circumstantial, social, or political factors. But on the other hand, it is because these concepts are contested that they can aim to achieve some "pragmatic" universality by becoming a new language of global politics: they are acceptable to most if not all parties; they can be easily adopted because they have a capacity to accommodate different if not diverging interpretations; they can be put to use for different aims. Democracy and human rights, indeed, provide a common idiom for idealists and realists alike, a language that both neoconservatives and liberals can share. They are "hegemonic" concepts in the sense discussed earlier: they have the form of universality but, at the same time, they lend themselves to being instrumentalized by particular interests and national security objectives.

The emergence of a structured field of human rights with its professional standards, its leading organizations, and its learned debates is therefore a more complex phenomenon than suggested by recent academic discussions. It owes as much to liberal activist networks as to their opponents who elaborated contending doctrines of human rights.[8] The fact that some political circles close to the Reaganites considered that the United States needed a democratic ideology just as the Soviet Union had a Communist ideology to export was an important factor in the institutionalization of this field. More or less at the same time, the emergence of a relative consensus on a restrictive definition of human rights as civil and political freedoms excluding social and economic rights also played a role in making this language available to foreign policy planners.

There is some kind of "winner-takes-all" bias, therefore, in explaining the institutionalization of a human rights agenda exclusively by the sole role of brave activists and their liberal networks. This common methodological bias in political science and international relations theory has its own reasons: if academics have identified themselves with practitioners and activists and have been eager to adopt their viewpoint, it is because they are often the same persons, or at least very close to each other as they participate in the same networks. The struggle to impose human rights as a principle of U.S. foreign policy was indeed closely matched by a struggle to carve a specialized niche within international relations theory and to impose, against old-style security studies and the Neorealist school, transnational networks and normative practices as a legitimate field of research. Rather than a neutral and detached observatory, academia has been indeed one of the arenas where the institutionalization of human rights has taken place, through the production of theories, doctrines, specialized curricula, democratization experts and human rights professionals — in law departments, of course, but in political science or international relations departments as well. No account of the emergence of democracy and human rights as new principles for the reform of states and international politics would therefore be complete with-. out including a reflexive analysis of the place and the role of academics and academic discourse in the paradigmatic shift this book is concerned with. From the outset, academic products have been constantly recycled in international circuits for strategic purposes and used in the construction of colonial or postcolonial empires (Simpson 1998). The same holds true today about the learned discourses on human rights or democracy. They are part of the context which needs to be explained, not explanatory elements themselves.

A Sociology of Transnational Symbolic Power

I have gone at some length over these established approaches to the subject because I think their respective shortcomings are instructive and they have contributed to shape the approach followed in this work. In the first case (international political economy and neo-Gramscian approaches), the field of democracy and human rights is subsumed under the structural logic of global capitalism in the world-system; its specificity, its agents, its internal evolution and its history are almost irrelevant to the overall theory. In the second case (the literature on issue-networks and advocacy groups), the empirical focus is biased by an insider's view and almost a hands-on approach. But the precise position of this viewpoint within the structure of the field under consideration is precisely what is not analyzed. An idealistic ethical commitment takes the place of a social scientific explanation for the emergence of these networks and of the struggles around which they are organized. In short, we have either an abstract structuralism lacking empirical grounding, or an idealism masquerading as empirical analysis.

The challenge is therefore to integrate both in order to neutralize their respective blind spots. They both point at different dimensions of the field of democracy and human rights: one emphasizes processes of domination and instrumental rationality, the other stresses idealism and the power of communicative action or ideas. But these are not only two ways of conceiving or theorizing this field between which one has to chose. They are actually elements embedded in it, and mobilized by different actors under the form of strategies or justifications for their actions. The task at hand is to show how these opposed logics, far from excluding each other, coexist within the field: realism and idealism, interest and disinterestedness, professionalism and moral commitment are as many repertoires pragmatically mobilized by the actors involved. They must be related to specific positions within the overall structure of this field and to specific institutional contexts, and at the same time they must be analyzed as the products of particular histories.

Such a sociological approach, I reckon, can make a valuable contribution to our understanding of this field. In part because, unlike political science or international relations, sociology is a discipline which has remained so far external to this field and which has not been mobilized as a symbolic resource in the struggles for or around human rights, democracy and foreign policy. In that sense, it is more apt to avoid endorsing this or that view of democracy, this or that theory of human rights, and better equipped to understand that each of these viewpoints makes sense only in relation to the others, and in relation to the structure of the field in which they are often used as powerful symbolic resources. It is better equipped to understand that these repertoires are also the product of a history which is one and the same with the history of the social construction of the field of democracy and human rights. The paucity of sociological approaches to the subject (but for a few exceptions discussed below) is largely due to the nature of this field, which benefits from the moral appeal of the values it promotes. This makes it all the more difficult to question the motives of those who operate in the name of democracy and human rights, and to analyze their practices in sociological terms. For sociology as an intellectual enterprise is primarily concerned with the notion of interest (Coleman 1990; Bourdieu 1997). The sociological analysis of forms of action which are justified by disinterestedness and driven by universals or moral ideals is immediately viewed with suspicion, as if its aim was to tarnish the motives of the actors and to aggravate this offence with the fact that it seems to deprive them of the definitive interpretation of what they are up to. Needless to say, this is not my intention in this book. The point is not to reduce ethical constructs to the fig-leaf of gross material interests but rather, following Weber, to understand disinterestedness as a form of interest, more precisely as interest in values or ideas, and to look at the social conditions of its emergence. The task is all the more urgent in that this specific form of idealist discourses and moral commitment have become the main idiom of global politics and of a new form of rule.

In writing this book, the approach that I found most useful was certainly to think of human rights and democracy as constituting a "field," in the sense of sociologist Pierre Bourdieu.[9] This means considering that democracy and human rights do not exist outside a dense network of activists, practitioners, institutions, bureaucrats, documents, monitoring technologies, normative practices, legal doctrines, styles of activism and learned credentials, and that the task of the research is not only to describe these various elements, but also to analyze their mutual relationships to the extent that they form a distinct, coherent and relatively autonomous sphere of social activity, a "field" of practices. In particular, this approach puts an emphasis on the differences and hierarchies internal to the field that are too often concealed in the literature on the subject, and relates them to various forms of "capital" (social, economic, scientific . . .) that have currency in it and to the pattern of the distribution of such capital among actors and institutions. It is particularly well suited, therefore, to analyze the social production of the international expertise on democracy and human rights which today fuels the production of global norms.

Another point of departure, related to this sociological tradition but focused on international processes having to do with democracy, emancipation, and human rights, is the work of Yves Dezalay and Bryant Garth (2002) on the promotion of the "rule of law" in Latin America and on the hegemonic imports-exports of legal or economic models between the United States and its South. Against functionalist views of globalization or disembedded theories of international norms, Dezalay and Garth have shown that the internationalization of U.S. regulatory models and economic recipes is not the result of some grand design but rather the internationalization of a certain type of conflicts around the role of the state and its transformation. Participants in these conflicts mobilize international instruments and resources (knowledge, expertise, contacts, policy templates, etc.) in local contexts, thus acting as facilitators of the international circulation of policy models. In this approach, local interests and institutional policies as well as the strategies used to pursue them are easily reprocessed into universalistic discourses and idealistic prescriptions. Thus, it becomes possible to trace the genealogy of these global constructs, whether they concern the reform of the state, the mode of economic growth, the rights of the individual, the environment, or democracy, which seems to float in an international limbo and to be detached from any specific social context.

Recently, various scholarly contributions have thus revived an interest in international interactions and exchanges as the primary context for understanding local change (e.g., Rogers 1998). Taking stock from these different views, I try to emphasize the importance of some international influences on the construction of global democratic prescriptions made in the United States: the experience of "democratization" of postwar Germany, the intellectual and ideological consequences of European intellectual migration to the States, the critique of U.S. policy in Latin America, or the role of liberal academic networks in the same region appear as some of the international building blocks of an global ideology of democratization that is today one of the faces of "Americanism."

What distinguishes this book from related endeavors is a matter of emphasis in its focus. While they often succeed in contextualizing the production of universalistic discourses on the economy, the environment, or human rights, they usually pay relatively little attention to the knowledge which is invested in these discourses and to the transformation of the underlying academic disciplines. Knowledge, by contrast, is a central character of the stories which follow. As noted, academic products and academics themselves have been central to the construction of a new global discourse on democracy. The construction of tools for democratization and the justification of this new form of international activism have proceeded both on political and academic ground, and it is impossible to understand the genesis of the field of democracy and human rights without carefully considering how it also took place as an essentially intellectual operation. Along with law or economics,[10] political science is one of the main "disciplines of power" concerned — not only because it defines an area where various modalities of government and the exercise of power are elaborated, codified, and justified, but also because it is a traditional training field for national and international elites. The transformations of this disciplinary area echo the major transformations of national and international rule. The emergence of a global paradigm based on the notions of democracy and human rights has been no exception.[11] The development of new forms of international activism promoting these values has been matched by the parallel development of a vast literature on democratization, the rule of law, or transnational networks. Whether from the perspective of area studies, comparative politics, or international relations theory, scholars have started to study processes of "transition" to democracy, the relationship between economic and political liberalization, elections, new civil societies, but also the role of transnational actors in these processes (on this aspect, see Whitehead 1996; Diamond 1996; Crawford 1996). If these learned developments have contributed to the institutionalization of the field of democracy and human rights, it is not only by turning it into the subject-matter of scientific discourse, but also because they were part of it. The mobilization of academic communities and their knowledge has been from the outset a crucial element of this new transnational activism. In some cases, it is impossible to distinguish between academic and political aspects: that is the case, for instance, of Latin American studies in the 1970s and 1980s, which made possible the emergence of an advocacy coalition between academics and liberal policy entrepreneurs that articulated a credible policy alternative to what was then the current practice of U.S. intervention in the region. For understanding these important political changes, therefore, it is necessary to consider the subordinate position occupied by such disciplines within the overall division of academic labor and their specific exposure to the effects of U.S. policy in Latin America — that is, their relation to the field of power.

The role of expertise in this field where skills and competence are important factors served to reinforce the links with academia. The discussion of which technologies of political change are most adapted, the evaluation of existing programs and projects, the assessment of the impact of political conditionality attached to foreign aid, have opened occasional or permanent professional outlets for many academics, allowing them to convert their knowledge into an expertise that was suddenly sellable on an expanding international market. At the same time, issues related to democratization represented a formula for the reform of the state that was more appealing and less narrowly technical than other successful global prescriptions, in particular regarding economic liberalization. In other words, the field of

democracy and human rights has allowed many political scientists to compete with other producers of expertise, and in particular with economists.
Discussions regarding in particular the relation between democratization
and neoliberal economic reforms must also be understood in this light: that
of professional turf battles waged by proxy. This means that the struggles
around such encompassing questions also conceal more petty fights internal
to academic politics and disciplines.

Conversely, these theoretical products have also been mobilized by foreign policy planners as weapons in their political battles. As one "realist"
and conservative foreign policy analyst explains: "What is really under discussion are not pragmatic judgments about what works and what doesn't,
nor even the best way to weigh competing objectives. . . . Debate over democracy promotion is really just a proxy for a larger war over the overall
direction of American policy abroad and at home" (Kagan 1998, 2–3). Indeed, as just noted, it is no coincidence that democratization studies
emerged as a subdiscipline in the 1980s, in the context of a liberal offensive
against the policies pursued by the Reagan administration in Latin America
in particular. Many such academic products are used as weapons in the
internal struggles of the foreign policy establishment because they are actually the products of its history and of its own efforts, through philanthropic
foundations and academic networks, to generate knowledge and expertise
deemed necessary for the conduct of foreign policy (Cumings 1998; Seybold
1980). In the same way that modernization theory was to a large extent
devised as an "antirevolutionary doctrine" (Smith 2000, 147) meant to deal
with the process of decolonization and with what was perceived as the threat
of socialism, democratization studies have been shaped according to specific
international strategies — devising technologies of smooth regime change
that would ensure some degree of stability in a context where national economies were also radically transformed and liberalized. In that sense, the new
academic discourse on democratization, human rights and the emerging
world order appear indeed as the continuation of a hegemonic project
(Cammack 1997) — and this seems to be supported by the fact that they have
taken the dominant position thereto occupied by modernization theory, often with the help of the same sponsors, whether the Ford foundation or
other philanthropic institutions and policy centers. But this should not conceal the fact that the academic foundations of this new policy wisdom have
been constructed against modernization theory, often with critical and heterodox intellectual resources. In the same way as democracy and human
rights activism has imported within foreign policy a range of critical and

emancipatory repertoires, democratization studies represent the successful conversion of critical knowledge into a new dominant expertise. In other words, the genealogy of the field of democracy and human rights must include a sociological analysis of its scientific foundations. It is important to understand in which contexts and from which perspective these new questions have arisen. In dealing with this issue, Wright Mills' statement that "we cannot very well state a problem until we know *whose* problem it is" (1959: 76) can be taken as a reliable methodological guideline.

Organization of the Book

The book analyzes individual evolutions, institutions, and discourses that have shaped the field of democracy and human rights and contributed to its emergence. It is organized as a series of short studies analyzing and relating to each other parallel but sometimes independent developments that have contributed to this process. Chapter 1 traces the origins of contemporary "democracy promotion" to earlier cold war crusades and in particular to previous attempts to establish a sort of "international of the free world," modeled after the communist international and capable of competing with it on ideological terms. Such earlier projects as the Congress for Cultural Freedom found their best promoters among the anti-Stalinist Left. The first chapter traces the evolution of this group of "double-agents" from its early involvement in radical politics to, ultimately, their rallying the Reagan administration where they created the National Endowment for Democracy.

Chapter 2 analyzes this organization in greater detail. The NED was the outcome of the struggle between liberal human rights activists and neoconservative ideologues to define the notion of human rights and the type of foreign policy which could be based on it. It also analyzes the networks of policy advocates and academics which contributed to and legitimated this transformation of earlier fights for human rights into a global program of "democracy promotion."

The following two chapters deal with the rather different profile of other activists, who ended up in the same networks or institutions, but tend to come from a more liberal and academic background. Chapter 3 switches to the genealogy of the current political science of democratization. It traces it back to various scholarly and political critiques of the paradigm of modernization and political development which was dominant in the 1950s and 1960s. It argues that these learned critiques of modernization theory paradoxically fulfill its political goals (in sum, change and stability), in particular by producing a prescriptive theory of gradual change that not only takes for granted but also asserts the importance of capitalistic relations and property rights.

Chapter 4 looks specifically at the transformation of these critical and structuralist theories of political change, fashionable in the 1970s, into a theory of "transition to democracy" in the 1980s and into a "political economy" that thrived around the World Bank. It resituates these theoretical products in their institutional and academic contexts, and underlines their role as weapons mobilized by liberal policy entrepreneurs in their opposition to neoconservatives. Chapter 5 leaves comparative politics and scholars of Latin America and turns to international relations theory. It focuses in particular on the role of so-called "social constructivist" approaches in producing an emancipatory narrative of global human rights and transnational activist networks. It also stresses the purposes and effects of this discourse within a broader strategy of legitimation pursued by NGOs and other moral entrepreneurs.

Finally, Chapter 6 is concerned with the internationalization of the new paradigm of democracy and with its relation to the global economy. By focusing on the World Bank, it intends to analyze how the earlier doctrines of development have been toppled by this new prescriptive discourse. It follows the sinuous path that led to the adoption of a new international agenda articulated around the notion of "good governance" and the rule of law, replacing earlier formulas for social progress. The World Bank acted as a powerful mechanism for the internationalization of the new agenda and its twining with specific economic prescriptions. Starting in the 1980s, the Bank combined its attack against previous developmental strategies with symbolic openings toward NGOs. It sealed the alliance of democracy, human rights, and capitalism within a global "business of empowerment" (Wade 2001, 131) that it contributed to legitimize. The adoption of a very activist pro-democracy, pro-participation agenda by this institution traditionally identified with pure economics and technocracy was also the result of less visible struggles among different types of international expertise.

1   From Cold Warriors to Human Rights Activists

"Some may prefer the term 'freedom' or 'democracy' to 'human rights' — but whatever the name, the United States needs to have a response to Communism on the level of ideology"

— Joshua Muravchik, *The Uncertain Crusade: Jimmy Carter and the Dilemmas of Human Rights Policy* (Washington, DC: American Enterprise Institute, 1986), p. 223.

"Neoconservatism is the final stage of the Old Left, the only element in American politics whose identity is principally derived from its view of Communism"

— Sidney Blumenthal, *The Rise of the Counter-Establishment: From Conservative Ideology to Political Power* (New York: Times Books, 1986), p. 130.

A human rights group in Cambodia receives $50,000 to train NGO personnel; an offshoot of the American Chamber of Commerce receives $124,612 to organize a workshop for African think tanks; an organization of indigenous women of the Peruvian Amazon receives $33,200 to enhance women's participation in local community groups and local elections.[1] There are many more examples. Today, there exists a global infrastructure network that encompasses and influences a variety of NGOs, local groups, political movements, and lobbies of all kinds. Its very existence represents a constant and enduring challenge to the claims to sovereignty and the power of authoritarian states. It binds together numerous local struggles for political emancipation or participation. Despite its limited impact this is a considerable achievement. Yet, by linking activist groups to remote foundations in Washington or elsewhere, by channeling financial assistance or sending political advisors or organizers, by promoting opposition forces which are not necessarily the most representative but fit the wider strategies or the worldviews of their sponsors, this emerging global network also contributes to the transformation of politics into a field that is less the expression of local, historical, and social developments than the reflection of global trends and practices. It does not only make possible all sorts of interference and occult influence, but it also coats them in the glorious appearance of progressive struggles and solidarities.

This new form of internationalism is, in other words, highly paradoxical, and it still awaits a description that grasps its ambiguity. This ambiguity pertains both to its functions and its genealogy. For some scholars, a genuine and dedicated commitment to democracy worldwide became possible only after the end of the cold war and is the work of activist networks, NGOs, and various actors that obey principles other than reason of state.[2] Earlier, the antagonism between the two superpowers ensured the success of "realism" as the main doctrine of foreign policy, which legitimated all kinds of accommodations with authoritarian regimes as long as they had chosen to side with the "free world." In this perspective, only the end of the conflict could open the way for the participation of civil society, with its NGOs and its activists, to international politics and the ensuing pressure toward democratization.

There is another view that by contrast insists the promotion of democracy has essentially an American character — one that has been the beacon of U.S. foreign policy since the origins of the nation (e.g. Smith 1994). Born out of an anti-colonial revolution and built upon a universal conception of human rights, the United States is in this view considered as a country whose history is that of a constant pursuit and defense of freedom abroad, from the war with Spain in 1898 to date. From such a perspective, the cold war was also a battle fought in the name of ideals and universals. This type of interpretation is usually linked to an idealist historiography which essentializes American history and transforms it not only into the unfolding of a progressive idea, but also, as we shall see, into a conservative project built on the confusion of national interests and universalistic values, which has consistently used the latter to further the former.[3]

Although they differ in many respects, these two genealogies of the field of democracy and human rights are actually closer than they appear at first sight. The first claims that U.S. foreign policy has become ethical under the pressure of activist networks, while the second asserts the intrinsic benevolence of American power. This kind of history of ideas is not very useful for understanding the emergence of a field of democracy and human rights, with its professions of "regime change," "transitions to democracy," "nation-building," "conflict-resolution," "privatizations," and so forth. Here I draw attention to the continuities — rather than the breaks — between this field of transnational activities and the cold war, during which many of the skills and technologies for political change were honed. In addition, many of the networks that shifted to "democracy promotion" in the 1980s are the result of complex ideological realignments that are intimately linked to the historical situation of the cold war, a continuity visible at a more conceptual level. It is highly significant, for instance, that a political scientist and advisor involved in the early construction and legitimation of democratization programs could theorize them as components of a democratic "campaign," a term that refers to a military notion and that implies an enemy (Gastil 1988).

Labels such as "democracy promotion" and "human rights" do not, however, refer merely to the overt continuation of political operations that were once covert.[4] Sure enough, as some advocates acknowledge, this has been one of the rationales behind the government's endorsement of institutions or programs claiming to promote democracy.[5] But the "democracy industry" of the 1990s cannot be seen as a mere extension of the institutional structures and operational experiences of the cold war. It has organized a worldwide market for the trade of political technologies, models of collective action, and economic prescriptions. Furthermore, the cold war was about maintaining stability and the status quo. To promote democracy is fundamentally to promote change. It aims at restructuring societies from the grass-roots level of civil society to the formal structures of power, transforming their economies as well in the process. There is something intrinsically revolutionary about it.

It should come as no surprise, then, that the field of democracy and human rights has been an important professional outlet for — and to a large extent the creation of — a cadre of political activists who have moved from left-wing anti-Stalinism to cold war anticommunism and who later found in neoconservatism a way to put their earlier involvement with revolutionary internationalism in conformity with the dominant political order. In the view of many of these policy activists, U.S. foreign policy should be a "liberation doctrine," as suggested by a document some of them drafted for the Bush Sr. 1988 presidential campaign (Fairbanks 1989: 623).[6] From the beginning, they were eager not to leave to the Soviet Union the monopoly of ideology and progressive values, and thus to fight the cold war on the ideological and cultural front. Democracy and human rights were to be the counter-ideology opposed to Communism. As former Trotskyists, socialists, and social-democrats belonging to the non-Communist left, they were also used to fighting political turf battles with Communists, and saw the cold war as an extension of these earlier battles and, therefore, as "their" turf. At the same time, they remained people for whom politics should be fought in a Marxist-Leninist manner, but without all its goals. This collective conversion and the recycling of leftist language and skills in a hegemonic policy constitutes one of the central aspects of the social history of this field. But the legacy of the cold war is also more complex, as many of its participants come from the other side of this ideological conflict, from the anti-imperialist campaigns that sought to oppose U.S. policies in Latin America in particular, and more generally from a liberal intelligentsia. These disparate groups converged into the same institutional networks during the 1980s.

The first phase of the project of building an international network to promote democracy began in the early years of the cold war. That phase ends about the time of the Vietnam war and the crisis of liberal internationalism — a crisis, that is, of the very ideology which underpinned such a project. This crisis also affects the foreign policy establishment and the social mechanisms of its reproduction. In this context of deep changes in the social and institutional fabric of U.S. politics — characterized in particular by the emergence of a "marketplace of ideas" and the resurgence of foundations, policy research centers, and ideological entrepreneurs as key political actors — can be traced the social and political trajectory of the advocates of an international ideological offensive focusing on democracy and human rights. This project came to fruition in the 1980s, with the creation of the National Endowment for Democracy (NED), although some unsuccessful attempts to create a similar institution had already been made in the late 1960s.

While the NED is by no means the only or even the most important organization involved in "democracy promotion," and while many other similar institutions have since emerged both in the United States and abroad, the NED stands out as a pioneering institution. With its mandate exclusively focused on political issues of democracy, it has contributed decisively to structure a distinctive field of democracy and human rights, in particular in the way it has assembled a wide-ranging network of political and scientific actors and has fostered the development of a "political science" of democratization along with an entire academic enterprise centered around these issues. The context of its creation is also significant: it was established in 1983 by the Reagan administration, at a moment when such struggles for democracy and human rights were not separate from an effort to raise the level of confrontation with the Soviet bloc and to revive the cold war. The NED thus offers an opportunity to observe, in the making, the conversion of cold warriors into human rights and democracy activists.

The Cold War, the Fight Against Totalitarianism, and the Congress for Cultural Freedom

The notion that democracy is not simply the product of a specific level of historical development but rather an *idea* that must be defended and promoted through modern means of communication and propaganda, political technologies, and cultural productions did not appear with the contemporary practices of democratic engineering in countries undergoing "regime change" or "transitions to democracy." This notion actually goes back to the configuration of the cold war as a struggle — and to a large extent as a *cultural* and *ideological* struggle — between liberal democracy and totalitarianism. The idea that it is possible, desirable, and even necessary to actively promote democracy, indeed, takes shape at the same time as the concept of totalitarianism is entrenched into intellectual and official political discourse as the symbol of a pervasive threat, both international and domestic.[7] With the onset of the cold war and the adoption of a policy of containment in 1947 — what came to be known as the "Truman doctrine" — the United States framed its opposition to Soviet policies not in terms of divergent interests (for different interests are equally legitimate from a moral point of view) but in terms of a radical opposition between two models of civilization and value systems, between democracy and totalitarianism.

The opposition between the West and Soviet totalitarianism was often presented as an opposition both moral and epistemological between truth and falsehood. The democratic, social, and economic credentials of the Soviet Union were typically seen as "lies" and as the product of a deliberate and multiform propaganda. In that sense, the cold war was also a battle of ideas, waged in the realm of culture, pervading also artistic and scientific productions. In this context, the concept of totalitarianism was itself an asset, as it made possible the conversion of prewar anti-fascism into postwar anti-communism.

The genealogy of this concept cannot be dissociated from the social history of its producers and brokers: the first analyses of the Soviet Union as a "totalitarian state," it should be recalled, were not produced by the political scientists of the cold war but, much earlier, by the anti-Stalinist strands of Marxism (Salvadori 1981). The subsequent success of the term "totalitarianism" during the cold war ensured the promotion of this small group of intellectuals who had entertained since the 1930s a critique of the Soviet Union as a totalitarian power, even when such criticism was played down during the war by U.S. governmental circles eager to maintain a unity of purpose with their most powerful ally. While the notion was prevailingly used in anti-fascist circles that were rather favorably disposed toward the Soviet Union, heterodox Marxists or former Communists — usually very close to the European émigrés who imported the concept to the United States — had used it at an early stage to denounce the degeneration of the modern state in general, including the state born out of the Bolshevik revolution. In progressive magazines such as *The New Leader*, founded in 1920 by Menshevik émigré Sol Levitas, or *The Partisan Review*, formerly a Communist publication which broke with the party in 1937 and attracted a modernist literary intelligentsia (Philip Rahv, Sydney Hook, Mary McCarthy, Dwight Macdonald, as well as many European intellectual refugees arriving in America), the concept of totalitarianism was acclimatized in a new environment, dominated by influential exponents of the anti-Stalinist left who had broken with Communism.[8] The Menshevik writers among the *New Leader's* staff, for instance, (in particular Boris J. Nicolaevski and David Dallin) regularly denounced the totalitarian nature of the Soviet Union and of other Communist countries including China. In 1947, seemingly with behind-the-scenes help from prominent labor leaders George Meany and Jay Lovestone, David Dallin even managed to publish as a supplement to the *New Leader* a map of concentration camps in the Soviet Union, presumably the first one ever published.[9]

The success of the notion in these intellectual circles was due to no small extent to its capacity to solve the political dilemma in which most members of the noncommunist left found themselves, as critics of both capitalism and Stalinism. Totalitarianism linked these critiques and rationalized them. In this way the notion that had originally referred to the mobilization of society by the fascist party-state came to be used within a critical diagnosis of the evolution of the modern state by prominent anti-Stalinist intellectuals. The sociologist Daniel Bell, for instance, writing in 1944 in the *Socialist Review*, saw in the wartime alliance of the state and large capitalist groups for the sake of war production the embryonic form of a "monopoly State," i.e., an appropriation of the state apparatus by capital, that prefigured a totalitarian evolution in the United States (Brick 1986: 94–95).

Justifying the initial opposition to U.S. involvement in the Second World War by the *Partisan Review* intellectuals, Dwight Macdonald wrote that "the first result of a war against foreign fascism will be the introduction of domestic dictatorship" (Cooney 1986: 169). A similar view was held by the philosopher John Dewey, who assumed that one of the main dangers of the

war was that it favored totalitarian tendencies in all states, including democratic ones (Dewey 1939). James Burnham, another heretic who would be
one of the first intellectuals of the noncommunist left to adopt conservative
positions, denounced in his book *The Managerial Revolution* (1941) a similar trend leading to the rise of the bureaucratic state based on the rule of a
technocratic elite of planners and administrators, a trend represented in its
most extreme form by Fascism and Stalinism, of which he nevertheless perceived some signs in Roosevelt's New Deal, for instance.[10]

In other words, the concept of totalitarianism allowed the non-Communist
left to criticize in the same breath both the capitalist state and the degenerate
nature of the Soviet state. Trotsky's prestige and his influence over vast areas
of American socialism, due in particular to the close ties existing between
the "old man" and the New York intellectuals but also to the charismatic
leadership of Max Shachtman over some of the Trotskyist currents in the
anti-Stalinist left, also contributed to make the interpretation of Soviet developments through the lens of "totalitarianism" a legitimate analysis among
these circles. The Bolshevik exile, who arrived in Mexico in 1937, had developed relations with important figures of the anti-Stalinist left such as John
Dewey, Sidney Hook, and Herbert Solow when they established a commission to denounce the 1937 Moscow trials as a farce and to prove Trotsky's
innocence (Wald 1987).

Trotsky's analysis of the Soviet state as a degenerate and oppressive bureaucracy, which since the mid-1930s made increasing use of the concept
of "totalitarianism" to refer to the Stalinist regime, was also very influential,
as demonstrated for example by his intellectual guidance over the circles
close to the *Partisan Review*. Obviously, the concept did not yet have the
theoretical depth or the rigidity it gained later on, in the course of its academic development. In particular, it did not yet imply a strict equivalence
between Fascism and Stalinism, of the kind it would later produce through
its comparative use.[11] Thus, while using the notion polemically to attack
Stalinism, Max Shachtman could hold at the same time that "the difference
between capitalism — be it Fascist or democratic — and Stalinism [is] fundamental and irreconcilable" (Shachtman 1962: 2).[12] Nevertheless, the
notion became firmly established in the intellectual arsenal of the non-
Communist left and was used to denounce the oppressive nature of Stalinism in the USSR and in the Communist parties across the globe. In fact,
Shachtman himself suggested that the term was synonymous with his own
analysis of the Stalinist regime when he wrote that "its social order . . . is
bureaucratic or totalitarian collectivism" (ibid., p. 29 — emphasis mine).

This very strong stance against Communism had the effect of uniting further the scattered currents and the various factions of the non-Communist left. Their opposition to the strategy of the "Popular Front" contributed to shaping a common political identity. After years of hostility toward social-democratic forces, which it had denounced as "social fascists" or "social felons," the Comintern did a turnabout and, in 1935, declared a policy of alliance between the Communists and all the progressive forces on the left in the name of anti-fascist struggle. This is called the "Popular Front" strategy. The Popular Front strategy contributed to increase the popularity of Communists and of the Soviet Union among liberals, a development much resented by the non-Communist left, which considered it a victory for Stalinism.

The prospects of international collaboration with the Soviet Union in the postwar world, widely discussed among Popular Front forces, was equally upsetting to the non-Communist left. Straying from the mainstream left, the anti-Stalinists accentuated their opposition to the Soviet regime, even more so after the pact with Germany and the Soviet invasion of Finland. In 1940, Max Shachtman, the Trotskyist leader of the newly created Socialist Workers Party, broke with Trotsky on the issue of whether or not their followers should join the war effort: while Trotsky considered that the Second World War was not simply a traditional war between imperialist powers, and that the workers state in the USSR, no matter how degenerate, ought to be protected at all costs, the Shachtmanites regarded it as a conflict between capitalism and Stalinism, that is between American and Soviet imperialism, and went on with wildcat strikes and "business as usual" while most of the left and its working-class components accepted negotiated discipline and sacrifices for the sake of military victory. This estrangement from the political mainstream, however, did not last for long.

The concept of totalitarianism facilitated complex political realignments. It did so by becoming an encompassing notion involving not only an abstraction of central features of the Nazi or the Fascist state, but also a historical trend transforming the modern state in general, including the Soviet Union and Western democracies. As Enzo Traverso observes in his historical study of the notion, the elevation of totalitarianism to a central concept of postwar international politics entailed a radical transformation of its meaning: "rather than fulfilling a *critical* function toward existing regimes — as it did in the thirties — the concept of totalitarianism then started to have an essentially *apologetic* function toward the Western order, that is, it turned into an *ideology*" (Traverso 2002: 87). This conceptual transformation is indistinguishable from the conversion of the anti-Stalinist left into an efficient supporter of the liberal consensus of the 1950s and an aggressive opponent of Communist organizations — that is, from its becoming actively engaged in the cold war.

When the former enemy, Germany, became an ally in the struggle against the former ally, the Soviets, the once-marginalized anti-Stalinist left suddenly found itself propelled into a strategic position. The early proponents of the notion of the Soviet Union as "totalitarian" now were in line with the principles guiding U.S. foreign policy toward the cold war. In this new context, the experience of opposition to Communism accumulated during the 1930s by the non-Communist left and, in particular, its capacity to fight Communist influence on the left and, even better, among leftist intellectuals, became a crucial strategic asset. Their ideological skills became particularly valued as the opposition to Communism began to take a cultural and symbolic dimension. As Peter Steinfels observes, "well drilled in Marxist texts and socialist history, blooded in the tribal wars between Communists, democratic socialists, and fifty-seven varieties of Trotskyists, they were already trained and in motion when the cold war put their skills at a premium and promoted them to the front lines" (Steinfels 1979: 29).

Historian Alan Wald also notes that "the skills and experience they had acquired as polemicists and ideologists during their radical years . . . enabled them to move rapidly into seats of cultural power" (Wald 1987: 8). In fact, one of the most striking features of their paradoxical political trajectory is the preservation and the stability of a militant and ideological political culture specific to the Old Left, in spite of its subordination to the imperatives of the cold war and of its eventual migration toward the right. Far from being lost in the process of their conversion from socialist anti-Stalinism to liberal anti-Communism (and, later, to neoconservatism), the Marxist-Leninist conception of politics and, more broadly, the ideological *forma mentis* of these activists remained the same while it was put to new uses.[13] It is precisely this specific political culture that made the anti-Stalinist left a key player of the cold war: nobody was better equipped to fight Communism than these "democratic socialists" who firmly belonged to the Marxist tradition but most of whom had already abandoned, by the 1950s, the perspective of class struggle and had embraced reformism, thus joining the fold of the liberal consensus.

Paradoxically, while the non-Communist left represented a marginal political force that still considered itself part of the revolutionary tradition, it became the very social foundation of the main anticommunist strategies

articulated by the State Department and the CIA in the late 1940s. According to Michael Werner, an in-house historian of the CIA, the sponsorship
of this group represented nothing less than the "theoretical foundation of
the Agency's political operations against Communism over the next two
decades" (Stonor Saunders 1999: 63). Peter Coleman, a former member of
the Australian section of the U.S.-backed, anticommunist International Association for Cultural Freedom, also writes in his history of the Congress for
Cultural Freedom that the "belief that the non-Communist left could be
the most effective response to the totalitarian left" had spread "from the
intellectual ghetto to high government office" (Coleman 1989: 8). It included numerous intellectuals, which gave it a certain ideological clout, and
it was able to penetrate mainstream institutions and political movements,
and in particular the labor movement.

In this respect, the rapprochement that had taken place during the war
between anti-Stalinists and trade union bureaucracies certainly played an
important role in defining the containment of Communist influence on the
field of labor as a crucial stake of the postwar struggles, domestic as well as
international. The war had made possible some degree of convergence between isolationist, "bread-and-butter" union officials opposed to the no-strike
pledges in certain industries and Trotskyists or other anti-Stalinists opposing
the war and denouncing both U.S. and Soviet imperialism. Some ex-Communists, such as Jay Lovestone, gained positions from which they could exert
a more direct influence on international affairs and foreign policy. A protégé
of Bukharin, who was then falling in disgrace in the Kremlin, Lovestone
had been expelled from the Communist Party in 1930 under the pressure
of orders coming from Moscow. He then joined the International Ladies'
Garment Workers' Union (ILGWU), a union affiliated with the CIO and
close to the *New Leader*, before moving to the American Federation of Labor
(AFL) in 1944, where he was put in charge of the Free Trade Union Committee (FTUC), the international branch of the AFL created the same year
in order to fight Communist influence among trade unions in Europe and
elsewhere.[14]

George Meany, the violently anticommunist boss of the AFL, and Lovestone seemingly managed to convince State Department officials of the
crucial importance of labor in the confrontation with international Communism, and to have numerous "Lovestoneites" appointed as labor attachés
in U.S. embassies, while the FTUC benefited from CIA funds for its operations (Muravchik 2002: 252–253). At the same time, the assessment of
recent European development by some influential State Department ad-

ministrators with some international experience (Dean Acheson, George Marshall, James Byrnes, George Kennan) made the administration sensitive to such arguments. *The Vital Center,* Arthur Schlesinger's political manifesto of cold war liberalism, gives a cogent account of this convergence of views: according to this direct witness, the State Department actively supported the non-Communist left, considering that "the only realistic hope for a bulwark against Communism in Europe lay in the strengthening of the democratic socialists" (Schlesinger 1970 [1950]: 166). It was thought that the ideological promotion of socialism would both demonstrate the capacity of the West to carry out social reform and thus lure important target groups away from Communism, in particular important fractions of the intelligentsia.[15]

The importance of democratic socialism as a strategic element of the cold war doctrine of the State Department would prove long-lasting, and it would still inform its operations in the 1980s, under the label of "proximate criticism," which was based in part on the promotion of socialist or Marxist critiques of Soviet Communism (Gastil 1988). In 1949, the exclusion of Communists from the CIO completed the articulation of a political alliance among the State Department, the conservatized upper strata of the labor hierarchies, and exponents of the anti-Stalinist left, thus giving birth to what became known as "State Department socialism."[16] This strategy was made possible because the anti-Stalinist left was revising its analysis of the social and political situation as it abandoned a revolutionary perspective and moved toward the endorsement of "democratic socialism." In a 1947 issue of *Partisan Review,* summing up the position reached by many on the anti-Stalinist left, Sidney Hook wrote that "the future of socialism depends upon the preservation to the last ditch of political democracy" (Hook 1947, 33).[17]

By 1950, Max Shachtman, who had refused as many other leftists to support U.S. intervention in the Second World War, had also considerably revised the political priorities of the Trotskyist movement and made the "fight for democracy — for all democratic rights and institutions" the primary goal of the working class (1962[1950]: 27). The whole postwar atmosphere accelerated this retreat of intellectuals toward more conservative positions and a gradual acceptance of the American social and economic model. For the literary intellectuals of *Partisan Review,* in particular, the stand-off with the Soviet Union was experienced as a situation of urgency that required choices, even if the alternatives offered were only second-bests. The vogue of existentialism, imported in particular by the same journal, only strengthened this feeling of urgency and responsibility.[18]

Thus, a division of labor emerged between the most enlightened and liberal fraction of the state elite and the anti-Stalinist left. While the former dealt with the general strategy, the latter were in charge of implementing specific tactics, in particular political and cultural ones, in the struggle against international Communism. As any division of labor, it was also a social division of labor reflecting class or status hierarchies: in this case, between the patrician, predominantly WASP, liberal establishment and left-ist circles comprising mostly former first- or second-generation immigrants, often Jewish, coming from Eastern Europe.[19] To the extent that it was purely instrumental, that is, not based on class or other forms of shared interests, this alliance would last as long as the ideological outlook of the non-Communist left would prove useful and fit the plans of the foreign policy establishment. The cold war thus ensured, at least in part, the *political* promotion (if not the social promotion) of these subordinate groups — paradoxically, in fact, of those who were a minority even in their political area — and also the inter-nationalization of their activities. Cosmopolitan, internationalist by creed, anticommunist, their most articulate and most committed exponents were thus perfectly equipped to play a discreet but nevertheless influential role in international affairs.

It is in this peculiar context that the theme of an international crusade for democracy gradually emerged within an ideological area straddling labor organizations and various socialist or Trotskyist movements. Even before the Truman doctrine, the very idea of containment was clearly on the agenda of some union officials worried by the influence of Communists within their own ranks or, even more so, among European trade union organizations in the process of reconstruction. The immediate postwar era thus saw labor abandoning its traditional isolationist stance and striving to become a major international actor. The creation of the Free Trade Union Committee was a direct offshoot of this evolution, and several Lovestoneites of the ILGWU strongly made the intellectual case for labor's involvement in the design of a new foreign policy. Widely publicized in the *New Leader,* these new ideas about the international role of labor were initially the expression of a fear of a "totalitarian" turn in politics, and an appeal to the defense of democratic values and institutions as the natural environment in which a strong labor movement could develop.

The need to defend New Deal conquests and to resist the attack on democratic liberties and the onset of a "militarized, regimented, enslaved, totalitarian world" also called for the alliance of progressives and liberals. In a June 1945 article, an ILGWU official wrote that "in this crucial moment, the ranks of liberalism and labor are thus drawn and bound together by a great need — to preserve and expand democracy at home and abroad" (Shore 1945: 14). Almost a year later, another major exponent of the ILGWU who had represented the AFL within the War Department published in the *New Leader* an article entitled "A Foreign Policy for Organized Labor," in which he analyzed the contemporary international situation and strongly asserted the need for labor to be at the cutting edge of an effort to defend and promote democracy abroad. The article stressed the need for "the democratic forces of all countries [to] work for a social, political, and economic program which will be more attractive and dynamic than the platforms offered by the defeated totalitarians of yesterday (Nazis and Fascists) and the surviving (and momentarily thriving) totalitarianism of today (the so-called Communists)" (Kreindler 1946: 9).

Previously implicit in the denunciation of totalitarianism, anticommunist motives became more explicit and more pressing, and they were used as a powerful rationale for the involvement of labor in international politics. The thrust of the argument laid in the emphasis that an exclusively political defense of democracy was insufficient to counter Communist influence, and that only intervention in other fields as well could thwart totalitarian advances and therefore avoid a direct confrontation with the Soviet Union: "The extension of democracy from the political into the social and economic fields is a life-and-death question for the postwar world" (ibid.). In other words, labor's traditional proposals for social reform and "industrial democracy," which were also shared by many socialist groups on the left, were framed as the best strategic asset of global cold war strategies. This whole line of argument, therefore, is nothing else than a formulation *ante litteram* of the doctrine of State Department socialism.

The proclamation of Truman doctrine crowned these efforts, although the democratic crusade envisaged by the non-Communist left within and outside labor was in some ways more militant and more confrontational, at least in the way it was fomulated, than the policy adopted by the administration in 1947. In fact, it recycled into the nascent cold war anticommunism the whole ideological legacy of anti-imperialism and some measure of revolutionary impetus. Soon after Truman announced his policy of containment, the *New Leader* opened its pages to a foreign correspondent close to the New York-based Liberal Party who advocated almost a roll-back strategy in terms directly borrowed from this tradition: "I have condemned American imperialism and shall go on condemning it. I would be a hypocrite, therefore, if I did not also condemn Soviet imperialism. . . . Americans who call themselves 'progressives' and 'liberals' have no right to those names if they support Soviet imperialism, or any imperialism. A true liberal has not favorite imperialism. . . . The only way to combat Russian nationalistic expansion and Bolshevik totalitarianism is through internationalism and real democracy. We must convert the negative, defensive Truman Doctrine into an assertive crusade for the brotherhood of free men who do not suffer want and will not therefore be lured by the false promises of dictators" (Fischer 1947: 8 — emphasis mine).

This predicted conversion was far from wishful thinking. It would soon take place. In October of the same year, Melvin J. Lasky, then a young foreign correspondent of the New Leader stationed in Germany, published an account of his disruption of the Writer's Congress organized by Soviet authorities in Berlin. Born in the Bronx in 1920, Lasky graduated from the City College, as had many other young radicals of the anti-Stalinist left, before joining the League for Cultural Freedom and Socialism in 1939, an anti-Popular Front group created by Dwight Macdonald, which defended artistic freedom against totalitarianism, but was still firmly anchored in the socialist left. He joined the staff of the New Leader shortly before being drafted into the army, sent to France and Germany, where he was finally demobilized.

Lasky achieved some degree of celebrity by making a passionate speech defending the rights and the freedom of expression of artists submitted to censorship in the Soviet Union during the Communist-dominated Writers' Congress held in October 1947. Reporting the episode in the New Leader, he elaborated on what he saw as a lack of understanding of Communist tactics by Western powers. "The policy of containment against Soviet expansion is, unfortunately, understood only in 19th-century terms of diplomacy and military force," he wrote, before suggesting a more confrontational strategy which reflected a lot of the ideas circulated within labor organizations, anti-Stalinist journals and the non-Communist left: "The West will lose Europe, slowly but surely, unless an international campaign is mapped out — in terms of political warfare, psychological warfare — which will carry the 'cold war' into European politics, into the labor movement, into the conflict of ideas" (Lasky 1947: 8).

At the same time, within Trotskyist ranks, where Shachtman even envisaged the creation of "a liberation movement against Soviet domination in Eastern Europe" (Drucker 1994: 208), the theme of an activist defense of democracy was developing. The search for a "third camp" siding neither with American imperialism nor with Soviet expansionism was indeed giving way to a qualified acceptance of capitalist democracy and to the forsaking of revolutionary strategies. The construction of socialism involved the defense of democracy as the natural environment of a strong labor movement. Writing in 1950, Max Shachtman explained that "the socialist movement . . . can be restored to a decisive political force if it realized that, today far more than ever before, *the all-around and aggressive championing of the struggle for democracy* is the only safeguard against the encroaching social decay, and the only road to socialism." Despite the recurring anti-capitalist rhetoric in his writings and speeches, the statement was resolutely anti-Communist: "The main obstacle on the road not to socialist power, but simply to the reconstitution of a socialist working-class movement, are not the parliamentary illusions of the proletariat. They are the illusions of Stalinism" (1962[1950]: 27 — emphasis mine).

Circulated among the various political families of the non-Communist left and resonating with the preoccupations of a new generation of liberal anti-Communists who brought their international experience within the postwar administration, this set of converging ideas about an active engagement with Communism in Europe and elsewhere would soon find a first institutional form with the creation of the Congress for Cultural Freedom. While the U.S. state was in charge of what Lasky had described as "diplomacy and military force," this seemingly private initiative would deal with the most militant aspects of the ideological crusade against Communism, the first of which was indeed to present it as a movement for democracy. By the same token, this institution would allow the non-Communist left to internationalize its own intellectual agenda as well as its privileged strategies for contrasting Communism.[20] While the trade unions, through their international branch, were doing political work with their European counterparts in the field of labor politics and industrial relations, the Congress for Cultural Freedom sought to oppose Communist influence in the field of culture — that is, to vie for the minds of the European intelligentsia — by using the same means of propaganda and organization. Over the years, the Congress would organize academic conferences, concerts, exhibitions, finance seminars, publish journals and magazines on the five continents, and considerably expand the networks of the American anti-Stalinist left abroad, until 1966, when press revelations about the role of the CIA in establishing and financing the Congress would start its terminal, albeit protracted, crisis.

To a great extent, the political culture of these various progressive movements that identified themselves with the Marxist tradition but were virulently anti-Communist was recycled into cold war projects in general and into the Congress in particular, along with their personnel. Even the organizational forms typical of the Marxist-Leninist conception of politics informed these international projects. In an elated letter to Arthur Schlesinger written in 1950, shortly after the first meeting of the Congress for Cultural Freedom in Berlin, Melvin Lasky tellingly asserted that "all that remains is really to build the democratic international," in direct reference to the equivalent international Communist organization (Ninkovich 1981: 66). From the very beginning, the model of a "democratic Comintern" was central to the emergence of an international field structured around the promotion of democracy. The organizational form taken by the U.S.-led democratic crusade of the 1950s was indeed the reflection of the enemy it was meant to defeat; it was itself a distant product of the same history and, in an indirect fashion, deeply shaped by the culture of Communism. It is no coincidence, therefore, that the concept of *propaganda* was also central to the whole effort. The defense and the promotion of democracy worldwide was based on the premise that, if the West represented a genuine form of democracy and guaranteed the rights of the working class better than any Communist regime, as the "democratic socialists" and the rest of the anti-Stalinist left firmly believed at the time, these qualities needed to be strongly upheld and contrasted with Soviet claims to a superior form of democracy and to a better defense of the interests of the working class.

In other words, as it was commonly argued at the time, truth needed propaganda.[21] It was not enough for the United States to be democratic or progressive or egalitarian or labor-friendly, one had to *persuade* others that this was the case. In that sense, the effort aiming at promoting democracy and, later, human rights, defined from the outset a field of *ideological* practices — a characteristic so deeply ingrained that it would continue to shape democratic efforts well after the collapse of Communism. It involved both the need to rebuild an ideology that could be defended, exported, discussed, circulated — the rediscovery of the tradition of liberalism in the late 1940s was indeed part of this process — and the need to deconstruct Soviet claims and Communist ideology in all its guises. In fact, the major achievement of the democratic crusade of the 1950s was certainly to pitch the conflict between the two dominant powers at the level of ideas, science, culture, or even the arts, thus tainting a vast array of cultural productions by subordinating them to the higher imperatives of the Great Game.

The Social Sciences and the Defense of Democracy

In this context, the social sciences became a strategic playing field, where societal models could be discussed, criticized, legitimated, or delegitimated.

It was also a field in which criticism of the Soviet Union and deconstruction of its social and economic claims could be done indirectly but very effectively, with the hope of achieving maximum impact on a social stratum usually well disposed toward Communism: intellectuals. Another reason explains the importance of science in the struggle against Communism. To a large extent, the cold war was also experienced as an opposition between truth and falsehood. The geopolitical conflict took immediately a moral or even epistemological dimension. In fact, the experience of the Moscow trials in the late thirties, during which various factions of the Bolshevik party were accused of conspiracy and treason by Stalin, represented a founding experience in this respect and contributed to shape the view of Communism as a regime based on deception among many intellectuals. The Trotskyist leader Max Shachtman, for instance, recalled in retrospect that "it was in the fight against the Moscow Trials, which occupied a good deal of the second half of the thirties, that so many American radical intellectuals learned to understand the modern communist state and movement" (Simon 1967: 42).

For many in the non-Communist left, therefore, the image of the Soviet Union was fixed during this episode and the need to denounce systematically the discrepancy between Communist discourse and Communist reality became an important aspect of political struggle.[22] In this context, contrasting validity claims in the scientific domain became a natural extension of the strategy of contrasting truth claims in the political domain. The sociological composition of the non-Communist left, which was more urban and elitist than the Communist organizations and comprised far more intellectuals (James Burnham, Sidney Hook, John Dewey, Seymour Martin Lipset, Daniel Bell, for instance, were all university professors) also contributed to the adoption of this strategy and to the extension of the cold war in the scientific and academic field.

In fact, throughout the cold war, the social sciences would serve strategic purposes, and countering Marxism was among the most important. The thread that runs from the early efforts aiming to impose the scientific method as a model for "empirical," "applied" social sciences to the quantitative and "behavioral" turn of the 1950s is indeed a consistent effort to oppose Marxism by fighting historicism in the academic field. These strategies made a major contribution to the production of a scientific ideology of "modernization," apt for exportation and deliberately conceived as an alternative to Marxist theories of social development. The major philanthropic foundations, such as the Rockefeller foundation, the Carnegie Corporation, and the Ford foundation, served to internationalize this learned anti-Communist strategy. By financing research programs abroad, in Europe and in developing countries, their aim was to "prevent Marxism from becoming the theoretical reference of all the advocates of social change" and, by opposing "ideological" or "globalizing" intellectual traditions, to "foster . . . institutional changes and policies deemed necessary in order to immunize [European countries] against the Communist temptation" (Pollak 1979: 56).[23]

Furthermore, the programs developed in occupied Germany by American authorities in the fields of science and culture had convinced foreign policy planners in Washington that academic and scientific policies were central components of a wider strategy of democratization.[24] These scientific programs were not separate from the wider political agenda of "State Department socialism." The promotion of empirical pragmatism in the social sciences was the external epistemological shell of a political ideology favoring social compromise over the development of social conflict and class struggle — in other words, of the very ideology of "democratic socialism" that most of the heterodox Marxist left had come to embrace in the 1950s, when it joined the fold of the anti-Communist liberal consensus and contributed its organizational skills and ideological talents to the internationalization of this consensus. In fact, it is no coincidence that socialist or social-democrat scholars, such as Paul Lazarsfeld, played a prominent role in these philanthropic strategies.

All these lines of thinking — the forsaking of revolutionary politics, a reformist strategy to improve working class conditions in a liberal democratic setting, the acceptance of the capitalist nature of the economy, the participation in the construction of the Welfare State, the indictment of Stalinism, the promotion of empirical social sciences as a tool for democratic and progressive social reform, as well as the vision of a movement that would point beyond capitalism and toward a co-managed welfare society — culminated in a thesis that probably captures best the political *Zeitgeist* of the 1950s and underlines the influential role of the leftist Cold Warriors in shaping it: the "end of ideology." What ended up as a commonplace of the social sciences was actually a carefully engineered ideological product, specifically crafted to be disseminated and discussed internationally. In that sense, its transformation into a topos of scientific discourse at the time was an undisputed sign of success.

Even though the topic emerged within the first discussions held by the Congress for Cultural Freedom at the time of its creation in 1950, the theme of the end of ideology was for all intents and purposes launched in 1955 at a conference the Congress had organized in Milan entitled "The Future of

Freedom." The participants were primarily drawn from the ranks of the various intellectual currents of the non-Communist left (Bell, Lipset, Hook, Schlesinger for instance) while their European counterparts came from a variety of political horizons, from ex-Communists (Arthur Koestler) to liberals (Raymond Aron) as well as conservatives (Friedrich Hayek).[25]

The end of ideology emerged as the consensus: as its core argument went, the process of modernization in the United States and, to a lesser extent, in Europe, resulted in the attenuation of ideological conflict. With the increasing rationalization of social life and the emergence of a welfare state mitigating and mediating between collective interests, class struggle was thought to be subsiding, and the clash of antagonistic worldviews tended to appear as a remnant of the past.[26] "The fundamental political problems of the industrial revolution have been solved," wrote Seymour Martin Lipset in his report on the conference: "the workers have achieved industrial and political citizenship; the conservatives have accepted the welfare state; and the democratic left has recognized that an increase in over-all state power carries with it more dangers to freedom than solutions for economic problems" (Lipset 1960: 406).

In such a context, class conflict and ideological discourses were bound to be transcended into a form of politics where the basic agreement on social ends made possible a rational analysis of the best means for attaining them. For the "end of ideology" thesis was the counterpart of a faith in the possibility of pragmatic social and economic reform carried out under the guidance of "value-free," applied social sciences. To a certain extent, it represented the spontaneous professional ideology of social scientists who conceived of themselves as key actors in the birth of the "good society," who embraced the Welfare State and got involved in the production of the knowledge necessary for implementing redistributive policies in an egalitarian society. It illustrated the nascent alliance of the social sciences and government that would culminate in the reformist administrations of Kennedy and Johnson, before being fundamentally challenged in the aftermath of the Vietnam war. The modern and responsible figure of the social scientist was directly opposed to the archaic one of the radical or revolutionary intellectual in need of "ideologies" or "utopias" for articulating his political action.

This technocratic ideology of the social sciences and the corresponding trend toward the professionalization of social reform also fitted perfectly the agenda of the philanthropic foundations which had sponsored such efforts since the early twentieth century in order to contain Socialist or Communist influence (Fischer and Forrester 1993; Dobkin Hall 1992). The end of ideology thus overlapped with a deliberate effort to de-ideologize Americanism by presenting it as a form of social modernization that was democratic, pragmatic, and rational (in fact, *the only* form of modernization), as opposed to Communism which was ideological — in other words, it was nothing other than the theory (and the ideology) of the liberal consensus.

If it reflected the new role assigned to the social sciences as a bulwark against Communism, the end of ideology also reflected the political evolution of most of the participants to the 1955 conference organized by the CCF. It was directly related to the situation of the non-Communist left in the 1950s, whose major political and intellectual leaders — whether they were Trotskyists, ex-Communists, Socialists, or something else — had come to embrace a form of social-democratic laborism as the only viable strategy for the American labor movement, and considered the participation in and the defense of democratic institutions as a political priority. The end of ideology thesis allowed the intellectuals linked to these political areas to rationalize this political evolution. Certainly, its main achievement was that it allowed most of them to read socialist meanings into the development of the postwar U.S. state. For some, like Lipset, it amounted to nothing less than "the very triumph of the democratic social revolution in the West" (1960: 406). As he would argue later, in the second edition of his work *Political Man*, he still "considered [himself] a man of the left," but added that he thought of the United States "as a nation in which *leftist values* predominate" (1963: xxi).[27] Americanism, in other words, made socialism superfluous, and leftists could therefore embrace it without any hesitation or regret.

For others, like Daniel Bell, the end of ideology implied a more ambiguous and skeptical view. As Howard Brick has shown in his superb study of Bell's social thought, the end of ideology reflected not only the retreat of the intellectuals into the political mainstream, but also an awareness that the ongoing crisis of both liberalism and socialism since the 1930s had not found a satisfactory political answer (Brick 1986: 194ff). Whether it was enthusiastic or clouded with doubts and contradictions, however, the endorsement of liberal democracy by the anti-Stalinist left represents the real social and political basis of the struggle for democracy and human rights.[28]

While the U.S. state apparatus was busy doing the "diplomatic and military" share of labor, to use Melvin Lasky's words, in Korea and elsewhere, the State Department socialists and their allies in the non-Communist left were in charge of organizing a global agitprop campaign for democracy and against Soviet totalitarianism. By joining the liberal consensus, even if their support was often qualified, they contributed their distinctive skills to the building of this international arena. All the defining characteristics of the field of democracy and human rights stem from this foundational moment: a strong internationalism, a faith in social progress through reform, a rhetoric of extending democracy in the economic sphere (or, as one would say today, in civil society), an ambiguous relation to capitalism, the constant denunciation of totalitarianism, the cult of political opposition and dissidence, the need for a democratic ideology, a political strategy buttressed by a strong intellectual agenda, an important role assigned to the social sciences in political struggles.

A Temporary Setback

And yet, this democratic crusade was a failure. The project of building a sort of Comintern in reverse was relatively short-lived, and defunct long before the dissolution of the International Association for Cultural Freedom, the CCF's successor, in 1977. Indeed, the crisis of the Congress for Cultural Freedom certainly represented the most visible symptom of this failure. In 1967, following the revelation by *Ramparts* magazine and the *New York Times* that the Congress was actually set up and secretly financed by the CIA, the organization lost its legitimacy as well as many prominent members, especially abroad. Although it survived for another ten years, as the International Association for Cultural Freedom and under the aegis of the Ford foundation, which replaced the CIA and its phony foundations as source of funding, it never really recovered from the blow. However, the crisis of the main international instrument used to further the cold war "democratic" campaign of the non-Communist left and the State Department reflects deeper, more structural contradictions in the overall project. This international project rested on the tactical alliance between the socially subordinate groups and the political sects comprising the anti-Stalinist left and the elitist and patrician governmental circles of the foreign policy establishment representing liberal anti-Communism. This alliance was sealed not only by a shared view of Communism but also by the complementary character of the strategic resources wielded by these two groups: state power on the one hand; intellectual, ideological and cultural hegemony on the other. In other words, the international democratic campaign to which the Old Left contributed its political know-how and its ideological talent rested entirely on the institutional advantage it drew form its association with the global strategy pursued by the U.S. administration and on its capacity to exert some degree of inside influence in the formulation of an ideology of U.S. foreign policy (as it had done at the time of the Truman doctrine). In that sense, and contrary to most of the assumptions found in political science and international relations theory, the field of democracy and human rights developed from the outset as an appendix of the field of state power.

Because of its precarious and exclusively tactical nature, however, this convergence of views was bound to be short-lived. It depended entirely upon the cohesion of the foreign policy establishment and, therefore, upon its capacity to reproduce itself socially and to preserve its political power. In the late sixties and early seventies, its ideological cement, liberal internationalism and the mechanisms of its social reproduction, were severely tested. The military escalation in Vietnam revealed another face of liberal internationalism and the involvement of the establishment in an atrocious secret war waged in the name of anti-Communism. The whole social and ideological structure of power was shaken, as the public realized that "the best and the brightest," to borrow the title of a best-selling journalistic account of the time, those who came from families which had provided generations of lawyers, bankers, or statesmen, who had been nurtured within the best educational institutions of the nation, who had embodied the solidity of the liberal consensus as a sort of national interest placed above the orientations of partisan administrations, were also the planners of massive high-tech bombings in a remote corner of the globe (Halberstam 1972; Bird 1998). In that sense, the Vietnam war shook the confidence in a whole system of policymaking. In addition, the administrative tools of benevolent social reform at home were now exposed as also those of mass killing abroad, thus calling into question the technocratic optimism that characterized the faith in the social sciences as a political and administrative instrument and the role of academics as policy advisors.

This crisis of the ideology of American foreign policy was also a crisis of its social foundations, as the democratization of higher education and the contemporary political radicalization of the campuses deeply affected the traditional circuits in which the policy elite was raised and trained. The "Harvard — Manhattan — Foggy Bottom corridor" ceased to function as the exclusive channel of recruitment for an elite whose privileged social status was thus converted into a merit-based entitlement to the exercise of government (Clough 1994). In many ways, the stability of the policy establishment previously reflected the continuity of its social domination. The government of the "wise men" was pretty much the government of a social caste. As David Halberstam wrote at the time, it was "a world where young men made their way up the ladder by virtue not just of their own brilliance and ability but also of who their parents were, which phone calls from which old friends had preceded their appearance in an office" (1972: 5). Such mechanisms of access to power fell apart in the late 1960s, in part under the pressure of structural changes in higher education. The 1960s saw the largest rise in university enrollment ever, with numbers surging from 3,639,847 in fall 1959 to 8,004,660 in fall 1969, a growth that would never be equaled thereafter.[29] The unrest and the radicalization of the campuses in the same period were one of the political expressions of this transformation, which accentuated further the crisis of liberalism. The demographic pressure exerted by these newcomers on the labor market also played a role, as a new generation of policy professionals, deprived of aristocratic entitlements but equipped with academic credentials, came to challenge the undisputed rule of an establishment made of enlightened amateur statesmen. All these changes converged and determined the crisis of the liberal establishment, which lost its cohesiveness, evolved into different political directions, and saw its composition change as it integrated a new generation perfectly aware that it could no longer operate in the global framework of the postwar struggle against totalitarianism. Anti-Communism ceased to be the cornerstone of foreign policy, or at least the ideology shared by foreign policy planners.

In this new context, the international crusade for democracy and against totalitarianism, as it had been elaborated and put into practice by the anti-Stalinist left, failed to keep pace with the changes in the field of state power and in the international arena. For the ideological cold warriors of the Old Left, the crisis of the liberal establishment resulted in the loss of their major institutional and political support — another powerful illustration of the subordinate position of the field of democracy and of its dependence upon the field of state power. The project of a global democratic campaign would eventually resurface in the 1980s, this time with the full support of the Reagan administration. Paradoxically, its promoters were the same individuals or, for the younger ones, the direct and legitimate heirs of the non-Communist left. Before analyzing the institutionalization and the professionalization of the field of democracy and human rights, therefore, it is necessary to take a step back and follow the complex political trajectory which led its early promoters from the prospect of revolution to that of neoconservative counter-revolution in the 1980s.

From the Old Left to Neoconservatism: The Leftist Condottieri of the Cold War

The emergence of an institutionalized field of democracy and human rights in the 1980s is the outcome of the successful reformulation of the old anti-totalitarian, anti-Communist ideological project in a completely new political context, dominated by the victory of Ronald Reagan, the military, moral and ideological rearmament of the United States, and the active dismantling of the social programs inherited from decades of liberal administration. In this context, a crusade for democracy was obviously characterized by a further emptying of its potential for economic and social progress, a complete disregard for any notion of egalitarianism (no matter how important it could have been in the 1950s), and an almost exclusive concern with the fight against Communism. Despite these important differences, the historical continuity with the old democratic crusade of the 1950s was extremely strong, both in terms of personnel and ideological outlook: it bore the unmistakable imprint of the old anti-Stalinist left. In order to understand the transformation of this global democratic project that runs from the late 1940s to the 1980s, therefore, it is necessary to analyze the social trajectory of the old anti-Stalinist left and to understand the internal logic of its paradoxical conversion to Reaganism.

This conversion is the endpoint not only of a long political trajectory, but also the ongoing political process which characterizes the history of the Old Left as a whole. All the historical studies on the subject — whether they are dealing with the "New York intellectuals" in general, or only a fraction of them, or the whole anti-Stalinist left — come to terms with this central aspect (Isserman 1993; Cooney 1986; Bloom 1986; Wald 1987). One could say indeed that the entire history of these political groups is merely a century-long conversion, a long rightward journey.

One of its peculiarities is that such a conversion did not take the form of a break with previous beliefs or of a sudden crisis — as it often does in the case of those who break with the Communist party and start a new career denouncing what they see in retrospect as a great "illusion."[30] Throughout their history and their political activity, on the contrary, members of the anti-Stalinist left have somehow remained constant and loyal to their ideals and they usually experienced their own trajectory as being entirely consistent and deprived of contradictions. In fact, the explanation of their conversion has not much to do with the abandonment of old ideals and the embracing of new ones: anti-Stalinism has remained an important principle guiding their political action and shaping the alternatives they faced, yet it has simply meant different things at different times. In other words, their move toward conservative positions was not so much programmed in their original political principles or in their social basis (as some authors have argued) as it resulted from the way they constantly reinterpreted the present situation with their theoretical and political instruments. Their principles of analysis, their political concepts, and their language remained formally the same, when their political meaning was changing. The peculiarity of this history is indeed, as Alan Wald notes, that "some elements of doctrine seem to remain identical from a formal point of view, precisely when their content is being transformed" (1987: 11). This point is fundamental for the purpose of our discussion, for it is the continuity of their political trajectory that made possible the preservation of a certain number of progressive political and ideological repertoires that would inform, at least rhetorically, their international practices even when these activists were already established neoconservatives.

The ideological matrix of the critique of totalitarianism and, later, of the international promotion of democracy in the whole postwar era originated in the anti-Stalinist Marxism that took root in the United States in the 1930s. New York, with its strong immigrant and working-class communities who had imported various strands of European socialism in their suitcases, was the intellectual and geographic center of radical politics at the time. With its socialist groups, its radical "soap-box" orators, its trade unions, its growing urban proletariat, the city was home to some of the most original political developments on the left during the interwar period. The conjunction of the economic Depression of the 1930s and the concentration of an immigrant labor force severely affected by it was the perfect breeding ground for various kinds of socialist and trade union movements. This is in fact the social background of many exponents of the old left. Seymour Martin Lipset, for instance, was the son of a printer and member of the typographical union. Daniel Bell was born in 1919 in Brooklyn; he joined the Young People Socialist League at 13, in part because his mother, as a worker, was away from home most of the day (Liebowitz 1985). Melvin Lasky was born in the Bronx, in an immigrant family (Coleman 1989: 16). Although he was born in Warsaw, Max Shachtman was taken to New York by his parents when he was hardly one year old, and grew up in Harlem, where his father made a living as a tailor (Drucker 1994).

In addition to their geographic concentration the attraction that socialism exerted on these working-class communities was the way it allowed the children of these immigrants to cope efficiently with their particular status as a minority in a country in which many opportunities were closed to them (in the 1920s and the 1930s, there were quotas in colleges and universities which were directly or indirectly aimed at limiting the number of Jews). Radical ideologies allowed them to combine a critique of American capitalism with a modernist critique of religion and traditional identities, and thus to refuse the dominant socioeconomic order from a position which did not imply a retreat into cultural particularism (Bloom 1986: 21–25). The Depression, in turn, brought many influential voices that did not belong to this background in tune with the 1930s radicalism of these outsiders.

The strong investment in education among these groups also furthered their politicization. At a time when most of higher education institutions had quotas and high tuition fees, young men from a Jewish immigrant background had not much choice as to where to study. In New York, however, some institutions had no entry quotas and were tuition-free, such as the Brooklyn College or the City College New York (CCNY). City College, in particular, played a crucial role in the intellectual formation of several generations of anti-Stalinist Marxists, among them Sidney Hook, Max Shachtman, Jay Lovestone, Irving Howe, Nathan Glazer, Irving Kristol, Daniel Bell, Seymour Martin Lipset, Melvin Lasky, and Alfred Kazin. In the midst of the Depression, CCNY functioned as a place of political socialization and radicalization. While Communists formed certainly the most important group at CCNY — reflecting their position on the left in general — the college was also home to "the much smaller but clearly visible and highly articulate Trotskyists" (Page 1982: 70).[31]

Usually gathering in alcove 1 of the cafeteria (the Communists could be found in alcove 2), the anti-Stalinists comprised indeed Trotskyists, but also Socialists and old-style Social Democrats. They debated the social and political issues of the day as well as the *vexata quaestio* of the nature of the Soviet regime, and looked to such mentors as Sidney Hook, Max Schachtman, Norman Thomas or James Cannon for political guidance. Both because of his brilliance and his involvement in the youth organizations of the socialist party, Schachtman, more than any other political organizer on the left, achieved intellectual influence at CCNY, where he occasionally gave a speech or participated in a debate, and managed to recruit numerous followers. In particular, because of this structural opposition between anti-Stalinist political clubs and the Communist students, CCNY turned the struggle against Communism into the founding intellectual and political experience for many of its alumni.

As we have already seen, the anti-Stalinist left of the 1930s contributed to the development of a critique of Soviet "totalitarianism" which led to the complete rejection of the Soviet Union as a political reference and to a shift toward liberal anti-Communism. Within the whole spectrum of the Marxist critiques of Stalinism, however, the analyses of Hook, Eastman, Burnham, or Shachtman already represented the "right-wing" (as compared to those of other anti-Stalinist Marxists, such as Otto Bauer or Leon Trotsky, who still considered that the Soviet experiment was, at least in part, socialistic). Far from being merely academic, the "Russian question," that is, the analysis of the nature of the Soviet state, was directly consequential in terms of political choices and orientation. In fact, the preexisting divergences around this issue would surface in 1940s, when Max Shachtman broke with Trotsky and decided to speak against the war — as Lenin had done before and during the First World War: because in his view the Soviet Union could not be described as a "degenerate workers' state" and had nothing socialist, it should not benefit from the support, however qualified and critical, of genuine revolutionaries. With the new course endorsed by Shachtman in 1940, the non-Communist left as a whole had completed its revision of the attitude to be adopted toward the Soviet Union, and moved to an uncompromising position. In that sense, the 1930s can be characterized as a decade of "anti-Stalinist radicalization" for most of the non-Communist left, to use Massimo Salvadori's apt expression (1981: 124). Outsiders politically, and often socially, the members of these groups would paradoxically move to the center of the political mainstream after the war, as a prelude to a protracted drift toward conservatism that would be completed in the 1970s.

There are several explanations for this political conversion. A more sociological one insists on the social origins of these leftists and on the gradual de-radicalization corresponding to their upward social mobility, while a more political one pays greater attention to the complex interplay between long-term political strategies and their translation into tactics fitting the present situation.[32] If the social background is obviously important in explaining certain characteristics of the various anti-Stalinist movements and, more generally, their position within the overall structure of American society, it certainly cannot be taken as a deterministic element mechanically imposing political choices or containing in a nutshell the whole future evolution of these circles. The Communist party, for instance, included many members with a very similar background — poor, lower- or middle class, immigrant background, etc. — who never evolved toward conservatism. Conversely, there exist social profiles in the non-Communist left absolutely similar to those of the future "neoconservatives" that nevertheless remained firmly in the liberal camp.[33]

If the social grounding of the non-Communist left is important, it is in a less direct fashion. A party like Shachtman's Socialist Workers Party (later simply the Workers Party before its merger into the Socialist Party), for instance, comprising mostly urban, well-educated, rather intellectual and politically elitist figures, and secondarily representing workers traditionally based on old trades, never really managed to recruit among the industrial working-class at large. It remained in fact pretty much a party of intellectuals, and the strategy of "colonization" of the industrial world launched by Shachtman in the 1950s merely meant in practice that some cadres of the Workers Party moved into the bureaucratic apparatuses of the AFL-CIO, where they often dealt with organizational work at the national or international level, joining Lovestoneites in the organizational warfare against Communism within and without trade unions worldwide.[34]

The move toward the "vital center" of American politics after the Second World War has also more political roots going back to the interwar period. For many members of the generation reaching political maturity in the 1930s, the Depression era was also that of a generalized crisis of progressive ideologies: liberalism was radically challenged by the economic crisis, while prospects for socialism were deeply affected by the failure of revolutionary movements in Europe and the degeneration of the Soviet regime under Stalin. This historical context certainly placed a premium on the more cautious strategies, those that sought to prepare the ground in the hope of an eventual reopening of revolutionary perspectives and to work on more immediate organizational or even material benefits in the meantime, even if that meant a certain accommodation with those aspects of the dominant order that served such strategies. This was, for instance, the strategy pursued by Shachtman's Workers Party and its followers in the Young People's Socialist League (YPSL — pronounced "yip-sel") throughout the 1950s: the institutional and legal framework of democracy was a precondition for building a strong labor movement and was therefore a crucial asset that ought to be defended.

Indeed, one of the factors accounting for the rightward evolution of the old left has to do with its changing relation with the liberal democratic order. Beyond circumstantial or tactical political reasons related to specific groups or individuals, the 1940s and the 1950s are characterized by a radical change in the dominant intellectual representations of liberal democracy. Not incidentally, this cultural shift has its center in the intellectual and academic strata of the non-Communist left, and it is reflected in their scientific production. At its most general level, it corresponds to an evolution from a position which sees democratic institutions as a mere instrument for working-class politics to a position which considers them as a progressive heritage with a normative, and no longer instrumental, value. This can be seen for instance in the case of Lipset, but Lipset's is actually only a single instance in a much broader and collective cultural passage.

A Democracy Worth Defending: Scientific Premises of Political Conversion

The postwar emergence of an internationalist discourse in defense of democracy among the anti-Stalinist left cannot be separated from a wider intellectual context characterized by an intense cross-fertilization between Marxism and the liberal tradition in the United States. In that sense, this international democratic project was not only dictated by the necessity of containing Communism, although this rationale was certainly important, but it also developed out of its own, internal dynamics. This episode was a direct consequence of a crucial event in the realm of the social sciences with far-reaching consequences for their subsequent development: the movement of intellectual and academic migration from Europe to the United States and, in particular, to the New York academic scene.[35] This migration had also a strong political content: it represented the migration of the Marxist and socialist European traditions and, what is perhaps the most important and paradoxical side effect, it helped to reconfigure Americanism as a progressive and democratic force in the eyes of a number of socialist intellectuals.

Throughout the 1930s and the 1940s, many Austrian, German, and other Central European academics and social scientists had sought refuge from Nazism in the United States. The safe haven they could hope to find there, as well as the active role of some institutions in providing support (among them the Rockefeller foundation, which developed special assistance programs in the 1930s) made the United States an obvious destination. In New York, scholars such as Franz Neumann, Karl Mannheim, Emil Lederer, and Paul Lazarsfeld left a lasting imprint on the institutions at which they found a provisional or permanent position — often at Columbia University or at the New School for Social Research. There, Marxists, socialists, social democrats, would often collaborate with trade unions, reformist political parties, or administrative agencies, these refugees represented the intellectual work-force of Weimarian social reform. Most of the time, they had been perse-cuted in their home countries for their political affiliations, but also as Jews, or as exponents of "non-German" scientific traditions in various disciplines, such as sociology, political science, law, or economics, and they were often barred from teaching when their life was not directly threatened.

In their new environment, and in spite of the support from which they sometimes benefited, these social scientists found a tight and relatively closed academic market. Their status as migrants (and for many of them as Jews) was a liability. As Paul Lazarsfeld would note later, U.S. academe at the time was not deprived of a certain "genteel anti-Semitism" (Lazarsfeld 1969: 300). They often had to accept positions inferior to those they had occupied in their home countries. Furthermore, the more established dis-ciplines in the social sciences, like legal and political theory, were the ex-clusive property of a homegrown academic aristocracy: as a result, the new-comers tended to concentrate in research areas that were subordinate and marginal to mainstream teachings. While the study of society and institu-tions was still dominated by a "legal-formal approach" mostly concerned with constitutional and historical erudition on politics, and overall very fac-tual and descriptive,[36] the refugee scholars usually dealt with less noble ob-jects (social stratification, market research, electoral behavior, broadcasting studies, survey research, and so forth) in a much more empirical fashion, importing new methods and tools such as the use of statistics or other quan-titative instruments.

Once again, the case of Paul Lazarsfeld is emblematic, since his name would soon be associated with the internationalization of empirical social sciences (Pollak 1979). But sociology was not the only discipline affected. In economics, for instance, they contributed to no small extent to the de-velopment of mathematical modeling.[37] These changes in the nature of social scientific work and in particular the empirical orientation of research were already well developed in the Weimar period. In part, they can be related to the type of research that these scholars had often done for trade unions or political parties. In part, however, it can also be related to a strategy for coping with the subordinate positions in the field of learning they found in the United States. The experience of exile was indeed an experience of adaptation to a substantially different cultural and academic context. As Lewis Coser rightly observed, adjustment was easier for engineers, physicists and other technically trained specialists for whom the mathematical lan-guage of the natural sciences remained unchanged across cultural boundaries (Coser 1984: 6). But for social scientists, more dependent on national academic traditions and institutional contexts, the obstacles were much greater. With a glance toward their colleagues from the natural sciences, the effort to make social science research more reliant on formal and mathematical instruments was to a certain extent an answer to the problem of insertion in a new intellectual environment.

But the contribution of these academic migrants to "empirical" and "applied" social science also stemmed from other concerns, specific to their own biographical and political trajectory. It was related, in other words, to a preoccupation with the danger of totalitarianism and with the role of science in a democratic order. In some disciplines, their role in developing such an empirical conception of social science research can be traced to the hope that reliance on formal hypotheses open to statistical confirmation would be a bulwark against the intrusion of political ideologies in scientific practice and discourse — to the "hope of building a *wertfrei* social science," as two historians of economics have put it (Carver and Leijonhufvud 1987: 181). In the investment in formal, statistical and comparative methods, the personal and professional strategies of adjustment to a new context thus linked up with the more general project of establishing the social sciences as autonomous from politics but also as a guide for democratic politics. Method, in that sense, was tightly connected to a process of substantive political interrogations.

In the fields which are most relevant to our historical reconstruction, such as sociology and political science, the refugee scholars imported a type of Marxist analysis that had been destabilized by authoritarian developments throughout Europe and by the experience of Nazism in Germany. A common effort to understand the role of the middle classes in the ascent of Nazism runs throughout their works and contributes to their specific outlook. What was at stake in their research was the possibility of developing instruments and concepts for understanding the social, political, and cultural identity of recently constituted classes that, as it turned out, did not fit the binary Marxist scheme. Well into the 1920s, indeed, the development of the new middle classes was still expected to validate orthodox Marxist theory, as their impoverishment was supposed to push them toward the proletariat and against the bourgeoisie. Instead, they provided one of the major social bases of the National Socialism and contributed to the collapse of democracy. The furthering of this research program thus evolved, at least implicitly, toward a critical reassessment of Marxism.

At the same time, the refugee scholars reflected upon the failure of Weimar democracy and the atomization of the middle classes into amorphous "masses" mobilized by totalitarian movements from a specific position — American academic institutions — which deeply informed their later outlook. Indeed, they continued their work in a country where these social strata had reached an unprecedented level of development but nevertheless coexisted with robust democratic institutions. The perspective of their political sociology was immediately *comparative*, and this comparative dimension was motivated by the fact (and sometimes the fear) that the Depression could trigger similar developments: are American middle classes comparable to the German ones? Can the economic crisis, unemployment, and social unrest determine a fascist turn? Are class structure and class conflicts comparable? Why hasn't the combination of a strong middle class and economic depression resulted into an American form of fascism? These questions dovetailed with the interrogations of many leftist intellectuals, as we have seen. They also implied a considered assessment of American society and democracy, and one of their consequences was to give currency to the idea that American society was somehow different, that its middle class played a central role in producing political stability and consolidating the democratic order.

From a cultural viewpoint, the U.S. middle class was thought to be cemented by a populist ideology and therefore opposed both to big business and to socialism. These social strata thus appeared as a bulwark against any concentration of monopoly capital or against any capture of the state by capital, that is, against the possibility of fascism. They were also perceived as progressive. All this strand of social research tended ultimately to configure the middle classes as the real social basis, the bearers and the defenders of democracy. This empirically informed discovery of the democratic virtues of the middle class also corresponded to the progressive political evolution of the refugee social scientists. By putting Marxist theory at the service of a democratic and egalitarian interpretation of the social structure in America, they actually opted for "liberalism as a guiding principle for social policies and political technologies" (Salvati 2000: 142).

The legacy of this scientific production found a very receptive audience within the anti-Stalinist left, and it resonated with its political and intellectual anxieties. Concentrated around Columbia University (which, at the time, had many students coming from City College or Brooklyn College) and the New School for Social Research, many émigré scholars occupied positions close to those of many exponents of the non-Communist left. Whether as students or colleagues, the latter were often exposed to their teaching — a teaching which opened a specific path out of political marginality and toward the dominant political culture. This intellectual affinity was reinforced by other common traits, such as a similar experience of the crisis of Marxism, an immigrant background, or a common political tradition.

The role that refugee scholars had often played in trade unions or social-democratic parties in their home countries was another characteristic that made the American Trotskyists, Socialists, or Social Democrats very much attuned to their theoretical production. The strong intellectual influence exercised, directly or indirectly, by the Austro-German émigrés on the left can be seen in the subsequent production of some socialist or social-democratic exponents of the academic generation coming of age in the late 1940s. It is reflected in particular in the topics — social stratification, revolution, class divides, radical politics, electoral analysis — and the instruments — surveys, statistics, and so forth — privileged by sociologists such as Seymour Lipset, Daniel Bell, or Alvin Gouldner. This whole line of research on democracy and class structure, originating in the intellectual migration to the United States, provides the background as well as the main conceptual articulations, which eased the non-Communist left into the liberal consensus of the 1950s. It made possible a "progressive" interpretation of postwar societal trends, which at the time fitted perfectly the political strategies of "democratic socialists" and Max Shachtman's Trotskyists.

In this respect, the writings of Lipset are highly revealing: not incidentally, his extolling of the virtues of the middle classes, characterized by a "belief in secular reformist gradualism" (Lipset 1963: 45) coexists in his work with the emerging theme of "working class authoritarianism," two topics that reflect the contemporary move away from working-class politics and the adoption of a very moderate stance. More fundamentally, and less explicitly, the encounter of the left with the middle classes and American exceptionalism (although this theme was exclusively academic, Shachtman's strategy, which consisted in building a labor movement taking American particularities into account, was nothing less than the translation of American exceptionalism into concrete politics) allowed the old left to discover the dynamic and reformist virtues of a form of capitalism deprived of feudal past, based on mobility and achievement rather than social extraction. In fact, one could say with Pierre Grémion that in the eyes of many leftists "America appeared as a society liberated from bourgeois obstruction to productive forces, a society where capitalism paradoxically gave a content to the idea of permanent revolution" (Grémion 1995, 315).[38] America, as Hannah Arendt would soon proclaim, was after all a revolutionary country.[39] By depicting postwar American democracy as pregnant with far-reaching reformist possibilities in the field of industrial democracy, redistribution of wealth and rising living standards of the working class — sometimes with radical or even utopian accents envisaging a near future where the "abundant society" would free everybody from the realm of necessity by satisfying needs (Brick 1998) — postwar social sciences produced a powerful rationalization for the simultaneous drift of the non-Communist left toward more conservative positions and for its involvement in the international fight against Communism in the name of democracy. For the sake of socialism, even if this reference had become purely nominal, American democracy was worth defending.

From Revolution to Counter-revolution

The 1960s and the Vietnam war shattered the strategic alliance between the anti-Stalinist left and the foreign policy establishment. The emergence of the New Left helped to marginalize further the remaining strands of the Old Left, demonstrating as well that the Old Left's agenda was out of touch with the deep transformations of American society. In fact, the main explanation for the drift of the Old Left toward conservative positions during this period lies in the opposition to the New Left (Isserman 1987).

In this respect, the evolution of most Shachtmanites from Trotskyism toward right-wing social democracy in the course of the 1960s is paradigmatic and highlights the structural problems encountered by the Old Left. While Shachtman's political strategy in the late 1950s and early 1960s had consisted in merging with the Socialist Party and working toward the constitution of an independent labor party attracting the progressive and liberal fractions of the Democratic party, his views changed by the mid-1960s, when he decided to work from within the Democratic party and in view of its stability, as his ties to the hierarchy of the AFL-CIO became stronger (Drucker 1994). The rise of social movements appeared as an opportunity to further this project. The "realignment" strategy, as it came to be called, sought to harness the civil rights movement and to link it to labor and to the liberal areas of the Democratic Party. This implied among other things that the social movements of the 1960s remain compatible with the conservative national and international political agenda of the AFL-CIO, a task which involved fighting any tendency toward radicalization — or, in other words, fighting the New Left. As a result, the generation of young activists who joined Shachtman in the 1960s, and in particular the Young People's So-

cialist League that was reconstituted in 1964 under the control of Shachtman's young followers (such as Carl Gershman, Joshua Muravchik, Tom
Kahn, or Rachelle Horowitz) actually joined a movement whose principal
preoccupation was to contain the New Left as it contained Communism.
"Newcomers," as Wald observed, "were assimilated into a group drifting in
a conservative direction" (1987: 11). They were also assimilated into a political movement which would soon support U.S. intervention in Vietnam,
which Max Shachtman interpreted as "a progressive war against Stalinism"
(ibid.: 328).

As the prevailing principle orienting political action, anti-Communism
had become the sole intellectual compass of the Old Left: the liberation
movements in the Third World, radical students movements, new social
movements, were gradually perceived as different expressions of the same
global Communist threat. "By the time Shachtman died in late 1972," writes
his biographer Peter Drucker, "he had helped define a distinctive organizational and ideological strand in U.S. social democracy, one that is almost
unique in the world. On international issues — the Middle East and Central
America, as well as Vietnam — latter-day Shachtmanites have consistently
been on the right-wing of international social democracy. But they have
combined their right-wing international perspective with a profession of
Marxist orthodoxy that is unusual among social democrats, founded on a
strong identification with the working class" (Drucker 1994: 289).

They were, in other words, double agents. By supporting the Vietnam
war and opposing Third World liberation movements or domestic forms of
resistance and rebellion, the social democrats reached the logical outcome
of their previous evolution and of their vision of democracy: they considered
that the extension of American institutions and structures was the necessary
precondition for the building of a strong labor movement and the organization of the working class. A long-standing ideological pillar of the anti-
Stalinist left, anti-imperialism itself started to become suspect. Instead, Americanism had become the intermediate stage of the transition to Socialism.

In this perspective, the crisis of the establishment after Vietnam and the
emergence of political expressions of the New Left was experienced not as
a mere setback but as a real felony perpetrated by the elites. The perplexities
which appeared within the foreign policy elite overlapped with the crisis of
the liberal ideology which ensured the ideological cohesion of these ruling
circles. The publication of *Foreign Policy*, a new journal created in order to
"revise" goals, means and responsibilities, shows how this revisionist challenge to the more traditional voice of the Council on Foreign Relations,

Foreign Affairs, actually emanated from the same ranks and expressed a widespread ideological and political disarray among foreign policy planners (Ehrman 1995: 24–25).

The wavering confidence in the principles that had guided U.S. foreign policy since the end of the Second World War meant that the functional relation and the division of political labor between the non-Communist left and the foreign policy establishment was starting to fall apart. The virulent anti-Communism of the old Trotskyists-turned-social democrats was no longer in line with a foreign policy agenda that was being entirely reformulated by a new generation of policymakers. The earlier exposure of the connections between the Congress for Cultural Freedom and the CIA had considerably weakened one of their main international ideological conduits (the other one being the trade unions). Furthermore, the philanthropic foundations started to sponsor alternative or heterodox political and scientific discourses in an attempt at understanding the crisis of liberalism. The Ford foundation, for instance, under the aegis of McGeorge Bundy, financed the work of Samuel Bowles and Herbert Gintis on post-liberalism or even neo-Marxist scholars abroad, such as some exponents of the dependency school of development economics in Latin America.

While these strategies illustrated the pragmatism of the foreign policy establishment and its capacity to adapt to changing situations, they were clearly at odds with the increasingly intransigent anti-Communism of the Old Left. The 1972 electoral primaries epitomized this increasing discrepancy between the right-wing socialists and the Democratic Party which had been for some time their natural political environment. While George McGovern, the candidate closer to the New Left, became the frontrunner, most of the socialists and social democrats behind Shachtman chose to support instead Henry Jackson (D, Washington), a candidate close to the military-industrial complex and representing a return to a Trumanian vision of global struggle against Communism. These changes within the party contributed to alienate the Shachtmanites from the new policy elites.

The new course in international affairs, the perspective of a new "world order" based on increased cooperation among nations, including the USSR, the political decision to pursue disarmament negotiations under the Carter administration, the recognition of social and economic progress as a basic human right, the perceived decline of American hegemony all seemed to converge into a general capitulation in front of Communism. There is a clearly visible nostalgia of the Trumanian tradition in the writings of the exponents of the Old Left. Paradoxically, the direct heirs of proletarian and revolutionary internationalism ended up extolling the virtues of the old foreign policy establishment of the cold war and, symbolically, reclaiming its ideological legacy. Daniel Bell, for instance, wrote in 1976 about the passing of the old establishment that had presided over the foreign policy and security issues in the postwar era, "an establishment which was confident of itself . . . [representing] a milieu for leadership — the Wall Street legal firms and investment companies" (Steinfels 1979: 248). Carl Gershman, one of Shachtman's latter-day disciples, expresses a similar attitude in an article published in *Commentary* in 1980: he deplored that "with the passing of this establishment, the bipartisan consensus which had sustained U.S. foreign policy and defined its purposes for a generation disappeared, leaving a paralyzing residuum of division and demoralization" (Gershman 1980: 13).

By becoming a majority within the Socialist party and parting with the anti-war currents gathered around Michael Harrington after the 1972 convention, the right-wing social democrats eventually gave birth to the small party Social Democrats USA, thus completing their odyssey toward conservatism. Although technically affiliated with the Socialist International, they already constituted a "neo"-conservative opposition to the Carter administration. This opposition took the shape of a domestic extension of the international fight for democracy that had been one of the political pillars in the ideology of these movements since the late 1940s. Indeed, the critique of the penetration of New Left ideas and personnel in the administration mobilized old themes inherited from the Trotskyist critique of Stalinism as the undemocratic rule of a bureaucracy, and in particular from Shachtman's re-elaboration of it under the guise of "bureaucratic collectivism." The idea that state power had been preempted in the United States by a "new class" of policy professionals and liberal intellectuals catering for themselves (as the Bolshevik state had been preempted by a "new class" of professional party bureaucrats) cannot be separated from this polemic context.[40]

Elaborated by a whole tradition of dissident Marxist critiques of Communist regimes (such as Milovan Djilas' in Yugoslavia), the theory of the New Class implied that democracy was under threat externally as well as internally. At home, the incumbent class was too liberal, too soft on Communism, not because it was naive but because it was itself suspect of totalitarian behavior. Even mild social reformism was thus condemned as a sign of "totalitarian temptation," which future Reagan appointee at the UN and ideological ally of the right-wing social democrats Jeane Kirkpatrick defined as the temptation to believe that "the institutions, the lives, and even the characters of almost everyone could be reordered" (Ehrman 1995: 119). The conceptual framework of the New Class also facilitated the identification of the anti-Communist champions of democracy with dissidents in the Eastern bloc. In the words of Carl Gershman, speaking about the group of activists from the Social Democrats USA who would later contribute to create the National Endowment for Democracy (NED), "today the NED might be looking for *the most authentic, devoted democrats in uncertain situations. We were those kind of people here*: marginal, in a way, because we were operating in a small political group, but we had access to important institutions, like AFL-CIO. And in a certain sense, also, to the broad political structures."[41] This analogy was reinforced by the actual relationships between these anti-Communist circles and Soviet or east European dissidence, developed through the mediation of Leopold Labedz, the editor of *Survey* magazine.[42] This subordination of domestic politics to the overarching framework of the international struggle against Communism bears witness to the considerable rigidity of this ideological scheme and of its role as a model for the neoconservative heirs of the Old Left.

The 1970s were a time of internal exile for these political outsiders whose heyday had gone with the heroic days of the Congress for Cultural Freedom. With their political influence waning, the perspective of a strong social and political build-up disappearing in the succession of internal splits, and being at odds with the administration, they moved toward positions of ideological and organizational work in the trade union bureaucracies and in the policy research centers and various think tanks, in particular the American Enterprise Institute (Nathan Glazer, Joshua Muravchik, Jeane Kirkpatrick). Changes in the policymaking context were certainly an opportunity for them. The end of the liberal consensus and the ensuing ideological fragmentation of the policy elite contributed to diversifying the supply of policy advice and research. The whole field of policy expertise moved toward a pluralization of expertise, as new foundations and think tanks mushroomed, updating the old model of the Brookings Institution or the Ford Foundation. A more adversarial style of policy research replaced the previous nonpartisan and nonideological model of expertise.

This new kind of policy advocacy sought to generate policy coalitions not on the basis of "nonideological, scientific, rational" problem-solving as before, but through ideological combativeness. The crisis of the liberal consensus had also affected the tools of policy reform, already weakened by new development in the social sciences underlying the epistemic uncertainty inherent to policy making (e.g. H. Simons). The previous model of societal modernization under the guidance of experts and planners came under attack, and this attack took the form of a critique of technocracy which dovetailed with the denunciation of a New Class of undemocratic liberal technocrats monopolizing governmental office.

The theme of the "technocratic takeover" of America, indeed, was frequently raised by the neoconservatives who increasingly considered themselves as a "counter-establishment" (Blumenthal 1986). Savvy and skilled ideologues, well positioned in conservative think tanks, close to a number of journals and magazines such as *Commentary, The American Scholar,* or *The Public Interest,* the heirs of the old left thus contributed to no small extent to the transformation of the "policy knowledge industry" in the 1970s and to the emergence of a competitive market for ideas and ideological productions, which Ronald Reagan would be able to tap successfully (J.A. Smith 1991; Stone 1996). After having entered the Democratic Party from the left, the Shachtmanites and their allies left it toward the right. By the end of the decade, they were posed for their discreet entrance in the new Republican administration.[43]

Coming from a political tradition strongly linked to the labor apparatuses, but having moved closer to the business circles which understood the political benefits they could make by financing the new think tanks and foundations at the cutting edge of the offensive against the political legacy of the New Left, this generation of political activists found itself in the best position to embody a revived form of classical foreign policy bipartisanship in the eighties. Cemented by a common ideological background, a sense of historical entitlement to preserve the legacy of early liberal internationalism, and a cold war camaraderie, these political networks imported their old international agenda of "democracy promotion" into government. The Social Democrats USA, as we will see in the next chapter, represented one of the main political channels through which the foreign policy culture of the "Old Left" was conveyed into the administration during the 1980s, shaping the most fundamental aspects of its crusade for "democracy." In particular, they represented a militant, fervently internationalist and revolutionary political culture, inherited from a leftist past. Although it was emptied of its substance, this culture transformed the style of foreign policy and contributed, in many respects, to making Reaganism a revolutionary or, rather, counter-revolutionary force — where counter-revolutionary should be understood not as a simple conservative return to things as they used to be but, literally, a "revolution in reverse" which leaves "nothing unchanged" and thrives on the same preconditions as revolution itself (Virno 1988: 638–669). The new centrality of "democracy promotion" in U.S. foreign policy is precisely a symptom of this. Trained in the Marxist tradition, having been "professional revolutionaries" was not the worst preparation for becoming dissident "policy professionals" in the 1970s and "democracy experts" in the 1980s.

2 The Field of Democracy and Human Rights: Shaping a Professional Arena Around a New Liberal Consensus

With the active support of the newly elected Reagan administration, the neoconservative strategy of a crusade for democracy based on cold war internationalism was essentially picked up from where it had been set down in the mid-1960s, when the behind-the-scenes role of the CIA in funding the Congress for Cultural Freedom was revealed. Indeed, the democracy promotion programs of the 1980s were created almost exclusively by networks of policy activists, organizers, and other cold war ideologues trained in the old political tradition of Trotskyism, "State Department socialism," and right-wing Social Democracy. In establishing the National Endowment for Democracy and in shaping Ronald Reagan's human rights policy, the specific contribution of neoconservative ideologues was to reformulate the old, traditional notion of national interest — in the narrow, Kissingerian sense of geopolitical interests — into the *idealistic and universalistic language of human rights*. As a result the traditional doctrine of realism took the new and powerful form of morality, while the deployment of American power became equated with progress in terms of human rights.

The new administration also created a continuum between an internationalist and progressive tradition, however perverted and conservatized, and Reagan's policy of global assertion of U.S. national interests. This alliance between political networks embodying a very ideological understanding of "democracy" or "human rights" and the state apparatus itself was similar to the one that had existed in the 1950s between the non-Communist left and the State Department or the CIA; it actually reproduced it under another form, albeit with different actors. The main difference, however, was that the democratic crusade of the 1950s was based upon the ideological cohesion of the foreign policy establishment. Of course, in the early 1980s, many of the anti-Communist policy activists coming from the Old Left, often affiliated with labor organizations or social-democratic groups, could be the symbol of a sort of bipartisan consensus once they were associated with the Reagan administration. But anti-Communism was not enough to cement this alliance, and their own drift to the right somewhat weakened their claim to represent a wide and far-reaching political consensus.

The real reconstitution of a functional equivalent to the consensus of the 1950s actually required, thirty years later, the elaboration of a new ideological framework that could encompass both the emancipatory aspirations of the New Left and the hegemonic projects of the incumbent Right. The twin pillars on which this new framework was based were democracy and human rights. Democracy, as we have seen, was an old battle cry for the imperial policies of the "State Department Socialists" since the early days of the cold war. Finally in office, their disciples were now in position to wage this battle. The issue of human rights had developed outside the cold war ideological apparatus, in a supranational context, and was often used to curb state power.[1] Moreover, as a principle informing foreign policy, human rights was associated with the Carter administration and therefore considered to be a political legacy of the New Left and of the 1960s.

The political strategy of the neoconservatives consisted in successfully capturing this theme and in contesting the virtual monopoly of liberals over human rights issues. By doing so, they sought both to deprive their adversaries of a critical weapon, and to capitalize on human rights as an instrument of legitimation for their own foreign policy. An informal network of philanthropic foundations, NGOs, and university research centers had been the site of a coordinated effort at institutionalizing human rights independently from and sometimes against U.S. foreign policy. With the emergence of a distinctive neoconservative human rights doctrine, human rights became, according to Yves Dezalay and Bryant Garth, "the stake of a political struggle between the incumbent holders of state power and a rather broad coalition that br[ought] together the most liberal fraction of the establishment and a more militant left coming out of the civil rights movement (ACLU, NAACP. . . .)" (Dezalay and Garth 1998b: 33). This struggle contributed to shape the options, the strategies, the definitions of human rights that the different participants invested in it, as well as the institutions and the activist networks they created. The whole field of democracy and human rights directly developed out of this struggle. Furthermore, for the neoconservatives, developing a human rights policy also meant situating their action in the continuity of the policy Carter had initiated — despite their very strong criticisms about the way in which that policy had been conducted.[2]

This symbolic continuity, which has been overlooked, contributed to the production of a hegemonic ideological framework around which a wide consensus could be articulated. The success of the National Endowment for Democracy and of similar initiatives was to mobilize not only cold war networks but also individuals coming from a militant, anti-imperialist, liberal tradition extremely remote from the political tradition which had produced the neoconservative movement. In other words, the field of democracy and human rights that took shape in the 1980s was the framework in which a new "liberal consensus" was possible.

These political and ideological struggles for the definition of human rights and the use of foreign policy in the defense of "democracy," however, are only part of the story. The powerful process of professionalization that has transformed and expanded these activities needs to be considered as well. With the creation of specific institutions and *ad hoc* university curricula, the production of a body of knowledge and techniques for promoting democracy or making human rights more effective, and the recruitment of personnel outside of the policy circles who pioneered these activities, the promotion of democracy has gradually moved away from its very ideological origins. In their own, distinctive ways, institutions such as the NED or Human Rights Watch have been at the cutting edge of this process of professionalization. Professionalism evokes images of neutrality, nonpartisanship, and value-free technical skills that are the opposite of the kind of ideological warfare that was first encapsulated in the idea of a crusade for democracy. Paradoxically, however, the ideological struggles opposing different conceptions of human rights have facilitated a shift toward professionalism. To a large extent, the development of the human rights movement was strongly correlated with its capacity to mediate between opposed conceptions, and to occupy a strategic position of equidistance between a purely instrumental conception of human rights which subordinated them to the needs of U.S. foreign policy and a substantive conception of human rights which put political/civil and economic/social rights on equal footing. It is on this strategy, for instance, that Human Rights Watch built its credibility, opposing the idea of economic and social "rights" as well as the selective denunciation of human rights abuse by the Reagan administration (Neier 2003: xxix–xxxiii). Without contested issues and debates about the nature or the political use of human rights, there wouldn't have been the same opportunity for building professional expertise. Political and ideological struggles, in that sense, are the ground on which and against which processes of professionalization take place.

In addition, professionalism often serves a strategy of social *reproduction*. For instance, the end of the cold war put an end to one of the main *raisons d'être* of an institution such as the National Endowment for Democracy and weakened its position in the field of foreign policy making, as the defense of democracy was an ideological issue that had arisen in the 1950s and that had been reformulated in the 1980s in the perspective of a global confrontation with Communism. It also revealed the political fragility of an agency created by activists whose trajectory and whose precise political stand were not clearly understood by everybody in the Congress.[3] The policy community in Washington, on the other hand, was divided over the question of whether such an agency should survive the fall of Communism.[4] By distancing itself somewhat from the anti-Communist struggle of the beginnings and focusing instead on the "technical" problems inherent to democratization processes, the NED contributed to the professionalization of the field of democracy and human rights. Among other things, this strategy of professionalism was also meant to stabilize this field and to allow for its reproduction beyond the generation of its pioneers.

The emergence and the institutionalization of a professionalized field of democracy and human rights appears to have been driven by the internal contradictions of the old cold war project of a democratic crusade in defense of the free world. Indeed, we can actually recognize the offshoots of different currents of the anti-Communist left of the 1950s and different interpretations of the fight for democracy if we analyze different segments of that professionalized field: on the one hand, there are the neoconservatives who provided the ideological workforce of the various "democracy" initiatives of the Reagan administration such as the NED; on the other hand one finds their liberal opponents in the human rights movement, and in particular in Human Rights Watch. In fact, in spite of their antagonism, however, these groups are less distant in historical and sociological terms than it might seem, as both come from the same political and militant areas around the Socialist party and its various youth organizations.

In this respect, the biography of the founder of Human Rights Watch and former director of the American Civil Liberties Union Aryeh Neier is very significant for it highlights the similarities existing between his own evolution and that of his future adversaries within the Reagan administration. He acknowledges the influence of the anti-totalitarian writers (Koestler, Silone, Orwell, etc.) in his early intellectual formation, and the attraction exercised by the kind of socialism embodied by Norman Thomas in the mid-1950s. In the wake of the Hungarian uprising against Soviet rule, Neier joined the Student League for Industrial Democracy, a social-democratic organization close to the trade unions and anti-Communist. Appointed executive director of its parent organization, the League for Industrial Democracy, he renamed the SLID "Students for a Democratic Society" in 1959, but soon found himself opposing the radicalization of his recruits Tom Hayden and Al Haber. At the same time, he "was unhappy about LID's rightward drift under the influence of the Shachmanites" and left the organization in the early 1960s, disagreeing with the strong support for the Vietnam war expressed by them (Neier 2003: xxi). He later joined the American Civil Liberties Union, before moving to human rights in 1978 and establishing Human Rights Watch. Therefore, while the Shachtmanites would later migrate toward neoconservatism and the ideological defense of "democracy," the more centrist fraction of the old anti-Communist left represented by Neier would play an important role in structuring the institutions and the networks of the human rights movement, the Vietnam war acting as the crucial historical divide.

Vietnam brought out into the open the internal contradictions of the cold war crusade waged in the name of democracy, and in particular the tension between a more ideological and combative understanding of the defense of democracy, and a more legalistic one. In other words, the field of democracy and human rights that took shape in the 1980s can be considered *as a whole* as an outgrowth of the different political shades of the anti-Communist social democratic left. This tradition appears as the real social and intellectual matrix of this field of international practices, as it encompasses both the democracy promotion projects subordinated to the logic of the cold war that the NED would inherit *and* their liberal opponents in the more institutionalized sectors of human rights movement.

The professionalization of these different political strategies represented by institutions such as the NED or HRW contributed to the overcoming of these divides and even, as we shall see, to the rallying of a more militant left coming from a radical opposition to U.S. imperial policies in Vietnam and elsewhere. The focus on political technologies for exporting democracy and enforcing global human rights standards rather than on ideological issues contributed not only to the institutionalization of this field, but also to the enrollment of scientific or "epistemic" communities in this global project.

From the Ideological Struggles Around "Human Rights" to the "Promotion of Democracy"

It is impossible to understand the rise of democracy and human rights as major policy issues in the 1980s without considering that what was at stake here were the views of different actors seeking to impose their own definition of human rights, or to legitimate their policies by invoking the term. The process which led to the creation of the National Endowment for Democracy must also be resituated in these initial debates around the notion of human rights. These struggles led not only to increasingly sophisticated arguments, but also to the establishment of practical or even normative standards and to the creation of new institutions which, in turn, served as the basis for the professionalization of this field. Depending on the position of the participants in these ideological struggles, the symbolic stake of these debates was nothing less than the capacity to legitimate — or to criticize — international or even global policies, in either case by referring to these powerful normative standards. As we shall see, the stakes were all the higher since the different approaches to human rights overlapped with contending conceptions of world order.

President Reagan announced the creation of the National Endowment for Democracy in a speech made in 1982 at Westminster, during an official visit to the United Kingdom. Describing a major initiative named "Project Democracy," Reagan outlined a global strategy articulated around the worldwide extension of democracy:

> The objective I propose is quite simple to state: to foster the infrastructure of democracy, the system of a free press, unions, political parties, universities, which allows a people to choose their own way to develop their own culture, to reconcile their own differences through peaceful means. . . . We in America now intend to take additional steps, as many of our allies have already done, toward realizing this same goal. The chairmen and other leaders of the national Republican and Democratic party organizations are initiating a study with the bipartisan American Political Foundation to determine how the United States can best contribute as a nation to the global campaign for democracy now gathering force.[5]

The speech, and in particular the emergence of the notion of "democracy promotion," should be considered as a strategic displacement of the center of gravity around which the human rights debate had previously revolved. In fact, the speech itself was meant to be the outline of a new *human rights policy*. A 1980 transition document already advocated a "battle of ideas" which was waged around the direction of U.S. foreign policy: "the President can wage the battle of ideas better than anyone else. He should make a major human rights speech defining his administration's policy and explaining how it differs from the previous administration's" (Fairbanks 1980a: 5).

In which way, then, did the new policy differ from the previous one? When human rights were introduced as a guiding principle of U.S. foreign policy under the presidency of Jimmy Carter, they were primarily equated with legal norms enshrined in international treaties and covenants. In that sense, human rights were part of international law, and U.S. human rights policy could be considered as an effort to strengthen international legality without any regard to ideological, political, economic, or geostrategic distinctions — at least according to official statements. By the same token, however, this policy was binding for the United States as well, to the extent that it required the conformity of its own foreign policy with such principles and a greater observance of its international commitments in general. In fact, the bulk of the neoconservative critique of Carter's human rights policy was that it placed severe constraints and self-limitations on American power, while facilitating attacks on U.S. foreign policy in the name of human rights.

The initial reaction of the Reagan administration was simply to dismantle this policy (a task for which Ernest Lefever was nominated assistant secretary for human rights, before the Senate refused to confirm this appointment under the pressure of human rights organizations).[6] Neoconservatives, most of whom had backed the Republican candidate, take credit for having persuaded a reluctant, if not actually hostile, administration to take up the issue of human rights. Their specific contribution to Reagan's foreign policy was to reclaim the human rights discourse instead of leaving it to their liberal opponents, as well as to produce a new interpretation of human rights or, better, an ideology of human rights directly opposed to a formal and legalistic conception of human rights. The thrust of this operation consisted in *shifting the focus of human rights from international legality to national institutions and social structures*. In the neoconservative view, human rights could not be equated with international standards, which they considered to be ineffective and deprived of enforcement mechanisms. Instead, human rights were primarily based upon a set of values embedded in existing national political institutions and legal structures, of which the United States were at once the best historical example and the model. In substance, a concern for human rights should be a concern about the political regime predicated on human rights, namely democracy.

Before examining closer this conception of human rights, it is important to consider the alternative notions that it sought to displace and their policy implications. A first conception of human rights can be related to the jus naturalist tradition, in which universal natural rights are pitted against positive law in general and, therefore, against existing legal structures or political regimes. In this perspective, to use the concise formula of Michel Foucault, "human rights are mainly what one opposes to governments." (Foucault 1994[1982]: 349). This tradition found its most developed institutional expression in the UN as well as American organizations created to monitor the human rights achievements of the Carter administration, such as Helsinki Watch and, later, its successor Human Rights Watch.

Against this liberal understanding of human rights, the neoconservatives put forward an interpretation in which human rights were "rooted in structure," (e.g. Fairbanks 1980a: 2; 1980b: 2), that is, in democratic political regimes and legal systems. This conception was based on the idea that, far from representing an absolute limit to state power or, in other words, something external to it, human rights could only exist as *the principled foundation and the moral substance of the state*. "The struggle for human rights," according to a major neoconservative analysis of this issue, "far from being, as Carter and his aides proclaimed, indifferent to political systems, is fundamentally a struggle about political systems" (Muravchik 1986: 59). Defending and promoting human rights meant defending and promoting political regimes having human rights as their premises. No longer considered a supranational norm, human rights were thus seen as a set of entitlements embedded in the classical, post-revolutionary, eighteenth-century constitutions and their modern equivalents — that is, as positive law. It is important to recognize that this theory was based on the primacy of the national level and directly opposed to the UN framework: it was an attempt at *"nationalizing" human rights*.

This conception, in addition to being pitted against any supranational conception of human rights, was opposed to another interpretation of human rights which also posited that they were "rooted in structure," but, this time, in economic and social structures. Next to the liberal conception, then, this more materialist understanding of human rights recognized that such rights include economic, social, or even cultural rights. In a report to the Conference on Development and Human Rights organized by the International Commission of Jurists in 1981, Philip Alston, then consultant to the UN Division of Human Rights, attacked the "structure blindness" of the traditional legal approach: "human rights initiatives have foundered because they have sought to treat the symptoms of repression without paying adequate regard to the deeper structural problems which gave rise to the symptoms in the first place. In many instances these problems are rooted in underdevelopment or maldevelopment" (Alston 1981: 33). In fact, this conception not only extended the scope of human rights to social and economic entitlements, but actually made progress in the field of political and civil rights dependent upon the improvement of social and economic conditions. The removal of "structural obstacles" and "inequities" at the international level was considered as a prerequisite (ibid.: 37–38).

Associated with the most progressive wing of the human rights movement and well represented within the UN, this notion of human rights was in part correlated to a global project aiming at reshaping the international order on the basis of more equitable relationships of exchange. For if human rights required minimal social and economic guarantees, then they ultimately implied a more egalitarian and participatory economic order that would not impair development. The "New International Economic Order" defended at the UNCTAD by Third World and nonaligned countries, which had sought to call into question the inequalities and the hierarchies of the global capitalist economy, can be regarded as the most developed political expression of this conception of human rights. In fact, UN General Assembly resolution 32/130 of 1977 clearly recognized that a structural transformation of the international economic order was a necessary preliminary for the promotion of human rights: "the realization of the New International Economic Order is an essential element for the effective promotion of human rights and fundamental freedoms and should be accorded priority" (ibid.: 83).

The more philosophical aspects of the human rights debate and the very definition of the concept, therefore, directly overlapped with different projects of world order. The intensity of the struggle between liberals and neoconservatives about human rights was directly connected to the issue of the U.S. relation to the UN and, beyond, of the place of the United States on the world scene.

In contrast with these UN-based international-legal or socioeconomic conceptions of human rights, the neoconservatives produced a theory of human rights that excluded social and economic entitlements and ensured the continued political and economic dominance of the center over the periphery, against any challenge to the capitalist world-system. Because it was central to these alternative conceptions of human rights, the UN became the main arena of ideological struggle over the definition of the concept. "Human rights," according to Tony Evans, "offered both sides considerable opportunities for engaging in the ideological struggle conducted at the United Nations. In particular, the struggle to win the hearts and minds of less developed states often focused on claims to self-determination, the right to dispose of natural resources and the demand for a more equitable international economic system" (Evans 1996: 9).

It is in this context that the composition of the U.S. delegation to the United Nations under Ronald Reagan should be analyzed, and that its ideological role should be emphasized. This institution can be considered as the fulcrum of neoconservative thinking on human rights in the early 1980s. It powerfully reasserted American hegemony and used the issue of human rights to raise the level of ideological conflict with the Communist bloc and the Third World (Gerson 1991). Headed by Jeane Kirkpatrick, who was allegedly appointed because of her famous 1979 article in *Commentary* making human rights a matter of distinction between right-wing authoritarian dictatorships and Communist totalitarianism, the delegation also comprised other neoconservatives such as Carl Gershman and Marc Plattner, both of whom would later contribute to the creation of the National Endowment for Democracy and occupy important positions in it (Gerson 1991; Finger 1988). The U.S. delegation thus represented a crucial articulation in the passage from a human rights policy to a global project which consisted in exporting democracy.

The neoconservative discourse on human rights entailed two major policy implications. The first was that if human rights were "rooted in structures" — "structures" hereby defined as the legal foundations of existing national political systems — there could be no conflict whatsoever between the preservation or the extension of these structures and human rights, since the latter depended upon the former. In other words, it meant that the pursuit of the national interest of "democratic" countries was entirely consistent, if not equivalent, with the international promotion of human rights. This "nationalization" of human rights at the service of U.S. foreign policy is recurrent in neoconservative writings on the issue. As early as 1980, a campaign document drafted by Reagan's future Deputy Assistant Secretary of State for Human Rights, Charles Fairbanks, stated in a quite straightforward fashion that "We have the right to say: what increases the strength of the United States and the respect in which we are held is good for human rights" (Fairbanks 1980a: 1). In his book on human rights, Joshua Muravchik, an American

Enterprise Institute fellow and right-wing Social Democrat trained in the Shachtmanite tradition, wrote that "the growth of American power encourages the growth of democracy (and human rights); the spread of democracy strengthens America's influence" (1986: xxix). Human rights, as Peter Berger observed in a symposium on "Human Rights and American Power" organized by *Commentary*, are nothing less than "the principle of legitimacy of the American nation-state" (Berger 1981: 27). "There is no conflict between a concern for human rights and the American national interest as traditionally conceived" wrote Jeane Kirkpatrick in the same issue (Kirkpatrick 1981: 42). By equating the defense of human rights with the assertion of national interests, this argument provided a strong moral legitimation for a policy of foreign intervention and confrontation with the Soviet Union. Previously conceived as a bulwark against state power, human rights thus became a crucial asset of power politics, functional to the exercise of hegemony. They were also reframed as a kind of positive morality best embodied by the values sustaining the U.S. political system, in a somewhat communitarian perspective. As a result, the increase of American power had a moral value. The circle was finally squared: traditional realism had been translated into normative, principled commitment.

A second implication of this reactionary human rights doctrine was that the nature and the form of foreign political regimes were brought within the legitimate scope of human rights policy. To the extent that human rights were considered to be determined and guaranteed by national legal and institutional traditions, "the big fight for human rights [was] a fight to create governments that have human rights as their premises."[7] In that sense, the emergence of various democracy promotion programs was a direct consequence of the neoconservative human rights doctrine or, better, the substitute for a human rights policy.[8] The policy which consisted in conforming foreign political systems to U.S. national interests by exporting political, legal, economic, and social technologies "made in the USA" could continue unimpaired under the human rights label. The "nation-building" programs, which would subsequently proliferate in the wake of post-conflict situations in the course of the 1990s, should also be viewed in this perspective, as an instrumentalization of human rights for the direct imperial control of foreign regimes. These developments contributed to secure these hegemonic policies by undermining the traditional critique coming from anti-imperialist movements and liberal human rights organizations. They promoted a conception of human rights with which this critique was inconsistent: global U.S. interests and the values in the name of which they were criticized were made to coincide. The discrepancy between principles and interests which had always fueled the critique of U.S. foreign policy was finally cancelled. But linking human rights with the nature of political regimes did not only prevent their preemption by critical and potentially hostile political constituencies. It also allowed the new administration to capitalize directly on the emancipatory and progressive imagination that human rights crystallized for many activists. The "promotion of democracy" opened new opportunities and new venues of participation for a variety of networks, organizations and activist movements.

While "human rights" tended to determine a certain degree of antagonism between activist networks and the state, democracy promotion organized their convergence. These actors suddenly found themselves operating within a field that was being transformed and subsumed under the logic of state power. Or, better, they became the new channels through which this power was now exercised globally. It is important to recognize that this situation was double-edged. On the one hand, it allowed activist organizations to increase their international clout because their activities fell in line with the stated objectives of U.S. foreign policy and no longer contradicted them. This allowed some of them to build their reputation by trying to influence foreign policy or by carrying out democracy promotion projects. On the other hand, and for the same reason, this also implied a revision of their strategies and of their *modus operandi*. Instead of acting outside the field of state power, they had to influence it from within, to work within the parameters of its policies, to adapt to its code and to develop a kind of expertise that was compatible, if not identical, with state expertise (Dezalay and Garth 2002). This process is what is commonly designated as professionalization. As we shall see, the strategy of opening toward academic communities followed very early on by the National Endowment for Democracy illustrates this phenomenon. By the same token, activist networks and NGOs have moved closer to the institutions they had traditionally sought to contrast. Their personnel have found it easier to move from nongovernmental positions to government or to international bureaucracies, where they dealt with increasingly similar policy knowledge and expertise.

By tapping this huge reserve of skills and competence, by redirecting transnational civic activism seeking to limit the powers of the state toward its own foreign policy goals, the promotion of democracy recycled a whole repertoire traditionally related to the critique of domination into a new instrument of global domination[9]. Such domination is no longer formal, exercised from outside, but direct and substantial: it is a transformative power that reshapes and refashions societies from within.[10] This new paradigm was identified very early by the new foreign policy planners. It provided the focus of the first Human Rights Report released by the State Department under Reagan, which clearly signaled the shift away from "human rights" and toward democracy promotion:

> It would narrow the range of action of our human rights policy excessively to limit it to responding to individual violations of human rights when they appear. This "reactive" aspect of human rights policy is essential. But it must be accompanied by a second track of positive policy with a bolder long-term aim: to assist the gradual emergence of free political systems (U.S. Department of State 1981: 5).

The document outlined the main features of this form of intervention, based on the administration of international programs seeking to generate the institutional, cultural, and legal infrastructure of democracy. It identified civil society as the field where this "soft power" could be exercised through a variety of intermediary institutions where alternative intellectual or technical elites could be identified, trained and assisted:

> The development of liberty is, in turn, encouraged by the emergence of areas within a political system where free choice and free expression can become familiar and respected, even while they are not permitted in other parts of the political system. Among these areas where freedom can develop are labor unions, churches, independent judicial systems, bar associations and universities. Where we do not have leverage over the shape of an entire society, we can nourish the growth of freedom within such institutions (Ibid.).

This strategy was not really new. Rather, it systematized the work traditionally performed by the philanthropic foundations in the field of education, by the Congress for Cultural Freedom in the field of culture, or by the international branch of the AFL-CIO in the field of trade unions and industrial relations. It also capitalized on the potential role that transnational professional networks could play in the exportation of policy knowledge and know-how. Democracy promotion thus served to organize a worldwide market for the diffusion of U.S. institutional models and policy prescriptions under the pretext of enhancing professionalism or "building capacity." America was going global again.

The human rights doctrine developed by neoconservatives and cold war social democrats in the early 1980s transformed human rights almost beyond recognition. What was once an international legal standard had now become an instrument for reshaping other nations to America's specifications or at least in conformity with her interests. Democracy promotion is the result of this *transformation of human rights into a modality of imperial control.* In retrospect, it is not surprising that the Reagan administration adopted a human rights policy instead of rejecting the notion altogether. Its hawkish policy agenda implied that America had to restock its military arsenals, but it also implied moral rearmament. In that sense, the notion of human rights was not merely imposed upon the new government by its opponents within the human rights movement: it was also internal to the logic of a policy seeking to rebuild American hegemony and to do so by mobilizing its moral resources — a fact often overlooked by human rights scholars. Human rights perfectly fulfilled this task once they were detached from international law and reformulated as *a moral concept of the democratic state.*

By turning human rights policy into democracy promotion, the new administration displaced the issue from the plane of law (where it was a weapon in the hand of liberal human rights lawyers and policy advocates) to the much broader field of transnational civic activism. In other words, it relocated it in the field of NGOs and activist networks, which turned out to be its paradoxical allies. The recurring argument in the neoconservative critique of human rights as international legality was that international law is insufficient to guarantee human rights, for it lacks enforcement mechanisms and ultimately rests upon consent. Instead, democracy promotion represented a human rights policy based not upon law but upon *struggles for rights* and *civic activism.* It was based, in other words, on the mobilization of nongovernmental advocacy networks and organizations. This activist edge was appealing to a wide range of NGOs and issue networks; it was more attractive than the narrow legal technicalities of human rights law; it also resonated with their own repertoire of collective action. In fact, the neoconservative human rights doctrine successfully turned to its advantage the "structuralist" approach advocated by the most progressive exponents of the human rights movement.

The "human rights and development" movement at the UN also entailed a strong activist component based on popular mobilization: "international efforts to promote awareness of human rights issues can play an important role in developing people's awareness of their rights and in mobilizing them for action" (Alston 1981: 68). Democracy promotion turned this progressive perspective into a conservative one or, rather, a counterrevolutionary one. This restatement of the state's foreign policy in the activist language of non-governmental actors blurred the line between the field of state power and the autonomous, self-organized forms of social empowerment. At the same time, this strategy contributed to the professionalization of civic nongovernmental activism. Empowerment thus became a specific aspect of state power. The rise of democracy promotion meant that empowerment technologies would now be indistinguishable from governmental policy techniques, as the field of democracy and human rights began to be organized around a new type of "democracy expert."

The Continuation of the Cold War through Other Means: The National Endowment for Democracy and the Rise of the Democracy Professionals

Created in 1983 with the support of the Reagan administration, the National Endowment for Democracy was a result of this new human rights policy. By its contribution to the conversion of cold war activism into a professional field of international practices, the organization played a crucial role. The genealogy of this institution brings us back to the old project of building a "democratic international" that emerged in the anti-Stalinist left of the 1940s and was sponsored by the State Department and other state agencies. In spite of its disruption in the mid-1960s, the attempt at reviving this project started in the immediate aftermath of the scandal provoked by the revelations concerning the use of CIA funds for covert interventions abroad, which involved the Congress for Cultural Freedom but also a range of other institutions such as the International Commission of Jurists or the National Student Association. In order to find alternative solutions, President Johnson established a commission, chaired by Nicholas Katzenbach, which recommended that the government establish "a public-private mechanism to provide public funds openly for overseas activities of organizations which are adjudged deserving, in the national interest, of public support" (quoted in Sklar and Berlet 1992).

In April 1967, Dante Fascell, a Democrat Congressman from Florida with close ties to the AFL-CIO tried in vain to pass a bill calling for the creation of an Institute of International Affairs that would run overtly international programs of political assistance of the same nature (Lowe 2000: 2). The failure of this early attempt at establishing the NED did not discourage the promoters of this strategy. Under the much more favorable political conditions created by the election of Ronald Reagan almost fifteen years later, they successfully placed it on the political agenda in the context of the struggle over the nature and the direction of human rights policy. The continuity between the international crusade for democracy launched from within the ranks of the anti-Communist left in the 1950s and the NED hinges in the first place on the continuity of the political personnel which has been the bearer of this project. Among the NED's founders or ideological designers, cold war social democrats occupy a prominent place: NED's president, Carl Gershman, was one of Max Schachtman's close aides within the Socialist Party; Joshua Muravchik and Seymour Lipset are both members of the NED research council and former activists of the Young People Socialist League; Albert Shanker, head of the American Federation of Teachers, Eugenia Kemble, of the Free Trade Union Institute, Tom Kahn, another AFL-CIO official, are other Shachtmanites who have all been affiliated in one way or another with this institution.

But the continuity is also visible at the level of the organizational forms. The NED is a "fuzzy institution" — neither a state agency nor really an autonomous private organization. The kind of power it wields is better described as "soft power." The way in which it was initially conceived still bears the imprint of the old project of building a "democratic international." (In 1998, the launching of the World Movement for Democracy, a loose network of funding organizations, lobbies, grantees, and donors placed under NED leadership was still a distant echo of this old template.) The creation of the Endowment was preceded by a six-month study sponsored by the administration and designed "to seek methods to assist in the effort to build democratic values and institutions abroad," called the Democracy Program. Charles Manatt, co-chairman of the Democracy Program and chairman of the Democratic National Committee, stressed that aspect in his statement before the Senate Committee on Foreign Relations:

> In recent years, many have commented on how they believe the Communist movement around the world has gained tremendous force from its formidable network of international parties, funds, and connections. While these same commentators have noted some promising developments in Western Europe which indicate that democratic nations are seeking to establish corresponding networks for the democracies, they have, nonetheless, been critical of what they regard as too little activity on the part of the United States, both governmentally and nongovernmentally (U.S. Senate 1983: 264 — emphasis added).

In fact, the continuity with "State Department socialism" also appeared in the close ties uniting the NED to the labor hierarchy. Lane Kirkland, George Meany's successor at the helm of the AFL-CIO, was instrumental in pushing for the creation of the Endowment. Close to Senator Jackson, staunchly opposed to U.S. withdrawal from Vietnam, Kirkland had been active in the creation of the Committee on the Present Danger, and in organizing support for Solidarity in Poland.[11] NED's affinity with the labor apparatus stems obviously from the prominent role of several labor bureaucrats in its creation, as well as from the fact that one of its main purposes was to channel funds for foreign operations to the international department of the AFL-CIO, a venerable cold war institution which had benefited from the CIA's generosity for years.[12] This background, as well as the role of the NED in favoring politicians or groups falling in line with the general purpose of U.S. foreign policy, has made the organization a perfect target for those denouncing U.S. imperialism (e.g. Cavell 2002).

The NED actually operates as a clearing house for Congress and State Department funds that it redistributes between four "core grantees," respectively the Free Trade Union Institute, the international branch of the AFL-CIO; the Center for International Private Enterprise, an offshoot of the Chamber of Commerce; and the international foundations of the Democratic and the Republican parties. These four institutional components, in turn, work with foreign organizations. Thirty percent of the NED's funds are directly distributed to overseas organizations in a discretionary manner. This institutional design is not very different from the multi-layered circuits of funding that were those of the Congress for Cultural Freedom. It allows the NED to present itself as stemming from American civil society rather than an organization situated in the field of state power. As a conservative critique expectably put it: "that convoluted organizational structure seems to be based on the premise that government money, if filtered through enough layers of bureaucracy, becomes 'private' funding" (Conry 1993). Indeed, the legislative Act establishing the NED, almost makes official this strategy of privatization when it stipulates, somewhat paradoxically, that "the Endowment will not be considered an agency or establishment of the U.S. Government" (U.S. House of Representatives 1983: 87 — Title VI, section 602[b]).

This structure is particularly appropriate for the kind of work performed by the NED, as it smoothly straddles the state / non-state divide and relates the realm of foreign policy to that of transnational activism. The activities of the NED range from financing "democratic" opposition forces to translating Western political literature, training pollsters, promoting human rights

education, fostering an entrepreneurial culture, easing the internationalization of neoliberal economics through symposia and textbooks, sustaining
independent news reporting, and briefing government officials on media
strategy. The organization, with a staff of about sixty, is located in Washington D.C., and receives a yearly budget that has varied between $15 and $35
million. This position as a fuzzy institution located on the margins of the
state and of the foreign policy establishment (well represented on its board
of directors which includes members of the Council on Foreign Relations,
of the House and the Senate, as well as fellows of influential foreign policy
think tanks such as the Center for Strategic and International Studies) but
operating within a nongovernmental framework and mobilizing an activist
repertoire was particularly well suited for contributing to the professionalization of the field of democracy and human rights.

Over time, the NED has expanded its activities and developed its role as
a quasi think tank sponsoring policy research on these issues, publishing a
quasi-academic journal and, occasionally, books. It has cultivated certain
academic communities — in area studies, comparative politics, political theory — which provided a strong element of scientific legitimacy to its activities
abroad and its role in engineering or assisting various "transitions to democracy." To a large extent, this investment in scientific credibility was meant
to compensate for the highly ideological origins of the NED, created in a
clearly anti-Communist perspective in the last phase of the cold war. However, it also served the purpose of a form of imperialism based not so much
on the exportation of specific policy prescriptions and institutional models
(although this also happens) as on the exportation of *a specific mode of
production of policy knowledge*. In other words, the enhancement of professional standards and the promotion of research and reflection on democratization processes contributed to turn the U.S. model of policy research and
advocacy as a universal model of political change. Itself a product of the
strong resurgence of foundations, think tanks, policy research centers, institutionalized lobbies and advocacy networks which deeply transformed U.S.
politics in the 1970s, the NED actively seeks to export and internationalize
this model. According to its Statement of Principles and Purposes,

> The emergence of public policy institutes in the United States and
> other Western democracies is serving as a model in developing and
> formerly communist nations. Independent and generally non-partisan
> centers for research and the development of alternative solutions to
> national problems have been established even in nondemocratic coun-
> tries, where they can serve as forums for dialogue among the various

political, economic and social forces. The Endowment is interested in assisting institutions of this kind, and will consider supporting programs that make informational resources available to public officials, in particular to legislative bodies.

As the statement clearly suggests, achieving influence in the realm of "policy institutes" and similar institutions gives substantial leverage over the definition of public policy. These institutions define an area where policy alternatives are shaped by professional "idea brokers" (J.A. Smith 1991) and other kinds of opinion-makers. By the same token, these policy alternatives are likely to be formulated in the technical language of these professionals and to derive their legitimacy from their conformity with the most orthodox kinds of policy expertise (in law, economics, administrative and policy sciences, or management). Training these professionals or building the institutions in which they operate ensures that a significant control is exercised over the process by which policies are fabricated and circulated. It also guarantees that social and political change will be gradual, smooth, and in line with the expectations of wider international epistemic and policy communities. The NED thus encourages the internationalization and the imitation of the U.S. policy industry by funding all kinds of research and advocacy centers abroad, as diverse (or alike) as a "Center for Liberal Strategies" in Bulgaria or a "Center for Dissemination of Economic Information" in Venezuela, or by sponsoring the publication of *Economic Reform Today*, a journal produced by Center for International Private Enterprise and the United States Information Agency and translated in many languages. This strategy extends the reach of the Washington policy community, as a variety of institutions built on the same U.S. model with NED support and funding eagerly adopt its know-how, its management techniques, and its culture of public relations. In the same breath, they often recycle its policy recommendations. As any other kind of imperialism, this one opens new foreign markets for the commodities produced in dominant countries — in this case for the policy prescriptions and recommendations emanating from national and international institutions in Washington.

From the Young People Socialist League to the NED

Before proceeding to analyze the role of the NED as a think tank, it may be useful to illustrate the continuity between the NED and the ideological framework of the old anti-Communist left by turning to an individual biography. The social trajectory of Carl Gershman, president of the NED since its creation, demonstrates well the continuity between cold war social democracy and the "democracy promotion" of today. Born in 1943 in New York, Gershman studied at Yale and Harvard. He obtained his M.Ed. in 1968, after a two-year break serving as a Volunteer In Service To America worker in Pittsburgh and, in 1968, as a member of the Anti-Defamation League of the B'nai B'rith. During this period, he started to publish political op-ed pieces in the *Pittsburgh Point* on the student movements, Communism and the New Left. He joined the Young People Socialist League (YPSL) in the second half of the sixties. While the YPSL had initially benefited from the momentum given by the civil rights movement and student mobilization, its influence had waned by the mid 1960s. A substantial number of members, finding themselves at odds with Shachtman's social-democratic strategy and alignment with the Democratic Party and the AFL-CIO, left to join more radical youth organizations.

In 1964, a diminished YPSL was reestablished under the tight control of the Shachtmanites. Within the organization, along with Tom Kahn, Rachelle Horowitz, Penn Kemble, and Joshua Muravchik, Carl Gershman was one of Schachtman's followers. He was active in a movement that, in spite of its leftist past, was now entirely devoted to ensuring the cohesion among the socialists, the AFL-CIO, and the liberal elites of the Democratic Party, and to keeping the social movements in line with this political strategy. Gershman played a significant role in enforcing that line. Still an influential YPSL cadre, he joined the union-funded A. Philip Randolph Institute as director of research in 1969, a position he held until 1971. The Institute had been founded and directed by civil rights activist Bayard Rustin, who was Shachtman's ally in the civil rights movement. It embodied the social-democratic strategy of ensuring social and material progress for the working class and the African-Americans in the framework of a democratic administration and in the respect of capitalist "responsible free enterprise" (Drucker 1994: 187).

During his years at the Institute, Gershman published his first articles in the *New Leader* and in *Commentary*, mostly political attacks on the New Left. He denounced the obsession of the New Left with life-style, its "anti-intellectualism," its lack of organizational capacity, its lack of a social basis outside of the campuses (Gershman 1969a). The underlying argument was that the "intensification of all the tendencies that lead to ultra-radicalism" (ibid.: 668) derived from this lack of a real social basis which, in turn, implicitly suggested that a radical movement could not be democratic. The

Students for a Democratic Society (SDS), indeed, represented "a new Thermidor" (Gershman 1969b). At the same time, Gershman continued his ascension within the political hierarchy of the YPSL. Between 1970 and 1974, he became successively vice-chairman, co-chairman, and chairman.

For the Democratic presidential nomination in 1972, he actively organized support for Henry 'Scoop' Jackson within the YPSL. Among the various aspects of Jackson's political agenda, his ties to labor and his anti-Communism stood out as the main arguments for considering him the "natural" candidate of the Shachtmanites. In Gershman's view, Jackson "st[ood] closer to the YPSL position on domestic and foreign policy than any other potential Democratic candidate" (Gershman 1972a: 1), in particular because he was committed to strengthening the "labor movements in developing nations — which can enable nationalist movements in these countries to resist totalitarian takeover" (ibid.: 8). This interpretation of Jackson's program already outlined the field of democracy and human rights activism in which many former YPSL and Social Democrats would find a professional outlet in the 1980s. Jackson's support to the military intervention in Vietnam war also brought him close to the YPSL position on this issue.

In contrast, McGovern was the devil incarnate: the South Dakota senator was "a spokesman for the revisionist view of history that places most of the blame for the cold war on the United States." (Gershman 1972b: 11). The fact that some YPSL members viewed McGovern with some sympathy located Gershman at the right wing of the movement along with Joshua Muravchik, Penn Kemble, Albert Shanker. After the 1972 election, this faction within the YPSL took control of the Socialist Party, thus leading to the defection of the left wing, led by Michael Harrington and the 'third camp' socialists.

With its center of gravity considerably displaced to the right, the residual political organization took the name of Social Democrats U.S.A., and Gershman became its executive director in 1974. The SDUSA placed a virulent anti-Communism at the core of their political agenda. On the international plane, the party saw growth opportunities in a context where liberal attitudes toward Communism have been changed by "the protests of Soviet Jews, [and] the remarkably courageous actions of Soviet dissidents such as Sakharov and Solzhenitsyn" (Gershman 1973a: 3). Domestically, anti-Communism fueled a critique of "liberal anti-Americanism," of the "new foreign policy establishment," and of the revisionist history of the cold war.[13] Orwell and Solzhenitsyn thus became intellectual icons for the social democrats (Gershman 1973b), while the party developed its ties with the exponents of the anti-Communist left (Melvin Lasky) or its international networks (the specialist of the USSR Leopold Labedz or the Spanish political scientist Juan Linz).[14]

The Social Democrats saw themselves in a position similar to that of the Soviet dissidents, as the only true believers in democracy, living under the rule of a totalitarian left: "liberalism," wrote Gershman, "has suffered a fate akin to that of socialism: it has been preempted by a political group that has perverted its meaning" (1976: 60). In line with the conservative evolution of the old left and its endorsement of American capitalism as the "natural" environment of social reform, the theme of the international promotion of democracy appeared as a component of a policy which subordinated social reform to the struggle against Communism: "Only out of the genuine motivation to reform, improve, and strengthen democratic society can there emerge that political will to defend it and to apply democratic values internationally. This revival will not occur unless social democracy . . . is guided by the view that Communism, not capitalism, is the main obstacle" (Gershman 1978: 45).

Gershman remained executive director of the SDUSA until 1980. He was then hired as Senior Research Fellow at Freedom House, a foundation today famous for publishing "indexes" measuring democracy on a country-by-country basis, but also a bastion of cold war liberalism of which Bayard Rustin was executive committee chairman. (Steinfels 1979: 148).[15] Gershman's record in terms of ideological work, of policy statements on international affairs, or on the "new" foreign policy establishment, his international networks (comprising Soviet dissidents as well as anti-Communist insurgents such as Jonas Savimbi in Angola) made him an obvious recruit for the neoconservative struggle around human rights and the political offensive at the UN. Close to the Social Democrats, the new U.S. Ambassador to the United Nations Jeane Kirkpatrick appointed him senior counselor. She also hired Marc Plattner, coming from the Twentieth Century Fund and former coeditor of *The Public Interest*, who would later go to the National Endowment for Democracy and contribute to shaping its intellectual agenda. The team at the US mission, in Gershman's own words, "became a center for lots of these ideas on the ideological confrontation with communist totalitarianism."[16] To a large extent, the National Endowment for Democracy would be the continuation of this confrontation through other means. Gershman's trajectory provides an example of the cross-fertilization between the cold war activism of the old left, state institutions, and militant nongovernmental structures such as the NED or Freedom House. It also underlines the structural proximity between these various institutions, and their complementary functions.

From Moral Crusade to Professional Expertise

The National Endowment for Democracy gave a permanent institutional form to the cold war project of an international crusade for democracy. This project developed from the anti-Stalinist critique of Communism of the late 1930s into the international policy of "democratic socialism" supported by the State Department in the 1940s, before becoming the backbone of an intransigent anti-Communism that would found a political expression in the neoconservative resurgence of the late 1970s and the victory of Ronald Reagan in the 1981 election. At the same time, the ideological struggle around the notion of human rights contributed to configure the new policy of democracy promotion as a *moral crusade*. Moral crusades, however, are not self-perpetuating and their institutionalization requires their transformation into a more professional trade (Becker 1963). To a large extent, the evolution of the NED from being a grant-making foundation to representing a more "intellectual" center actively organizing reflection and research on democracy and democratization processes is a response to this requirement. The involvement of academic actors in the construction of a form of policy expertise related to democracy and human rights was therefore tightly connected to this strategy.

From its very beginning, the NED was conceived as an institution that would not be confined to giving grants. It would also be involved in small research projects. Its *Statement of Principles and Objectives* specifies that "the Endowment also seeks other ways to develop close ties with the academic and policy research institutes," and that over time, "the Endowment intends to broaden its role as an intellectual as well as a programmatic center of activity." As a matter of fact, the very first grant made by the organization, in 1984, of $100,000, went to support research on democracy in the Third World undertaken by political scientists Juan Linz, Seymour Martin Lipset, and Larry Diamond, a researcher from the conservative Hoover Institution (Diamond, Linz, and Lipset 1988).[17] These academics were however closely related to the inner circle of the NED and, more than a purely academic work, their work was rather meant to provide the semblance of a theoretical framework for NED activities.

Throughout the 1980s, academic research remained a marginal issue and the NED was not really known outside of the foreign policy circles. The real development of academic activities came later, in 1989–90, when the *Journal of Democracy* was launched. Distributed for the Endowment by the Johns Hopkins University Press, this publication opened its editorial board to American political scientists and foreign contributors. While it is not properly peer-reviewed, it displays all the signs of academic respectability, allowing many academics to enrich their publications list with policy-oriented contributions.

The second major institutional opening toward academic communities came in April 1994 with the creation of the International Forum for Democratic Studies within the NED. The Forum hosts visiting fellows, organizes conferences on various topics related to democratic transitions and is also in charge of the publication of the *Journal of Democracy*. Its purpose is to be "a leading center for analyzing the theory and practice of democratic development worldwide. It serves as a clearinghouse for information on the varied activities and experiences of groups and institutions working to achieve and maintain democracy around the world." It is also a sort of meeting place for scholars, Endowment personnel, administration officials and the foreign policy community at large. Its activities are placed under the authority of a Research Council, which comprises approximately one hundred members presented as "scholars and other specialists of democracy from around the world" (NED 1998: 69).

The Research Council of the International Forum for Democratic Studies offers a valuable insight in the sociological structure of the field of democracy and human rights. The Council does not meet in official sessions nor has it institutional functions within the organization. Rather, it is a network of individuals who have been involved with the NED at some stage or who have regularly contributed to the *Journal of Democracy*, or who have just been approached for the purpose of lending their name, and therefore their authority, to the organization. It represents a significant social sample of which actors contribute to the production of a new global and normative expertise on democracy. All the members of the Research Council are indeed presented as "democracy experts" by the NED.[18] The analysis of the Research Council, therefore, provides an entry point in the process of social construction of such expertise. In other words, it allows us to flesh out the social structure of the field of democracy and human rights. (See the appendix for a list of these experts.)

Exactly like socio-professional categories, "expertise" is the result of a "work of *aggregation* and symbolic imposition" (Bourdieu and Wacquant

1992: 243), a work performed by individuals seeking to impose the certifi-
cation of their knowledge or their skills and to delineate a field over which
they become entitled to make authority claims. Scientific credentials —
diplomas, academic affiliations, etc. — are a common resource in this process of entitlement. Indeed, any process of professionalization implies the
mobilization of "a real technical skill that produces demonstrable results
and can be taught"; such skill must be "difficult enough to require training
and reliable enough to produce results"; at the same time, however, it should
not be so reliable that nonspecialists can assess its results (Collins 1979, 132).
In other words, the successful transition from cold war ideologies to a professional field of expertise therefore implied the mobilization of scholarly
communities. In the case of democracy and human rights, however, the
paradox was that those communities most able to provide a scientific legitimation for the technologies of democracy promotion were also those which
had been most opposed to U.S. imperial policies. As we shall see, democracy
or human rights had emerged as an issue within specific research traditions — comparative politics, Latin American studies, political sociology or
political economy — where they were often linked to a critique of domination and exploitation within the international system in general, and of U.S.
foreign policy in particular.

At first sight, the Research Council of the NED looks like a roster of
academic scholars specializing in various geographical areas or political issues (human rights, economic reform, comparative democratization, Chi-
nese politics, Latin America, etc.). From its list of members appearing in
various NED publications, 67 out of 95 members are academics. If we exclude those who occupy a position outside the United States — for the sake
of retaining an homogeneous sample in order to make comparisons — the
proportion is 52 out of 63, or 82.5 percent. Of course, such information is
provided precisely in order to validate the kind of expertise that the NED
seeks to establish. If we examine instead the various positions and affiliations
of each person on the list, one can generate a much longer list — one that
gives a more precise picture of the social composition of this field.[19]

This statistical treatment relativizes the weight of academic affiliations
(44%) and makes visible the other characteristics of these experts in democracy and human rights. The most salient are the affiliations with various
think tanks and policy research centers (32%), such as the Woodrow Wilson
International Center for Scholars (7 individuals), the American Enterprise
Institute and its offshoot the Center for Strategic and International Studies
(5), the Hoover Institution (3) or the International Institute for Strategic

Studies (3). Permanent or occasional work with the State Department (10) or with other state agencies related to defense or security (13) also appears as a relevant characteristic. To a lesser extent, consulting for the USAID (7) is another visible feature. Obviously, many members of the Research Council cumulate positions across these various institutions. In contrast, there are only few affiliations with NGOs (6), and among them Human Rights Watch predominates (3).

This brief overview already suggests that the academic circles involved in the production of "democratic expertise" are rather policy-oriented and socially very close to, if not part of, the foreign policy establishment. The fact that a substantial amount of members of the Research Council are also members of the Council on Foreign Relations (16) confirms this description. This analysis seems to be further borne out by the distribution of academic positions: Ivy League universities (21.1%) and universities located in the Washington, DC area (25%) are over-represented. This also tends to suggest that these networks of scholars and advisors are both socially and geographically close to the major power centers. A closer look also reveals that a number of the members are not simply faculty members, but directors of research centers or whole departments.

The analysis of the academic disciplines represented in this sample allows for a more detailed picture. What appears in the first place is that the scientific construction of this international expertise on democracy is primarily taking place in the field of political science (or departments or "government"): this discipline represents 92.3 percent of the academic affiliations of the members of the sample. The few exceptions are distributed across the disciplines of law, history, and sociology. The break down of the various specializations within the discipline, expectedly, reveals the importance of international relations, comparative politics, area studies, and public policy. A more precise analysis of the different sub-disciplines represented shows the predominance of Latin American studies (19%), followed by Asian studies (17.5%), and Comparative Politics (12.7%). Conversely, the under-represented approaches are Law (4.9%), Political Economy, African Studies and Middle Eastern Studies (6.3% each).

At this stage, we can already recognize some important structural characteristics of the field of democracy and human rights. In the first place, the expertise it seeks to impose and the political technologies for democratization it produces are all rooted in the discipline of political science. Political scientists provide both the scientific legitimation of this expanding field of activities and the tools for addressing its main problems and issues. It seems also that their discipline has been mobilized to a certain extent against more social and legal approaches — this reflects the fact that, as we have seen, democracy promotion was to a large extent created against a liberal interpretation of human rights and its political implementation. The picture is however more complex, for political science is not a homogeneous discipline and it is riddled with internal tensions and struggles. The different sub-disciplines which compose it are the outcomes of different histories, of consolidated methodological divisions, of different demands made upon scientific work by policy planners at different points in time, of past research programs promoted by philanthropic foundations, and so forth. They do not have the same "value" on the academic market, nor do they enjoy the same policy audience outside academic walls. In fact, the correlation between these sub-disciplines and the other social characteristics of the Research Council members (in particular affiliations with other institutions) vividly illustrates these differences.[20]

The sub-disciplines traditionally associated with the critique of the dominant scientific and political paradigms, such as African Studies and Political Economy, are usually associated with a preoccupation with development and they tend to be closer to institutions such as the USAID or the Overseas Development Council. They also tend to be less endowed with political capital — that is, remote from the world of think tanks and prestigious public policy research centers. In other words, these are subordinated disciplines, both in academic and in political terms. At the other end of the spectrum, we find disciplines more fully integrated with the foreign policy apparatus: East European Studies and, to a lesser extent, Asian Studies. The former, in particular, is a field that has evolved out of Russian or Soviet Studies — a privileged research program very well endowed financially and close to governmental institutions. Expertise in these areas tends to be less academic and more connected with important centers for the production of foreign policy analysis, such as the Center for Strategic and International Studies, or with the journal *Foreign Affairs*. It is also linked with state institutions, whether the State Department or other agencies dealing with security or foreign policy. For the same reasons, it tends toward the conservative side.

Although they are very different, both the more critical and the more policy-oriented sectors of area studies stand in contrast with the more dominant sub-disciplines of Comparative Politics and, broadly speaking, Social Theory. These fields of specialization tend to be dominant in academic terms. For the sample of individuals under scrutiny, they are associated with a high scientific prestige and a high number of publications (in fact, scholars such as Samuel Huntington, Seymour Martin Lipset, Peter Berger, Adam Przeworski, Juan Linz, Robert Putnam, Robert Dahl publish on a wide range of subjects and have established a reputation that goes beyond the boundaries of their discipline). Most often, however, these "theorists" have actually defended an empirical theory of democracy, in line with the methodological cannons of the most orthodox political science. Not surprisingly, these disciplinary areas also tend to be associated with the more prestigious universities.

As it is articulated through the National Endowment for Democracy, the field of democracy and human rights thus comprises wide-ranging academic and policy networks. Individual members of the Research Council more closely related to the ideological background of the NED — and in particular to the struggle against Communism — actually represent a minority (i.e., Joshua Muravchik, Charles Fairbanks, Seymour Lipset, Adrian Karatnycky or, in a more conservative than neoconservative vein, Samuel Huntington or Francis Fukuyama). Instead, what begs for an explanation is the very strong representation of Latin American Studies within these networks of "democracy experts." For sure, the study of authoritarianism and the obstacles to democratization have become a central focus of this branch of area studies during the 1970s and the 1980s. In that sense, it may seem logical that this knowledge could be tapped for generating policy expertise. But within the "epistemic community" of Latin American studies, more often than not, such topics were articulated primarily within the perspective of a more general critique of the subordinate place of these countries in the world economy and of their exposure to imperialist policies strengthening local ruling classes resisting popular participation. Within political science, this sub-discipline had attracted a generation of scholars strongly opposed to U.S. interventionist policies, whether in Vietnam or in the region they studied, and involved in the anti-imperialist and anti-authoritarian struggles of the 1960s and the 1970s. Paradoxically, many of them started to work on democracy and human rights in direct opposition to the imperial policies of support for right-wing dictatorships advocated by Jeane Kirkpatrick and her entourage, and theorized by the cold war activists and the right-wing social democrats who created the NED. The nascent political science literature on democratization was as much the outcome of developments internal to the discipline as a weapon in the construction of a liberal opposition to the ambivalent policies of which the State Department, the U.S. delegation at the UN and the NED were the complementary channels. The first collective volume on "transitions to democracy" (O'Donnell, Schmitter, and

Whitehead 1986), for instance, was thus connected to a counter-project supported by the Woodrow Wilson Center for Scholars and the liberal Inter-American Dialogue. Within the Research Council that we are analyzing here, this critical tradition is represented by scholars such as Wayne Cornelius, Terry Karl, Scott Mainwaring, Cynthia McClintock, Guillermo O'Donnell, Philippe Schmitter.

This paradox becomes even more striking when we consider the particular status of Latin America both as an academic object and as a geostrategic area. These scholars developed an interest in democratization, authoritarianism, and the politics of liberation in a region placed under the influence of American hegemonic policies and subordinated to the overarching logic of the confrontation with Communism. Their own experience of field research in the region, as well as the constraints bearing upon their discipline, explain the critical nature of their work. This critical outlook was institutionalized in the Latin American Studies Association (LASA), created in 1966, precisely when this province of area studies was trying to assert its specificity, to a large extent against the methodological pressure of mainstream modernization theory. Presided by relatively young scholars, in comparison to other disciplinary organizations,[21] LASA also captured much of the critical energies released during the 1960s and the 1970s. Its early development coincided with swelling enrollment in higher education in general and in Latin American Studies in particular. It was from the outset a politicized institution that contributed to channeling into political science the critique of an American model that political science itself was exporting into Latin America under the form of modernization theory. All these factors facilitated the politicization of research, and help to explain the proximity that developed for instance between LASA and the dependency school, which had enormous appeal for the younger generation of students and scholars (Packenham 1992). Politicized, open to neo-Marxist and *dependencistas* analyses, Latin American studies would be predominantly critical of U.S. imperialism in the region and of its local political clienteles.

This engagement with foreign policy issues proved to be a long-lasting feature of Latin American studies, as the region became one of the symbolic grounds — the main one, actually — over which the battle between different approaches to human rights was fought in the 1980s. Even before the election of Reagan, the Carter administration had been the target of criticisms coming from many Latin American scholars for whom the new human rights policy was an imperial instrument.[22] The opposition only grew when the Reagan administration took over, and when it sought to reframe its counter-insurgency policies as the promotion of freedom and democracy. LASA then stood openly as a political opponent of the new foreign policy planners.[23] Latin America therefore concentrated all the political oppositions on the issue of human rights, democracy and U.S. foreign policy. In fact, for all these reasons, dealing with Latin America was considered as a necessary step in the development of the political capacity of the human rights movement (Neier 2003: 153).

What explains the conversion of this intellectual activism based on the critique of imperialism into a professional expertise which paradoxically defines a new form of international hegemony if not a form of symbolic (e.g. legal, political, economic) imperialism? In many respects, the end of the cold war gave birth to paradoxical convergences which recall those which followed the Second World War. In the same way as the "democratic crusade" of the 1950s expressed the alliance between U.S. foreign policy planners and the socialist critics of totalitarianism and imperialism on the left, democracy promotion in the 1990s contributed to bring within the same institutional area the neoconservative heirs of the latter and academic networks which coalesced in the opposition to U.S. imperialism.

From the perspective of the sociological literature on the de-radicalization of the social movements of the 1960s, this development could probably be analyzed as part of a more general return of the New Left to the fold of a new consensus, and of the dilution of the critical energies initially concentrated on the campuses in society at large. This literature often stresses the professionalization of academic life as a factor of this evolution (e.g. Levitt 1984; Jacoby 1987; Katsiaficas 1987). While such explanations may indeed provide part of the answer, they remain too general for the specific issue dealt with here and, sometimes, too mechanistic. The role of professionalization is certainly more subtle than these explanations suggest, and comes into play in a quite different manner. Part of the answer to the above question, I think, must be sought in the similarity of the repertoires and of the strategies used for promoting different political agendas. In seeking to oppose Reagan's foreign policy, some of these activist academics moved closer to liberal policy entrepreneurs and to institutions such as the Woodrow Wilson Center, the Inter-American Dialogue, or the Council on Foreign Relations, in order to make their opposition more effective. By the same token, they were forced to adapt their strategies to more policy-oriented standards of research and advocacy. In fact, many LASA scholars within the NED Research council embody this more "professional" approach. Abraham Lowenthal, for instance, has been a critic of both the neoconservatives' policies in Latin America, and the academic activism which he considered as a "violation of professional norms" within LASA due to its excessive politicization (quoted in Packenham 1992, 175).

A similar process of professionalization of advocacy took place in other "critical" disciplines, such as Political Economy, where some critics of the political consequences of neoliberal policies managed to find allies within the World Bank, and gradually translated their critique into more policy-oriented prescriptions. In other words, the struggles around human rights and democracy gradually moved away from the political and ideological level to the professional one: these battle were waged *on both sides* with the same tools, the same weapons, and in the name of the same ideals. In fact, they tended to become professional turf battles. Moreover, in their effort to fight the reassertion of American hegemony, the liberal and academic opponents of the neoconservatives came to rely on the traditional institutions of this hegemony: philanthropic foundations, policy research centers, international issue and academic networks and other traditional exporters of conceptions of the polity and the economy made-in-the-USA. In doing so, they helped consolidate the role of these institutions as unavoidable actors in any project of social and political change.

Obviously, some important contextual factors have also made possible the emergence of this integrated field of policy expertise on democracy and human rights, as well as the convergence between previously opposed political constituencies: the collapse of Communism diminished the strategic value of authoritarian dictatorships in the South, and the administration as well as the National Endowment for Democracy endorsed a limited form of political liberalization as a viable strategy for the region, which made possible a certain form of cooperation.[24] But the transformation of ideological battles into a market for policy expertise and research was also determined to a large extent by the nature of these struggles and of the strategies used to fight them.

The changing position of the political scientists analyzing democratization processes influenced the evolution of their discipline. For many of them, the experience of research in and on subordinate countries had made them sensitive from the outset to the international dimensions of national politics. Now that they were themselves involved in international networks promoting democracy and human rights, they easily went on to theorize — and, to a large extent, to justify — the role of these new "international actors" of democratization. A whole body of academic literature has thus been produced which links democratization with the exposure to these transnational actors (e.g. Quigley 1997; Whitehead 1996). The evolution of "comparative democratization studies" is a direct outcome of these developments: "curricula were changed to reflect new global circumstances; syllabi were modified; a variety of new courses on NGOs, civil society, democracy, and related topics were introduced" (Quigley 1997: 566). Democracy promotion has thus connected social science research to the construction of a worldwide market for policy prescriptions and expertise, facilitating the circulation of methods, models, agendas. As one of its practitioners writes, "bureaucrats charged with mounting programs to support democratic transitions also appear to be more receptive and interested in what social scientists have to say, because they need answers to the same questions" (Barkan 1997: 376). The fabrication of this knowledge which today forms the basis of this hegemonic expertise will be the subject of the next chapters.

3 From the Development Engineers to the Democracy Doctors:

The Rise and Fall of Modernization Theory

The centrality of democracy and human rights in U.S. foreign policy discourse has been matched by scholarly efforts to generate a science or a "proto-science" (Schmitter 1994) of democratization. The institutionalization of "democratization studies" as a recognized curriculum in major U.S. universities is the outcome of a long process of theoretical renewal in political science. This renewal has developed against a previous body of theory, broadly speaking the political sociology of modernization which was a dominant research program of the 1950s and the 1960s. Against this academic tradition and the associated liberal ideology of social progress which endowed the particular historical development of Western societies with universal value, the political and scientific reaction against modernization theory overlapped with a search for a less structural, more voluntary and, ultimately, more political approach to democratization. At the same time, most of the exponents of the new political science of "transitions to democracy" approach (e.g. O'Donnell and Schmitter 1986; Whitehead 1996; Linz and Stepan 1996) came from the academic tradition of "comparative politics" which was the cradle of modernization theory, and they often belonged to a generation trained during the heydays of the behavioral revolution in the social sciences. They have however abandoned structural or functional types of analysis to focus instead on political agency and the "crafting" of democratic regimes (DiPalma 1990).

While modernization theory corresponded to the policies of development assistance and foreign aid, comparative democratization and the analysis of democratic "transitions" overlapped with the crisis of developmental ideologies, diminishing levels of foreign aid, and the emergence of a new policy of democracy promotion advocated by the neoconservative ideologues of a global U.S. hegemony based on the notion of human rights. Here I analyze this shift and explain the "fit" between academic social science and the main foreign policy doctrines, this time to examine its *scientific forms*, its theoretical and academic expressions. One way of explaining the fit between academic products and foreign policy needs would be to stress the subordination of the field of the social sciences to the field of state power. Law, economics, political science are disciplines that have been often tapped for policymaking purposes. The philanthropic foundations and the social, political, and intellectual elites associated with them have traditionally acted as the mediators of this relation of dependence and sophisticated subordination. The role of universities and international academic exchanges, the division of disciplines, and the nature of research programs in the social sciences represented important political stakes throughout the cold war and were actively managed by the major foundations (Berman 1983; Simpson 1998).

While this view of social sciences correctly reflects a well-documented reality, too often it remains steeped in a crude functionalism. It implies a simplistic image of the dynamics involved in the evolution of the social sciences, for at least two reasons: first, because this interdependence between the fields of science and state power does not mean univocal subordination. Scientific research does not simply mirror political factors or espouse their dictates. It converts them into internal scientific struggles, which follow a different logic, and scientific protocols present their own specific constraints that cannot be entirely reduced to external influences. In other words, the emergence of a new generation of theories dealing with democratization must be seen as a matter of tension between intradisciplinary developments and the evolution of the structural position of academics in the field of policymaking. Second, and more specifically, because the development of democratization studies and of the new technologies of democratization owes a great deal to a generation of political scientists who have distinguished themselves by their political opposition to U.S. foreign policy, in particular in Latin America. A picture of the social sciences as structurally dependent and subordinated to the making of foreign policy cannot account for this paradox. The convergence between social-scientific research programs and policy agendas in the 1980s calls for a different type of explanation, in particular because it was a convergence between policy actors with opposed political views.

What is needed, rather, is a better understanding of how even opposed strategies, pursued by actors located in different contexts, can end up converging or being functional to one another. The idea that there might be a sort of coherent grand design systematically subordinating political science research to policy objectives would not only lead to a weak form of conspiracy theory but would also prevent us from understanding the very real conflicts that have sometimes divided scholars or opposed them to the foreign policy establishment. And by the same token, it would preclude a proper understanding of how these conflicts have been functional to the emergence of different "discourse coalitions" between social scientists and specific political elites.[1]

Both the agenda of political modernization and, later, the agenda of transition to democracy have been promoted by such "discourse coalitions," the making and unmaking of which is analyzed in this chapter. I show that the changing conceptualization of the path toward democracy — societal modernization in one case, controlled demise of authoritarian rule in favor of limited democracy under neoliberal economic conditions in the other — did not signal a major change in the policy objectives of Washington. In both cases, the goal was to create international networks of political, technical, and intellectual elites promoting gradual conceptions of political change. Born out of the cold war, this project was justified by the academic narrative of "modernization": as they underwent functional differentiation, "traditional" societies evolved toward a form of political pluralism that would eventually translate into modern liberal democracy. Influenced by the structural functionalism of Talcott Parsons, the theory reflected the American understanding of American modernization, and transformed it in a universal model that could be exported and applied virtually anywhere. Yet, the scholars who contributed most to the demise of this hegemonic theory and who criticized its imperialist political implications actually provided the new social scientific framework of the interventionist policies of democracy promotion" that emerged in the 1980s.

Cold Thought: Modernization Theory and Cold War Policies

By "modernization theory," I refer to the literature on political development that prospered in the 1960s and the dominant research program on the comparative analysis of political systems that supported it. This research agenda, which shaped most of postwar American political science, was explicitly articulated in a series of publications. The best known were the Studies in Political Development published by Princeton University and the Little, Brown Series in Comparative Politics. It was institutionalized in 1954, with the creation of the Committee on Comparative Politics of the Social Science Research Council successively chaired by Gabriel Almond and Lucian W. Pye. Produced in prestigious universities and well-funded research centers, the voluminous literature on modernization was influenced from the outset by cold war considerations and in particular by postcolonial developments in the Third World.

After the Second World War, with the completion of European reconstruction, U.S. foreign and aid policy became increasingly geared toward the Third World, where the process of decolonization raised the stakes of the confrontation with the Soviet Union. It is in this historical context that the issue of "development" was first formulated (Bromley 1995). Development was primarily meant to address two sets of problems: to expand the international circuits for capital and to sustain American prosperity by allowing for the appropriation of overseas surpluses. Very early on, the more far-sighted sectors of the corporate and philanthropic world had identified the fragility of the U.S. economy and pushed for the increase in overseas trade and investment (Berman 1983: 44). On the other hand, the rise of anti-colonial nationalism in the Third World posed serious threats not only to the above objective, but also to the stability of the international order by raising the specter of Soviet influence.

If political independence supposed economic autonomy, as many Third World leaders thought (Mosley et al. 1991: 3), decolonization would undermine the liberal economic model that inspired foreign assistance by introducing state regulations on trade, investments, and foreign property. It was also feared that such development would bring decolonized countries closer to the Soviet bloc. These issues reshaped the logic and contents of development assistance. There was now a need to secure control over the processes of decolonization. The former strategy of criminalizing Third World nationalism was progressively substituted with a more positive approach that regarded nationalism, if well handled, as a potential defense against Soviet imperialism (Füredi 1994: 66ff). The United States began to support "legitimate" nationalism where it was clear that it would not fundamentally challenge the integration of the country into the capitalist economy and play into the hands of the Soviet Union.

The assistance to "state-building" processes in former colonies was also a

way of promoting capitalistic forms of development where possible, to develop political ties, and to stabilize the country. In this context, development
assistance was a major policy instrument, designed in order to promote what
Wood has called "defensive modernization." (1986: 76). The point was to
ensure that developing countries would reach socioeconomic modernity and
statehood without triggering major social upheavals that would disrupt the
geostrategic equilibrium of the cold war. The point of American-assisted
modernization was, as Rostow (1960) had theorized it, to provide a coun-
terpoint to communist revolutions. Since they feared that the widening of
political participation provoked by the process of modernization would disrupt traditional political institutions, modernization theorists were particularly interested in the structure of political authority (Huntington 1965;
Huntington and Nelson 1976; Pye 1966). If democracy was seen as an at-
tribute of modernity, developing in parallel with the economy, the whole
impetus toward democratization and liberal democracy posited by U.S. political sociologists and political scientists remained ambiguously intricate
with an attachment to strong authority.

   If modernization theory reflected the U.S. perception of the global context, it was because this research program had been created under the indirect supervision of the foreign policy establishment and its philanthropic
institutions. The need to train scholars informed about the political and
social realities in regions of the world that the United States would have to
deal with was identified early on by those in charge of thinking about postwar
foreign policy. In collaboration with the CIA and other security agencies,
the philanthropic foundations massively invested in the creation of academic
centers in area studies and comparative politics in the aftermath of the Second World War. The strategy was to produce "able young scholars," as once
said Shepard Stone, president of the Ford Foundation, who could contribute
reliable knowledge to the making of security policy. Combined together,
area studies and modernization theory represented a form of scientific imperialism or, in the words of Johan Galtung, of "scientific colonialism": "a
process whereby the center of gravity for the acquisition of knowledge about
the nation is located outside the nation itself" (Galtung 1979: 168–69).
Once it is processed in the North, this knowledge is then re-exported as
development strategies, policy prescriptions, or economic recipes in order
to be applied. The Russian Institute at Columbia University, the Russian
Research Center at Harvard, and the Far Eastern Association (later the Association for Asian Studies) were the first institutions created around the
cold war academic agenda.[2]

During the 1950s and 1960s, the philanthropic foundations used their munificent resources in order to create almost from scratch the subfields of area studies and comparative politics. According to Edward Berman, the Ford Foundation established the major area-studies programs in U.S. universities "almost single-handedly" (1983: 102). From 1953 to 1966, it spent an estimated $270 million in 34 universities on area and foreign language studies (Cumings 1998), thus establishing new disciplinary boundaries and shaping an entire field. By coining a "behavioral" agenda for the social sciences and creating the Center for Advanced Study in the Behavioral Sciences in Palo Alto in 1953, the Ford Foundation managed indeed to transform the disciplinary structure of political science and to separate it from political theory (Seybold 1980; Gunnell 1988).

This reorganization of the discipline was in line with a long tradition of promotion of "empirical" "applied" social science by the philanthropic foundations, traditionally supportive of all attempts to model the social sciences after the natural sciences in order to develop "social control." Intended to make the traditional teaching in area studies more scientific, behavioralism also promoted the training of a personnel that translated into social scientific language the very practical strategic concerns of the Foundation. Throughout the late 1950s and the 1960s, modernization theory thus institutionalized the convergence between the strategic tenets of foreign policy planners and the assumptions of political scientists. A largely inarticulate and liberal belief in the technical and institutional capacities to generate societal development was the common ground of this research agenda and of the policy framework of development assistance; it allowed for the overlap between (political) doctrines and (academic) theories that was characteristic of this period (Packenham 1973: xvii).[3] The conversion of views was aided by the circulation of the same personnel among academic positions, state bureaucracies, philanthropic boards, and international organizations.[4]

Philanthropic foundations therefore played a crucial role in agenda-setting. Between 1960 and 1967, for instance, the Ford Foundation made two grants to sustain the efforts of Pye, Almond, and their colleagues to provide a scientific framework for understanding modernization processes. The Studies in Political Development series was largely the outcome of this funding. The Carnegie Corporation, also active, sponsored in particular Lucian W. Pye's *Aspects of Political Development* (1966). Pye is certainly the scholar who expressed in the clearest terms this symbiotic relation between the foreign policy establishment and modernization theorists:

Those who feel a sense of responsibility for maintaining international stability are striving to facilitate the process of modernization so that all societies can become stable states while at the same time seeking to prevent this very process of social change from disrupting the stability of the international system. The resulting struggle explains the prime purposes of American foreign-policy efforts in this era (Pye 1966: 8).

The involvement of the foreign policy establishment in the scientific field certainly reflected the social proximity and the increasing interactions between academic research centers and policymakers. But it also corresponded to a real need for planning tools in foreign policy and especially in foreign aid, designed to facilitate economic modernization and avoid its political hazards. The group of John Kennedy's advisors in charge of long-term development aid — the so-called "Charles River" group, mostly recruited from MIT and Harvard — symbolized this search for "more specific, quantitative criteria for assistance" (Packenham 1973: 62) that would underlie the work of development agencies such as AID or the World Bank during the whole decade. With its stress on quantification, operationalization, and testability, modernization theory provided the perfect scientific ideology for a growing development technocracy that sought to combine a faith in technocratic solutions and a commitment to social reformism dictated as much by political convictions as by strategic pragmatism (Dezalay and Garth 2002). Progressive social reform was indeed a central component of the U.S. strategy toward the developing world. To the extent that achieving "take off" and reducing the "explosiveness of the modernization process" required not only economic inputs but also social change — land reform, tax reform, more voluntary organizations, greater political participation (Packenham 1973: 62), the cold war policy of modernization entailed the promise of more democracy, social improvement, and individual well-being. The multiple agents of this policy — a swelling body of technical advisors, development engineers, administrators, and social scientists — could legitimately consider themselves as the agents of a benevolent social reformism. This professional group was therefore endowed with moral attributes by a techno-political discourse functioning both as a standard of scientificity and as an emancipatory ideology. In the words of a leading exponent of modernization theory, "the problem of the American serving abroad is no longer that of representing American power but of learning how to be effective in helping others to achieve their ambitions of development" (Pye 1966: 4).

Modernization as a Disciplinary Stake

Reflecting the perception of the world from the standpoint of U.S. foreign policy planners and institutionalized in academic institutions that benefited from the financial support of the philanthropic foundations, modernization theory appears as a socially situated research program, in spite of the emphasis it placed on objectivity, formalism, value-free concepts and in spite of its apparent universality. As a recent assessment notices, "since it was American social scientists at elite academic institutions who contributed disproportionately to 'modernization analyses,' the model of modernization was to an important extent an unreflexive projection of the liberal, secular, individualizing values of 'establishment' intellectuals." (Tiryakian 1991: 170).

This context certainly was propitious to the establishment of modernization theory as a dominant research agenda. And it certainly explains the capacity of modernization theory to function as a political ideology, legitimating development policies and transforming the U.S. socioeconomic model into a universal one. What it cannot account for, however, is the capacity of this paradigm to function also as "science." The massive financial investments sustaining the growth of area studies and comparative politics do not explain the capacity of modernization theory to impose successfully its methods as scientific standards and to impose a semblance of conceptual unity over "area studies." In other words, while this academic agenda suited the purposes of the foreign policy establishment, that did not mean that it was apt to play the role of a real scientific paradigm in an academic environment. Michael Latham is right when he argues that the ideology of modernization functioned as a political weapon "in one surface-level sense," but that "it was also a cognitive framework that crystallized an underlying, firmly-held set of beliefs" (Latham 1998: 205–6).

The successful imposition of this research agenda across the major political science departments is all the more surprising, since area studies and comparative politics were initially subordinated and poorly considered subfields in a discipline dominated by a tradition of historical-legal erudition and political theory. Scholars associated with more traditional approaches to politics regarded area studies as intellectually deficient disciplines, kept alive by massive funding (which also caused some envy). More importantly, modernization theory contained the project of an orderly system of area studies: it imposed new disciplinary divisions which mirrored the geographical divisions defined by the cold war, but it also conveyed the promise of a methodological unification of these newly defined area studies under a single coherent conceptual framework. This project threatened the traditional boundaries of scholarly investigation and encountered resistance. In the words of William Fenton, the new area programs "faced fierce resistance from the 'imperialism of departments' since they challenged the fragmentation of the human sciences by disciplinary departments, each endowed with a particular methodology and a specific intellectual subject matter" (Fenton [1947] quoted in Cumings 1998: 163).

If modernization theory included much of the foreign policy establishment's fears and hopes under the form of scientific rationalizations, it also entailed the promise of a conceptual unification of political science. Conceived on the model of the natural sciences, it was expected to deliver the same degree of precision and rigor, in particular through a greater reliance on formalization, mathematization, measurement, etc. This project was pitted against the scattered historical erudition of regional specialization and the traditional teaching in political theory, considered to be vague and value-laden. In one of the most authoritative statements on the "modern" research agenda, Gabriel Almond enthusiastically wrote about the sound and constructive impulse "toward rigor and precision" and the "possibilities of applying formal logic and mathematics to the study of politics." The whole project of building the "probabilistic theory of the polity" that Almond puts forward aims at specifying the properties of the political system "in such form as to lend itself to statistical and mathematical formulation" (Almond 1960: 58–59). These very high expectations regarding the potential for social engineering based on the use of value-free concepts and scientific instruments pervaded the sociological and political literature on modernization. The need for "operational" definitions allowing for "tests" and "falsification," the perspective of a linear accumulation of reliable knowledge and the hopes placed in the contribution of social scientific disciplines to the management of public affairs constituted a new article of faith.

This scientific ambition is certainly a distinctive feature of modernization theory. In retrospect, these expectations are much more significant and more revealing than the actual achievements. Both critics and proponents of modernization theory have ultimately recognized the failure of this research program. In 1960, Almond observed that "the first efforts have not produced impressive results yet" (1960: 58–59). Six years later, Pye (1966) asserted that the field had still "little central coherence" and went on to distinguish painstakingly the various and confused meanings of "political development."

This diagnosis was not substantially different in the early 1970s, when the whole research program entered its protracted crisis. This has led critics of this literature (e.g. Cammack 1997) to emphasize its ideological functions over its status as a legitimate scientific norm within academic community.

While the ideological elements in modernization theory are clear, well-known, and quite central, they fail to explain the whole picture. It is precisely the imposing scientific pretensions of the theory that explain its successful institutionalization within political science departments. The "scientifica-tion" of politics promised by behavioralism and embodied in modernization theory was actually serving a strategy of professionalization of political science. The sophisticated comparative designs implied in this research program offered a way of revalorizing a field — "area studies" — that lacked scientific status and was poorly considered. Furthermore, the amount of research that was needed, the intellectual manpower that was to be consumed in this undertaking of monumental dimensions, fitted the simultaneous "massification" of higher education in general and political science in particular. In this respect, it is highly significant that Lucian Pye, for instance, was able to "sell" political development research to prospective students on the basis of purely professional arguments such as career perspectives, rather than scientific superiority: after taking notice of the lack of "central coherence" of the field, he immediately observed that "Students who do become interested in fundamental problems of the emerging states can expect to move to the frontiers of a discipline in a very short period of time and to contribute substantially to a great public policy problem of our time and to a significant advance in human knowledge" (Pye 1966: viii).

Modernization theory or political development thus offered fast tracks to academic tenure and prestige. Previously marginalized and confined to narrow geographical specialization, "area studies" political scientists could at last assert the scientific character of their work under a unified methodological umbrella. The tensions and the polemics between the champions of behavioralism and exponents of classical political theory are revealing of the professional stakes of this academic revolution. They signaled, within political science, a break with the traditional figure of the intellectual academic and the rise of a new profile: the professional technician. In fact, political theory would soon become a dominated sub-field of political science, from where the main critiques of the dominant liberal paradigm would be articulated, whether in a conservative perspective (Wolin, Strauss, Voegelin, etc.) or in a more radical one (the Frankfurt school). The establishment of more "scientific" standards for the comparative analysis of political systems paved the way for the professionalization of political science and for its integration within a wider policy environment. Under the cover of objectivity and formalism, it facilitated the convergence of methodological choices and political interests, thus ensuring significant amounts of funding and influential positions for a small number of leading scholars. The formal definitions of politics underlying behavioralism and the sociology of modernization "were functionally rational for serving the interest of the scholarly community within its larger environment" (Ricci 1984: 217).

The Economic Production of Democracy

There has been a debate within the literature examining the record of modernization theories about whether the democratization of developing countries was considered a desirable goal, or even envisioned at all (Cammack 1997). Alternatively, historians of this scientific paradigm often distinguish two periods in the development of the sociology of modernization: a first period, characterized by a strong optimism about the democratic perspectives of developing countries, and a second, much more pessimistic, dominated by concerns about stability rather than democracy (e.g. Huntington and Weiner 1987). As a matter of fact, the ideal goal of transplanting Anglo-American liberal democracy to developing nations was explicitly posited by modernization theorists, but in order to be immediately qualified. Most of the literature, while acknowledging that this goal was desirable, warned against the many obstacles that paved the road. At the end of a chapter-long discussion of this issue, for instance, Pye significantly acknowledges that "there is much truth in the often cynically advanced generalization that these societies are "unprepared" for democracy" (Pye 1966: 87).

Such doubts were also fueled by what a researcher of the Rand Corporation has termed the "unproductive search for middle classes in underdeveloped areas" (Halpern 1963: 51), driven by the parochial view of scholars whose conception of democracy was imbued with the American experience and with the idea that a large middle class formed the only possible social basis of democracy. This ambivalence of modernization and political development doctrines with respect to democracy is actually constitutive of this literature and of the political project behind it. This project was contradictory. On the one hand, ensuring stability in developing and decolonized countries could not be achieved without expanding political participation. Yet, this participation should also be limited in order to guarantee the continuous influence of pro-Western political elites. This dilemma lies at the heart of the "doctrine for political development."

One of the most significant illustrations of this nexus between democracy, stability, the requirements of the cold war, and the role of political scientists can be found in the writings of Seymour Martin Lipset. His works and his own biography shed an interesting light on the complex interactions among the international context, the development of an empirical theory of democracy, and the conversion to liberalism of the non-Communist left analyzed in chapter 1. While not a pure exponent of modernization theory — of which, however, he shares the main methodological orientations and in particular a strong comparative approach — Lipset has paid much attention to the relation between democracy and modernization. His 1959 essay on "Economic Development and Democracy" (Lipset 1963) is the starting point of a whole *genre* of studies on the social prerequisites of liberal regimes using statistical models and large data sets (Curtis, Vanhanen, Przeworski, etc.) and is still widely cited in the "transitions" literature. Simply stated, his argument is the following: liberal democracy is correlated with economic wealth and high levels of industrialization, urbanization and education. These aggregate indicators, on a closer look, actually capture the capitalistic nature of national economies and also a type of social stratification centered around the middle classes.[5] While this American bias is common to most forms of modernization theories, what is interesting is Lipset's underlying concern with the way in which economic development "determines the form of 'class struggle.' " Depending upon the path followed, economic development can give rise to democratic or authoritarian solutions to the social conflicts generated by the process of modernization. By improving the conditions of the lower classes, economic development also fosters among these classes "a belief in secular reformist gradualism" and leads them away from leftist extremism (Lipset 1963, 45). For this to happen, however, a relatively compact social stratification is deemed necessary. A strong middle class along with an emphasis on egalitarian values translating into relatively open redistributive policies are therefore the structural and ideological elements implicit in Lipset's tautological demonstration. His sociological concern with the political form of "class struggle" reflects the political concern with Communism he shared with other exponents of the anti-Stalinist left. In the same way as "democratic socialism" was promoted in Europe in the perspective of an ideological response to Communism, reform, development, and redistributive policies were promoted in the Third World — and for the same purpose.

In newly industrializing countries, the defeat of domestic Communists also required that the process of industrialization be kept slow and progressive, in order to avoid political upheavals. The integration of the popular sectors of society was considered as a necessity in order to avoid creating a receptive ground for Communist propaganda. Rather than a potential collective actor of democracy, the lower classes were in fact considered as potentially subversive and authoritarian. Lipset dedicated a long chapter of his *Political Man* to proving the social predisposition of the working class toward authoritiarianism (1960: 97–130), a theme that can be traced to the early socio-psychological analyses of unemployed workers, such as the *Marienthal* study conducted by Paul Lazarsfeld in Germany.[6] But while it initially denounced the reduction of the "life scope" created by unemployment, Lazarsfeld's study took a different shade once placed in a wider reflection upon the social bases of Nazism, and later again when it was imported to the United States. Lipset's treatment of the topic of "working-class authoritarianism" is explicitly related to the Communist threat, especially in less developed countries (ibid.: 130). In tune with a whole elitist tradition within American political science, running through Lippman and Huntington, the masses were thought to be better off when kept in a political apathy based on relative material welfare. In this elitist view, the intellectual classes bear the "responsibility to keep democracy representative and free" (1963: xxxiv).

"A Man on the Left": Seymour M. Lipset and the Political Meaning of Modernity

Lipset's biography sheds some light on the social and political uses of modernization theory. It offers a striking example of the relations between the social sciences and the "democratic" project articulated in the immediate postwar years that we analyzed in chapter 1. In particular, it shows the function of modernization theory as an intellectual bridge from a previous form of sociological analysis still inspired by Marxism and mainstream liberalism, ultimately leading a whole generation committed scholars to embrace "American values" and play an instrumental role in the legitimation of the cold war.

Born in 1922, in a Jewish working class area in the Bronx, Lipset was the son of a printer who was "a socialist of some kind" (Lipset 1996b), and a member of the typographical union. If this background was certainly important in determining his early socialist orientation — his father, as Lipset

recalls, had been unemployed on and off during the Depression and socialism was seen as a way of solving mass unemployment — the intellectual
atmosphere of his academic generation was at least as determinant. As was
typical for educated young men with his background, Lipset went to study
at City College New York, where he joined the groups of the anti-Stalinist
left and, later on, Shachtman's new Workers Party. Soon afterward, however,
Lipset left the party along with Philip Selznick and Irving Kristol in order
to join the Socialist Party and the Young People's Socialist League. This
political evolution toward Social Democracy was matched by a corresponding move away from Marxism. At about the same time, after obtaining his
B.S. (1943), Lipset enrolled in the Sociology Department at Columbia,
where he studied under Robert Lynd, but also got to know Robert Merton
and Paul Lazarsfeld.

Some of the works collected in *Political Man* offer a glimpse of this
intellectual evolution leading to the embracing of the "American proposition." If socialism had failed in the United States, according to Lipset, it was
essentially because America itself was an egalitarian, almost socialistic society. As a model of open society, where material progress, full employment,
and consumption guaranteed the insertion of the lower classes in the dominant life-style of the middle classes, the United States embodied the promise
of solving the "social question" (*la question sociale*). Making all these developments possible, rational social reform was superior to class-based ideologies. In fact, Lipset used the theme of working-class authoritarianism in
order to castigate "those intellectuals of the democratic left who once believed the proletariat necessarily to be a force for liberty, racial equality, and
social progress" (1960: 97). Not surprisingly, Lipset's explicit rejection of
socialism was related to his belief in the possibility of a social reformism
guided by the new empirical instruments offered by applied social sciences — instruments displayed most attractively at Columbia's sociology
department.

Encapsulating these arguments about the peculiarities of American society, the topic of American exceptionalism would remain at the center of
Lipset's reflection (e.g. Lipset 1996a; 1996b). To a large extent, the notion
of exceptionalism appears as the artefact that allowed a whole generation of
anti-Stalinist leftists to rationalize their reembracement of mainstream liberalism. In Lipset's case, it translated into "normative interest in gradual
change, political accommodation [and] in limiting the power of the state,"
as two of his student-disciples later noted (Diamond and Marks 1992: 3).

The rest of Lipset's political and intellectual career bears witness to the further rightward drift of the Old Left of the 1930s. In the early 1970s, he was among the founders of the Coalition for a Democratic Majority, an informal group headed by Ben Wattenberg and Midge Decter and composed of anti-Communist intellectuals in the Democratic party.[7] He later followed most of those future neoconservatives to the Committee on the Present Danger, an intellectual lobby opposing arms-reduction negotiations with the Soviet Union. In the 1980s, Lipset held positions in such institutions as the Woodrow Wilson Center for Scholars, the Council of Foreign Relations, the National Endowment for Democracy, and the United States Institute for Peace, which highlights the continuity between the new policy of democracy promotion, which was fabricated and implemented in these various centers, and the old project of exporting American democracy abroad.

Modernization theory therefore provided the melting pot for very different intellectual and political traditions. As the first byproduct of the fusion between Marxism and liberalism, it put the analysis of social structures at the service of a pragmatic form of social control associated with the scientific agenda of behavioral political science. Its more or less implicit acceptance of the American social order as a democratic order, based on the channeling of the middle classes in structured and orderly channels of political participation ranging from civic organizations to political parties, injected into the theory a Tocquevillian influence overlapping with its Marxian birthmarks. While the comparative study of democratization reproduced these features, it also conveyed a fear of the disruptive potential of massive political participation. This concern was fully complementary with the management of the cold war by the foreign policy planners and their strategic doctrines for developing countries. Lipset, for instance, ended his analysis of the "end of ideology" with practical counter-insurgency recommendations. While the end of ideology was useful in the West, in underdeveloped countries, there was "still a need for intense political controversy and ideology." In particular, it was necessary to recognize that in those countries, the West's allies "must be radicals, probably socialists, because only parties which promise to improve the situation of the masses through widespread reform, and which are transvaluational [sic] and equalitarian, can hope to compete with the Communists" (Lipset 1960: 416).

The convergence between the professional-intellectual transformations of political science and the interests of the foreign policy elite therefore ensured the institutionalization of the new research agenda and the prestige of its exponents. Initially frowned upon by a discipline dominated by legalistic and historical learning, the new emphasis on economic and sociological variables of political development was on its way to becoming the major influence in American social sciences. Sustained by newly devised empirical and quantitative research methods, the concern of this generation of political scientists for the social mechanisms of democratic politics — associational life, public opinion, voting — found the favorable attention of the philanthropic foundations which were in the process of expanding their involvement in research. It resonated positively with their own promotion of social reform at home and of modernizing elites abroad in the framework of a global anti-Communist strategy.

The role of the Ford Foundation, which contributed more than any other philanthropic trust to establishing the legitimacy of the "behavioral sciences" (Dahl 1961: 765–66), illustrates the complementarity between the social sciences and foreign policy objectives. Its Behavioral Sciences Division supported a wide range of research on modernization and democracy, ranging from Lipset's work on elections and class structure reproduced in *Political Man*, to such works as William Kornhauser's *The Politics of Mass Society* (1960) or Herbert Hyman's *Political Socialization* (1959). It also provided financial support for Almond, Coleman, and Pye for their publications on political development. All these efforts, however, would soon turn out to be vain, as the paradigm of modernization came increasingly under attack in the 1960s and 1970s, and as its strategic value diminished.

The Crisis of Modernization Theory and the Latin American Connection

To the extent that it reflected the concerns of the foreign policy planners, modernization theory rested upon the ideological cohesion of the foreign policy establishment. When contradictions appeared and became divisive, in the late 1960s and throughout the 1970s, the paradigm of elite-led modernization and democratization also entered its terminal crisis. The Vietnam War signaled the end of the consensus which this scientific ideology had successfully reflected so far. In a retrospective look at the whole effort aiming at producing a scientific theory of political development, Gabriel Almond pointed out that the research program was indeed fraught with internal divisions between scholars: "Politically, it included scholars with relatively naive expectations of democratization in the third world, as well as skeptics and pessimists who foresaw authoritarian regimes. It included "hawks" and "doves" as the Vietnam War divided American academic circles" (Almond 1987: 444). In fact, just as the liberal consensus would be challenged from within the ranks of the foreign policy establishment, the paradigm of modernization would also be attacked by some of its exponents.

Converging developments contributed to transform the scientific discourse on democratization. Democracy was initially built into modernization theory as a dependent variable. That is, it was supposed to be the outcome of structural socioeconomic evolutions that development policies tried to foster. Producing democracy, in that sense, was equivalent to promoting development. However, the establishment of authoritarian regimes throughout Latin America in the late 1960s and 1970s was a severe blow to the scientific narrative of modernization. Modernization turned out to be carried out by authoritarian modernizers — bureaucrats, technocrats, and the military. At the same time, it also became clear that the research agenda of modernization theorists had taken a significant turn toward a concern for security and stability rather than democracy (illustrated by Huntington, for instance.) The reformist strategy pursued by the United States, which tolerated for strategic reasons a certain dose of economic nationalism and considered positively the work of the UN Economic Commission for Latin America (CEPAL), was also at a dead-end. This fostered a series of radical responses in academic circles, both North and South, which were able to take advantage of the divisions within the establishment and of its lack of intellectual cohesion. The Ford Foundation, for instance, which had worked in symbiosis with the other sectors of the foreign policy machinery, came to play the role of a protector of alternative academic elites which were often radical — in a strategy that sometimes directly clashed with the objectives of the State Department. At the same time, it eased their insertion into a U.S.-dominated market of academic and technical skills, functioning according to different rules.

Paradoxically, the successful challenge to modernization theory and the renewal of the field of comparative politics around new issues contributed to building the international North-South networks that would function as sites of coordination for the "democratic" foreign policy agenda of the late 1980s and 1990s. The National Endowment for Democracy mobilized the same networks in its strategy of professionalization of the field of democracy and human rights. Far from disrupting the "U.S.-Latin America academic diplomacy" (Gil 1985: 10) that was part of the policy followed by the foreign policy establishment in the region, the activist scholars who rejected modernization theory and its ideological biases actually became the actors of new transnational policy networks that played a crucial role in the democratization policies of the late twentieth century. I now focus on the convergence between the Southern critique of modernization theory known as dependency theory and the Northern field of Latin American studies. It is in this context that the political science literature on "transitions to democracy" emerged and found a receptive policy environment.

By the 1970s, modernization theory could be considered a defunct research program. After a decade of massive production and publication, with no convincing results and no Grand Theory in view, the literature took a different turn. The last two volumes of the series *Studies in Political Development*, Charles Tilly's *The Formation of National States in Western Europe* (1975) and Raymond Grew's *Crises of Political Development in Europe and the United States* (1978), illustrate this shift. Initially meant to bring some historical grounding to the project of theorizing a typical sequence of political development, these volumes actually jeopardized it. The first, in particular, brought to light a split between the early political development theorists and the historians. Tilly denounced not only the illusory attempt at generating an ideal-typical sequence of political development, but also the "implicit policy aims of the models."[8] In addition, the problems that the editors identified in the political development agenda were related, in their view, to the fact that it had paid no attention to the international factors influencing domestic political developments (Tilly 1975: 620).

This internal critique, which came from within the ranks of modernization theorists, linked up with the external attack on the political development literature that took the form of "dependency theory." This current was inspired by the work of the Argentine economist Raúl Prebisch (1901–1986) who was associated with the CEPAL.[9] In spite of their differences, the approaches to development respectively embodied in the Alliance for Progress launched in 1961 by the Kennedy administration and the CEPAL were initially complementary. As a liberal response to the Cuban revolution, the Alliance for Progress rested on the sincere conviction that poverty was the root of revolutionary instability. Foreign aid was thus considered as a strategic policy, but the Alliance for Progress also placed the emphasis on social progress, and in particular on land reform — a position that struck a sensitive chord with Latin American left-wing economists and intellectuals. While the CEPAL implicitly (as a UN organization, it could not formulate openly political prescriptions) called into question the dominant conceptions of international trade with its theory of the secular deterioration of the terms of trade and a preference for import-substitution industrialization, the type of modernization by stages it envisioned for Latin America was perfectly in line with U.S. academic modernization theory.

The economic analyses produced at the CEPAL also translated into a political program which called for the building of developmental states and the rise of a national bourgeoisie (as opposed to a "comprador" class that benefited from the unequal terms of trade). The early sixties were thus characterized by the convergence between CEPAL, much of the Latin American left, and the Alliance for Progress. Dependency theory, instead, flowed from the "disillusion of former members of the CEPAL camp" with this reformist consensus (Lehmann 1990: 24). A group of South American scholars radicalized Prebisch's theory of unequal exchange and import-substitution industrialization into a structuralist analysis of dependent capitalism.[10] In this perspective, the process of industrialization in the Southern cone was consolidating the political power of the social classes which drew their resources from the system of unequal exchange and thus gave rise to a split between one the one hand a modern sector, co-opting the national managerial class and segments of the middle classes, and on the other a traditional sector. This split impeded balanced development.

This Southern dissent with the dominant framework of capitalistic modernization was influential because it was not isolated. Its impact was multiplied by its convergence with a simultaneous Northern critique of the academic rationalizations of foreign aid and security policies, coming mostly from scholars and students of Latin America. From the outset, the relationship between this specific field of area studies and the dominant paradigm of modernization theory had been an ambiguous one. Initially, the emphasis on method characteristic of modernization theory and comparative politics had eased the insertion within mainstream political science of this branch of area studies which was still regarded in the 1950s as "narrowly focused, ethnocentric, atheoretical" (Dent 1990: 2). In retrospect, Gabriel Almond wrote along similar lines that at the time, "Latin American social science studies in the United States were in their infancy" (1987: 454). They lacked the methodological rigor, the conceptual precision, and the predictive capacity of behavioral sciences. Modernization theory did not only direct research toward certain topics or certain issues, it also provided a conceptual framework which was supposed to bestow scientific legitimacy — or at least a semblance of it — upon a discipline still attached to the pre-World War II tradition of erudite learning and legal-historical chronicling, still in its "public law phase" (Valenzuela 1988).

Starting in the mid-1960s, intellectual and academic pressure built up to extend the methodology of "modernization and political development" to Latin American studies.[11] In parallel, there was a surge in quantitative and statistical research that extended the "behavioral revolution" to Latin American Studies (Smith 1995: 11). This disciplinary normalization of Latin American studies under the hegemony of modernization and political development was not exempt from tensions and problems. The experience of field research had often led political scientists to question the validity of the concepts and theories of political development they had been equipped with.[12] Even scholars of Latin America sympathetic to this project did not fail to notice that one of the conceptual pillars of this literature, namely the distinction between the Western and the non-Western political process, was highly problematic when it came to studying Latin America.[13] After initial attempts at using modernization concepts, Kalman Silvert — the first president of the Latin American Studies Association — came to the conclusion that "the exercise of standard American professionalism is incompetence in explaining Latin American politics." (Silvert [1975], quoted in Valenzuela [1988: 70]). In the view of these scholars, the vast political science literature on comparative politics failed to give serious consideration to the specific character of the continent. As a result of the Western / non-Western dualism that pervaded comparative politics, "Latin Americanists . . . have sought in vain an acceptable and useful way of incorporating their area of interest into a broader scheme" (Martz 1966: 57).

The crisis of the modernization project that led in the 1960s and 1970s to the coming to power of authoritarian and military governments throughout the continent only contributed to making manifest these contradictions already present in the U.S. academic field and to radicalizing them. Initially a factor of professionalization and legitimation of Latin American studies, modernization theory and political development soon became targets for a generation of scholars and students who rejected their political implications. Their political radicalization was due largely to the repressive atmosphere following the establishment of "bureaucratic-authoritarian" regimes, which made field research increasingly difficult.[14] The existence of these authoritarian regimes also compromised the classical research agenda of comparative politics, which included interest groups, parties, or elections, as these institutions were controlled or simply disappeared. Instead, it opened new avenues of research on the colonization of the state apparatus by private interests and on the political economy of dependent development. The research agenda came quickly to reflect these internal crises and, by 1982, Jorge Dominguez — a president of the Latin American Studies Association — could argue that the literature presented more points of divergence than of consensus (Dominguez 1982). At the same time, North American scholars and students came to share the political mood of their Southern colleagues who were often in the line of fire of the authoritarian governments. The mass of academic refugees out of Latin America who ended up in U.S. universities facilitated this rapprochement.

The role played by American foundations in Latin America also facilitated the conjunction of this Northern critique of modernization with the Southern one. Under the military regimes, many South American academics who were not in favor with their rulers and encountered difficulties in their universities found havens in the various think tanks and research centers set up by U.S. philanthropic funds (Puryear 1994). Faithful to its liberal creed and to its strategy of investment in alternative elites, the Ford Foundation helped to promote research institutions such as the CEDES in Argentina or the CEBRAP in Brazil, where a generation of social scientists managed not only to continue their work but also to familiarize themselves with the American way of doing research, including certain methodological standards enforced through a competitive market of publications, the constraints of reporting and "project management," and so forth. In the late 1960s, the Ford Foundation spent an average $27 million per year on Latin America — approximately 23 percent of its budget (Smith 1995: 19). The Rockefeller, Tinker, and Mellon foundations were also active in Latin America and especially in the academic field. The Fulbright program and the Title VI of the National Defense Education Act also provided resources for scholarship and travel (Gil 1985: 11).

This process of transnationalization of Latin American socioeconomic research traditions had far-reaching effects. It facilitated the emergence of a North-South transnational network of academics sharing similar professional standards and a political concern with democracy. In his handbook of political science research on Latin America, for instance, Dent notes the "dramatic growth in qualified academics . . . , many trained in the United States and Western Europe, who are making important contributions" through the Latin American research centers supported by Ford funds (Dent 1990: 3). But beyond professional issues, the transformation of Latin American research also contributed to change the politics of social science research. The initial concern with the perverse effects of dependent modernization and of the exposure to an imperialist pattern of trade which motivated a radical democratic project gave way to a concern with a more limited form of democracy or political liberalization and to a discovery of the "democratic" virtues of international actors. As they generated new policy knowledge on the authoritarian state and the strategies for democratizing it, the former critics of imperialism became the producers of new imperial policies.

The Ambiguous Demise of Modernization Theory

While the alliance of these Northern and Southern critiques contributed to the demise of modernization theory, already discredited by political developments in the Latin America, the process was ambiguous. Indeed, the attack on this dominant academic paradigm and on its political implications was not completely external to the institutional contexts that had supported it. Nor was it completely independent of the very institutions that had been at the forefront of the development of modernization theory and comparative politics. The Ford Foundation, as we already mentioned, was at the cutting edge of a policy of shielding alternative elites (mostly academic ones), who were *de facto* critical of the modernization project that generated "bureaucratic-authoritarian" responses in Latin America. U.S. universities and research centers also showed that they were rather receptive to the new, more radical, approaches, provided, however, they fitted within established canons of method. This suggests that rather than constituting a break with the grand strategy which consisted in building transnational networks of scholars, intellectuals, and politicians around an ideological project, the demise of modernization theory was merely an internal adjustment of this strategy required by a new political context. It merely changed the personnel of the "U.S.-Latin American academic diplomacy" without fundamentally altering its structure. That is, the collusion between social science research and foreign policy was not brought to an end, but redefined along new lines.

This hypothesis receives further confirmation if we look at the professional and political trajectories of the critics of modernization. Their reaction was initially an activist one, motivated by political concerns, often overlapping with personal experiences of life under dictatorship. This politicization of research was also an implicit rejection of the ethical and normative indifference posited by the functional approaches to politics dominant in mainstream political science and typical of modernization theory. In methodological terms, this reaction was often associated with structuralism, Marxism, and a focus on the structure of class alliances and its political economy in order to underline the systemic character of repressive regimes and their intrinsic collusion with the project of modernization. Yet, the terms in which this critique was formulated were at odds with the empirical conceptions of social science that the philanthropic foundations were exporting in Latin America at the time. According to Gabriel Almond, for instance, dependency theory represented a "backward step, a movement away from the hard-won rule of evidence and inference in social studies." This methodological criticism, it should be clear, overlapped with a political one: dependency theory "involved the adoption of unfalsifiable concepts of the state as a part of class domination" (Almond 1987: 455). It has also been argued that the structural analysis of authoritarian modernization has been gradually dropped because it did not provide directions for political action (Lehmann 1990: 51; Przeworski 1986).

I argue, however, that the kind of structural analysis of the state which evolved out of dependency theory directly contributed to generate the policy knowledge that was invested in the analysis of "transitions to democracy" and that was used to theorize democracy promotion. As Lehmann argues, this current "rediscovered the democratic strand in Marxist theory and emerged in the late 1980s as a supporter of social democracy" (Lehmann 1990: 51). It emphasized political agency and theories of action, while the political activism of these political scientists was converted into a concern with "the question of democracy" (O'Donnell 1979) and the question of the transition to democracy. By the end of the decade, this academic knowledge would become a quasi-official doctrine supporting the new international crusade for democracy launched by the neoconservatives in Washington.

Modernization, Dependency, Democracy: The Intellectual Journey of Guillermo O'Donnell

O'Donnell's work, which spans more than three decades, provides a good basis for understanding the dynamics of the demise of modernization theory, the subsequent intellectual and political evolution of its critics, and their historical role within U.S. academic diplomacy. O'Donnell's professional career also illustrates the convertibility of roles and positions made possible by the U.S. strategy of support for alternative elites in Latin America. Before coming to social science, O'Donnell was indeed a "child prodigy" of Argentine politics (Lehmann 1990: 52) who emerged as the leader of the anti-Peronist University Students Federation at 18, in 1954, before obtaining his lawyer's diploma at the University of Buenos Aires in 1956. O'Donnell opted for a political career and, in 1963, was appointed *Sub-Secretario del Interior*

in the interim government which took over after the overthrow of Frondizi —
thus becoming the youngest deputy minister in the history of Argentina
(Lehmann 1989, 1990). Following this stint into politics, stopped by the
coup which brought Onganìa to power, O'Donnell spent three years (1968–
1971) at Yale University, dedicating his research to the economic and political evolution of Argentina. At that time, the department of political science included leading scholars of the discipline such as Robert Dahl, Alfred
Stepan, and Juan Linz. By O'Donnell's own acknowledgement, the influence of David Apter was also crucial (O'Donnell 1973, ix).

The outcome of this experience with U.S. political science at the time
was a complex attempt to cope with the nexus between modernization and
authoritarianism from the perspective and with the tools of behavioral social
science as taught in American universities. *Modernization and Bureaucratic
Authoritarianism*, published in 1973, bears testimony to this critical endorsement of the modernization literature. Lehmann notes that the reference list
resembles "the sum of every 'pol.sci.' reading list at Yale in the early 1970s"
(1990: 51). While paying tribute to the established canons of behavioral
political science, employing large sets of aggregate data, statistical indicators,
and testing the classical modernization hypotheses regarding the correlation
between socioeconomic modernization and democracy (especially Lipset's),
O'Donnell used these tools in order to show that "it is in those South American countries where modernization has proceeded furthest . . . that there
have been the only successful attempts to implant a new type of authoritarian
political system, which [he] labeled 'bureaucratic authoritarianism' "
(O'Donnell 1973: vii).

Inverting the relation between modernization and democracy, O'Donnell
showed that it was precisely the modernizing elite, the technocrats, with the
support of the oligopolistic and transnationalized fractions of the bourgeoisie
and the armed forces, who carried out the modernization of the country
through a political arrangement based on the exclusion of the lower social
strata (the "popular sector," *lo popular*) Although couched mostly in the
language of modernization theory, the substantial argument was therefore
closer to dependency theory than to conventional political science. It indicates the influence of the critical Latin American literature that O'Donnell
discovered during the same years, and in particular of the writings of
Cardoso, Furtado, Sunkel, and of other CEPAL members.

As it stands in *Modernization and Bureaucratic Authoritarianism*, modernization theory is ambiguously employed. It is obviously subjected to a
fundamental critique of its major assumptions. But this critique also left

intact the procedures and the methodologies on which the legitimacy of the "behavioral sciences" was based. It is indeed highly significant that such a virulent opponent of dependency theory as Almond could praise O'Donnell—though after the latter had achieved academic fame—for the fact that in this early work, his argument "was presented as an empirically testable hypothesis" (Almond 1987: 464), contrarily, in Almond's view, to most dependency theorizing, based on "unfalsifiable" assumptions. In order to be credible and legitimate, therefore, the critique of the hegemonic project of U.S.-inspired modernization had to be couched in the terms associated with this paradigm.

This selective use of modernization theory, which sought to meet the accepted standards of falsifiability and empiricism, was however short-lived. In the 1970s, O'Donnell's works definitely leave behind the remnants of U.S.-style comparative politics and take on board a strong version of structuralism along with the major tenets of dependency theory. Written between 1971 and 1975, his book on Argentina *Bureaucratic Authoritarianism* reflects the discredit of liberal reformism and the strong influence of structuralism and class-analysis among the generation of intellectuals and academics to which he belongs. Rather than "operational definitions" and "classifications," it starts with a theory of the capitalistic state as the guarantor of "capitalist relations of production" and of "the ensemble of social relations that establish the bourgeoisie as the dominant class" (O'Donnell 1988: 2). Light-years away from the comparative politics jargon, the language stands in sharp contrast with the earlier technical sobriety, even when O'Donnell goes on to analyze bureaucratic authoritarianism as a specific form of the capitalistic state, based on an equally specific class alliance.

Paradoxically, however, the departure from the dominant cannons of political science and the development of a more radical and politicized analytical framework took place concomitantly with the internationalization of research in Latin America and the growing influence of U.S. philanthropic foundations. In June 1975, O'Donnell created with some of his colleagues the Centro de Estudios de Estado y Sociedad (CEDES) in Buenos Aires, with the support of the Ford Foundation and the Swedish development agency SAREC. The purpose of the center was to secure an institutional space of intellectual freedom in the perspective of the impending coup, which took place the following year (O'Donnell 2003: 7). Leaving Argentina for Brazil in 1979, O'Donnell would subsequently spend four years teaching at Rio de Janeiro, and four years occupying Cardoso's position at the CEBRAP, another research center supported by the Ford Foundation (Cardoso had by then started his political career and had left the position almost vacant). While the emergence of bureaucratic authoritarian states had convinced part of the left that the only way out of such dictatorships was a revolutionary break with the logic of capitalist domination, the reflection on the "BA state" elaborated in these various independent research centers sponsored by North American donors tended to evolve toward a more centrist position advocating a gradual liberalization, and even negotiation with the most enlightened segments of the ruling elite. Analyzed by various political scientists, the experience of liberalization in Spain, Portugal, and Greece also played a role as it was slowly being codified into a universal model, a protocol for the transition to democracy that could be replicated elsewhere.

The funding and the support that these critics of the modernization paradigm received from U.S. foundations is not as paradoxical as it seems, therefore. In the first place, it was in line with the more liberal attitude of the Ford Foundation throughout the 1970s, as opposed to the more intransigent and conservative views of the State Department.[15] It also corresponded to a global revision of the strategic objectives of U.S. foreign policy. If the project of enlightened, elite-led modernization as it was formulated by the foreign policy planners and the establishment intellectuals since the fifties had begun to raise doubts in Washington,[16] it was because in many places it had failed to produce the stable regimes it was meant to foster. In Vietnam, it had led to a "quagmire." In Latin America, it had created a situation of polarization between authoritarian regimes and radical oppositions — a situation clearly at odds with the hopes placed in modernization and potentially threatening to U.S. national interests. A more realistic interpretation of philanthropic policies in the 1970s suggests that the shifting patterns of funding for social science research indicates a search for alternative strategies for stabilizing the region. By sponsoring scholars who might be "socialist in their political orientation" but who combined "both rigorous quantitative methodologies with a conflict model for interpreting social phenomena," the point was to "diagnose what went wrong with reforms grounded in the liberal worldview, a perspective that by definition avoids recognition of power and conflict and is thus unable to explain its failures," noted a former Ford foundation officer in Latin America (Arnove 1980: 320–21).

Research on the BA state, on the international factors leading to authoritarian regressions, on dependent development, and on its political forms, was in position to generate novel insights, better informed than previous ones because grounded in local realities. As a social scientist educated at

Yale and with an insider's knowledge of Argentine politics, O'Donnell represented the type of intellectual elites that fell in line with the objectives of the Ford Foundation. He had "a rare insight into the workings of the military 'mind,' and of the military institution" (Lehmann: 1990: 52) — a quality that made him a good investment in a period during which empirical work on the politics of bureaucratic authoritarianism was rare and therefore precious (Valenzuela 1988). At this level, whether the approach was closer to dependency theory, neo-Marxism or behavioralism did not make much difference in terms of strategic benefits.

However, the transformation of Latin American social sciences under the influence of U.S. philanthropic and academic institutions also changed the policy knowledge that such research generated. Its major effect was to foster an evolution away from the structuralism typical of dependency theory and political economy toward a focus on political change and political agency. On a closer look, O'Donnell's writings reflect this evolution in their conceptual and linguistic ambiguities. In spite of its structuralist accents, *Bureaucratic Authoritarianism* also reflects, in the words of Lehmann, an overlapping concern "with intention, preconception, ideology, and blunder — in short, the paraphernalia of political agency" (1989: 187). The perceptions of the main political actors, their strategic concerns, and their tactical calculations indeed occupy the center stage of an analysis that constantly oscillates between a structural sociology of the state and a psychological approach to political rationality.

O'Donnell's 1979 article on "Tensions in the Bureaucratic-Authoritarian State and the Question of Democracy" illustrates this new course. Significantly, it was also included in a volume edited by David Collier intended to serve as the academic platform for exponents of a democratic activism linked to the liberal elite. This time, O'Donnell dwells on factors "which have previously been insufficiently analyzed: i.e., *strictly political factors* and, in particular, the problem of democracy" (O'Donnell 1979: 285 — emphasis mine). While the analysis still reflects a certain structuralist rhetoric, it serves an argument basically concerned with political agency. O'Donnell's concern is to underline the fundamentally unstable nature of the system of class alliance supporting the bureaucratic authoritarian state. In his own words, still drawn from a left-structuralist lexicon, bureaucratic authoritarianism "is a suboptimal form of bourgeois domination" (1979: 309) because it undermines the legitimacy and the basis of consensus for its policies, and because it also entails deep contradictions between the upper classes and the military (which take the form of tensions between the transnationalization of the economy and the expansion of state activities). This type of state, therefore, is stabilized only in periods when the threat posed by the popular classes or the opposition is strong. Otherwise, it is open to uncertain evolutions and plagued by internal tensions. And the weakening of the original alliance supporting the implantation of the bureaucratic authoritarian state only increases the need for legitimating its policies. The only way out of this situation, O'Donnell argues, is "the very thing that BA has radically denied: democracy" (1979: 313).

According to this analysis, then, democracy evolves out of the bureaucratic-authoritarian state. It becomes the endpoint of a process of politically managed *transition*, not a political form determined by the degree and the form of social development. Once this idea was formulated, macro-structural approaches or various forms of class analysis appeared as relatively useless, because they were too deterministic to provide courses of action (Santiso 1996: 49). Establishing links between the GNP, economic growth or consumption patterns and the degree of political liberalization was a purely academic activity, utterly useless to democrats.

When political scientists adopted the standpoint of political actors as an epistemological basis for theorizing transition to democracy, this became the starting point of the literature on democratic transitions. Adam Przeworski, for instance, observed that in spite of its severe limitations, an approach in terms of strategic choices made by political actors on the basis of expectations and risk-assessments was preferable "on pure grounds of utility" (1986: 50). Practical commitment to democracy, in other words, was taken as a guideline for theory-building. Yet, by emphasizing opportunities and expectations in dynamic contexts, the perception of risks, costs and benefits by political actors was seen as a more predictive factor than the class interests they represented. The approaches favored "on pure ground of utility," therefore, quickly appeared as superior also *in theory* to structuralist or class analyses.

The Journey from Structuralism to Palace Strategies

The analysis that took shape in the late 1970s led to a positive reassessment of the "abstract, but not insignificant equality" (O'Donnell 1979: 313) on which "bourgeois democracy," criticized a few years earlier, had been based.[17] It also shifted the attention from the macro-social structures and the patterns of state-society relations to the internal developments of the authoritarian state and, more specifically, to its agents prone to open the political system to popular participation. The idea that democracy could unfold from within the inner circles of the authoritarian state and did not depend from the level of socioeconomic development was again directed against the idea of "modernization," often used as a justification for the undemocratic rule of technocrats. The critique of modernization theory was the critique of the "'social engineers' who offer their expertise" (O'Donnell 1979, 315) on the assumption that economic modernization will foster democracy. One of O'Donnell's arguments is indeed that the rise of authoritarianism was also the rise of technocrats considering democratic politics and disagreement as irrational and as an obstacle to sound economic policy. Challenging the BA state thus meant challenging this elite of modernizing technocrats.

At the same time, however, the emerging perspective of a democratization from within, negotiated with "the most enlightened actors in this system of domination" (ibid.), led many political scientists to pay a greater attention to these actors. A whole vein of political science research eventually redis-covered the democratic virtues of these technocrats who understood the necessity to build support for their economic policies both at home and abroad, and who therefore contributed to opening up the political game. The figure of the "technopol" later encapsulated this positive assessment of the democratizing role of technocratic elites generally trained in economics and usually in U.S. universities (Dominguez 1998; Williamson 1994). As Latin American countries had to negotiate loans and adjustment programs with the World Bank and the IMF, the technopols strengthened their posi-tions within the various governments of the region. They represented a neo-liberal economic orthodoxy which, as we shall see in chapter 6, increasingly required some degree of political openness, the rule of law, and transparency. In the 1990s, their rise within governmental administrations was considered to be related to the wave of democratization sweeping various countries. Even though many of these economists had only recently been converted to democracy, sometimes for purely instrumental reasons, they embodied the democratic virtues of the Washington consensus and its neoliberal agenda. At the same time they "made democracy safe for neoliberal eco-nomics" (Centeno and Silva 1998, 12; see also Dezalay and Garth 2002).

The intellectual opposition and the technopols represented two distinct aspects of the passage from authoritarian modernization to market democ-racies in the 1980s. The former was an opposition from without, motivated by a socialist or social-democratic project. The latter was an evolution from within, motivated by a neoliberal project. The former was formulated in the language of the social sciences, the latter in the language of economics. Yet, these important differences should not obscure the similarities. Both mobilized skills and assets acquired abroad; both mobilized their connections with prestigious institutions and their U.S. credentials; they traded on different types of expertise validated in prestigious universities; they often shared the same cosmopolitan education and training; both had a privileged relation to politics (while the technopols were "politically engaged" (Domiguez 1998, 101), many social-scientist protégés of the Ford Foundations had an experience with politics as O'Donnell or Cardoso). In other words, both groups mobilized their international and their scientific capital in the reshaping of Latin American states in the 1980s and 1990s.

This only seems to confirm the crucial role played by the transformation and the internationalization of the policy knowledge in generating the intellectual framework in which democratization was conceived and implemented. In his study of Chilean intellectuals, Jeffrey Puryear (1994) has extensively documented the foreign investments in "modern social science research" during the dictatorship and the high "political dividend" they later yielded—in particular those made by the Ford Foundation.[18] These investments deeply affected the methodologies and the intellectual posture of social sciences in Latin America, by fostering a "dollarization" of research (its subordination to dominant agendas set in Washington and in the U.S. policy research industry). The private research centers where most social scientists spent the period of authoritarianism needed to raise funds in an international and very competitive market for donor support. These donors tended to privilege "empirical, applied studies over work on theory or ideology" (Puryear 1994: 53). The dependency of social science research on these sources made the enforcement of new methodological standards effective. As José Joaquín Brunner recalled, researchers developed compliance with three North American academic rules: " 'publish or perish,' 'no nonsense' and 'accountability.' "[19] Combined with sustained interactions with politicians-turned-researchers—a process also encouraged by foreign donors—these influences fueled the emergence of a pragmatism in the social sciences, of which the new theories of democratization as "transitions" would be the most significant example.

The strategy which consisted in "transforming dissident thought" (Puryear 1994) facilitated the "movement of ideas . . . between the metropolitan center and the periphery" (Arnove 1980) through the transnational networks of scholars and politicians created during the 1970s. The progressive move away from structuralist analysis was also facilitated by the local conditions. As researchers experienced increasing difficulties in gaining access to aggregate data sets, reliable official statistics, they gradually turned their attention to different objects. These difficulties, impinging as they did on the possibility of analyzing processes of modernization, also affected the capacity to analyze unequal trade, dependent development, or social stratification.[20] This situation contributed to a shift from structuralist orientations toward micro-level issues that involved a whole generation of political scientists who "began to pay close attention to the microcontexts of the social world": "This occurred in part because of the impossibility of obtaining adequate aggregate data due to the secrecy imposed by harsh authoritarian rule, and also because of genuine emotional and intellectual need to understand those microrelations" (O'Donnell 1999: 51).

A second factor was the self-critical mood of many Latin American intellectuals and social scientists on the left which led them to reconsider their own ideological and theoretical posture in the aftermath of authoritarian coups. They saw their impotence in front of the political changes as a failure of their theoretical choices and generated a "collective sense of responsibility" (Puryear 1994). This led to a positive reassessment of democracy — however "formal" — as a safeguard of human rights. The generation of social scientists who transited through these centers was, as Brunner and Barrios write, "the generation of *post-Marxism*, which however 'went through' Marxism at some point and found in it a set of concepts and a critical inspiration, subsequently transformed by the encounter with democracy and the adoption of a certain relativism vis-à-vis the different sociological focuses" (Brunner and Barrios 1987: 195).

By the early 1980s, the landscape of "U.S-Latin America academic diplomacy" had radically changed. Social scientific endeavor had moved irreversibly away not only from modernization theory, but also from dependency theory, Marxism, and the critique of capitalistic modernization toward a broad concern with democracy, political reform, and statecraft. In the 1950s and the 1960s, the strategy of investment in the social sciences pursued by the U.S. establishment had aimed at creating "a worldwide network of elites whose approach to governance and change would be efficient, professional, moderate, incremental, and nonthreatening" to the economic order (Berman 1983: 15). The disciplines of comparative politics and area studies were created in order to support this strategy and generated its academic rationale under the form of modernization theory. The crisis of this paradigm in the 1970s, particularly clear in the case of Latin America, opened the way for the exploration of alternative means of reaching this goal. Paradoxically, it is the abandonment of the paradigm of modernization that made possible the fulfillment of its political goals. Supported by academic institutions and foundations, it is mostly radical critics of this paradigm, both in the United States and in Latin America, who finally provided the backbone of these transnational academic and political "networks" furthering a professional and moderate conception of political change. In their retreat from structural theories, they honed concepts and tools which sought to reproduce as closely as possible the rationality of political action. Their democratic activism, formed within a radical or leftist matrix, ended up generating policy-oriented science in line with the canons of academe and the needs of the political elite. Their political science became a kind of capital valorized within the field of state expertise and reformist politics. Political change was thus reduced to the manageable format of palace revolutions, discussed behind closed doors and under golden stucco. Social change took the format of round-table talks.

The complexity of these changes should not be underestimated, nor should they be reduced to the compromise of an earlier activism. On the contrary, the democratic credentials of this generation of scholars are undeniable; and they paradoxically provide a real continuity in their political and intellectual development. As they abandoned structuralism and mainstream political radicalism, these political scientists would channel their leftist political legitimacy into their opposition to Jeane Kirkpatrick's policy of qualified support for Latin American dictatorships. Often, they would also denounce the collusion of this policy with the extension of Reaganomics to the South through the mediation of the Chicago school's teaching. But it is also in this professional competition with economists that they converted their own knowledge into at least an equally valid source of policy advice in a booming international market of expert knowledge on state reform. A good example of this ambiguous competition is O'Donnell's article "Do Economists Know Best?" (1995). If political science has taken "a back seat to economics" in the growth industry of state reform advice, O'Donnell argues, it is because political scientists have not managed to develop the equivalent of the "Washington consensus" in their own discipline. Intended to fulfill this function, the frantic search for a consensual definition of "democracy"[21] — on which much ink is still spent — must be resituated in the context of disciplinary competition for the political dividends of scholarly efforts.

In this politically motivated competition, however, the search for a consensual concept of democracy that would give political science the credibility of neoclassical economics had the effect of giving the premium to empirical and minimalist conceptualizations, explicitly inspired by Schumpeter or

Dahl, which tend to be associated with elitist conceptions of politics. The search for a formal consensus thus ended up having substantive effects. By the same token, it contributed to make their policy-oriented knowledge functional to the institutional state reforms of which the "Washington consensus" was only the economic side.[22]

This complex picture shows the extent to which the trajectory of activist scholars and the transformation of political science in the 1980s does not represent an ideological U-turn, but a logical outcome of strategies deeply shaped by a complex environment. The main research orientations of the sub-discipline of "democratization studies" that they contributed to establishing are as much the result of scientific choices as they are also resources invested in extra-disciplinary struggles, both political and professional. These struggles proved all the more ambiguous in that they fostered a complementarity between the antagonists.

In any case, the research on transitions to democracy, surrounded by an aura of democratic activism and a militant history, developed successfully in academic terms. At the same time, paradoxically, this research agenda converged with the interests of the ideologues in the Reagan administration who used the notion of human rights in order to initiate an imperial policy of democracy promotion.

4   Democratization Studies and the Construction of a New Orthodoxy

In his analysis of the cultural Pax Americana that the Establishment sought to impose in Latin America and other continents after 1945, Edward Berman wrote that one of the aims of the educational and philanthropic policy it pursued was to create "a worldwide network of elites whose approach to governance and change would be efficient, professional, moderate, incremental, and nonthreatening to the class interests of those who, like Messrs, Carnegie, Ford, and Rockefeller, had established the foundations" (1983: 15). Because it reflected the same, deep-seated "set of beliefs, anxieties, prejudices, and values" (Latham 1998: 206), modernization theory was an integral part of this project, of which it was both the theory and the vector. Through its secular arm, the Alliance for Progress, or through its own internationalization in foreign universities, modernization theory furthered this conception of social change and its adoption by the relevant actors. We have seen in the previous chapter how it was progressively called into question, contested from within and from without.

The crisis of this scientific and ideological paradigm, however, also signaled the paradoxical success of its built-in political purpose. It succeeded not in spite of the failure of modernization theory, but precisely because of this failure. Its demise was indeed the result of an attack by scholars denouncing the collusion of dependent development, authoritarianism, and, often, U.S. foreign policy. Ironically, it is these scholars and their political and intellectual allies who ended up generating an international "network of elites" not unlike the one envisioned by the old establishment. Initially associated with rather critical positions, their political commitment to democracy evolved toward a pragmatic and moderate posture, more compatible with the concerns of their liberal sponsors, but also of the U.S. administration and major international institutions. Severing the link between democratization and more encompassing conceptions of social change, the literature on "transitions" to democracy that they produced rested on a conception of negotiated, orderly and, ultimately, manageable political change, kept distinct and separate from socioeconomic transformations. Their scientific productions emphasized, as Metin Heper put it, "gradual and controlled regime change" (Heper 1991: 193), thus echoing the long-sought goals of the establishment.

The advocacy of such gradual change explains why the development of contemporary democratization studies, and especially the approaches based on the concept of "transition," have often been regarded as a revival of modernization theory. Both critics and exponents of the political development literature stress this continuity. This is, for instance, the perspective adopted by Cammack (1997) in his work on the evolution of the literature on political development from the 1950s to the 1980s. He sees the transition approach as "taking further" a doctrine that was already in the making, without solution of continuity. In a completely different vein, Pye, in his presidential address to the 1989 meeting of the American Political Science Association, argued that research on transitions to democracy showed the fallacy of dependency theory and, instead, "vindicated" modernization theory, which had identified early on the "key factors" that would play a role in the democratic transformations of the late twentieth century (1990: 7).

In the field of area studies, and especially in African studies, the contemporary discussions on the relation between the rule of law and economic performance, or on democratic governance, is perceived by many scholars as a resurgence of modernization theory (Barkan 1994). More generally, it has been acknowledged that the epochal transformation of 1989 called for a new macro-paradigm in political sociology that would combine structural aspects of societal change with a "stress on agency" that would also "renovate the *voluntaristic* basis of action theory" (Tiryakian 1991: 172). Tiryakian has suggested calling it "neo-modernization." By analyzing democratization as the outcome of strategic choices actively made by a political elite in a context of structurally determined opportunities, the new approach to transitions to democracy fully fitted that nascent research agenda.

This characterization is partially misleading. It ignores the very real struggles between different factions of the political science community. In particular, it ignores the tensions that opposed modernization or political development theorists and those who would later embody the transitions to democracy approach. These struggles often entailed a political dimension that cannot be underestimated. An account such as Cammack's, for instance, in spite of its wealth of documentation and its solid argument, is too seamless. Theories of transition to democracy are not a mere outgrowth of modernization theories, even if they may fulfill the same political functions. Yet, as we shall see, they were ultimately used as the scientific ideology of a new foreign policy articulated around democracy promotion. The capacity of this scholarly discourse on democracy to generate consensus, illustrated by the existence of an organization such as the NED, and to accommodate simultaneously different meanings and different agendas has certainly contributed to its successful institutionalization. All the paradox of this scholarship, which is also a democratic discourse on democracy, is that it began as a heterodox critique of dominant paradigms but ultimately contributed to creating a new orthodoxy.

This "continuity within change" is an important aspect of the evolution of political science doctrines of democratization. The theoretical oppositions, the scholarly discussions and struggles between "transitologists" and modernization sociologists, between *dependencistas* and behavioralists but also between liberals and neoconservatives, paradoxically furthered the political goals that the search for a scientific theory of moderate, elite-driven and capitalistic change was supposed to legitimate and facilitate. I illustrate these processes by focusing on the research program on "transitions to democracy" that emerged in the late 1970s as a critical contribution to the debate on U.S.-Latin American relations, before becoming a major subdivision of political science. This success story — a critical approach that became institutionalized in a discipline that is traditionally close to the field of state power — is also the story of the transformation of this knowledge. In particular, I focus on the conversion of what I call a "critical knowledge of the state" — broadly speaking a political economy of the state inherited from dependency theory, or the critical functionalism specific to the theories of neocorporatism (e.g.. Schmitter 1974) on which the analysis of authoritarianism and transitions to democracy was based — into a dominant policy expertise on democratization.

With powerful institutional resources at their disposal, the scholars who "invented" democratization studies in the 1980s sought to oppose neoconservatives by showing that democratization processes would not lead to socialist regimes mushrooming next door, but to democracies preserving the influence of "notables" — regimes that would maintain the power of those that Weber has called the "economic *honoratiores.*" They thus reinvested a structuralist analysis of the state in these moderate prescriptions which conformed with the expectations of foreign policy institutions and, more broadly, with the policies encapsulated in the Washington consensus. Another paradoxical outcome of the same theoretical legacy has been the development of a "new international political economy" which analyzed the political stakes of economic policies (in particular of structural adjustment) and ended up being adopted by the World Bank in the early 1990s.

Scholarly Institutions, Liberal Networks and Transitions to Democracy

The multi-volume work on democratization published in 1986 by Guillermo O'Donnell, Philippe C. Schmitter and Laurence Whitehead is at the center of these transformations. It has become the foundation stone for the subsequent — and burgeoning — literature on democratization, and required reading in scholarly discussions on the matter. It offered the first major comparative study of contemporary processes of democratization. In doing so, it somehow vindicated the subordinated position in which Latin American Studies had been confined by giving them a central position in the revival of comparative politics. As a critic argued, the collapse of authoritarian regimes that motivated this academic enterprise "added a new set of impatient area scholars to the ranks of comparative political scientists" (Hagopian 1993: 464), and it substituted a discredited modernization theory.

Never really at ease with the main assumptions of modernization theory, Latin American Studies scholars finally managed to break away from it at the time when developments in Latin America put their discipline in a position to renew the field of comparative politics. A generation of scholars whose names had been directly or indirectly associated with dependency theory and structuralist approaches to politics came to replace a more conservative "old guard." By the same token, the fall of authoritarian regimes in the context of intensified capitalism led these political scientists to revise a number of assumptions of dependency theory. In particular, they thought it necessary to break with its alleged determinism and a political pessimism which, it was supposed, was its practical consequence. The attention to macro-structures progressively gave way to a concern for what the Chilean sociologist Manuel Garretón has called "the less predictable and more fluid elements of politics, political creativity and collective action" (Garretón

1988: 358–59). As we shall see, this transformation of scientific discourse entailed major consequences not only for the discipline of comparative politics — which abandoned the study of social change in favor of political change, reduced however to the dimensions of palace revolutions — but also for the nature of emancipatory politics.

Transitions from Authoritarian Rule also offers a perfect illustration of the type of studies produced by the transnational networks of activist scholars that were analyzed in the previous chapter. This scientific production was deeply influenced by the international context in which it developed and by the political commitments of its authors. In particular, the essays collected in the *Transitions* series raised to the level of theory the practical commitment in favor of democracy that animated the political and academic networks of protégés of the liberal establishment, at the same time that it stripped it of its more radical connotations. From a methodological point of view, this translated into a progressive detachment from the paradigm of dependency and, more generally, from structuralist explanations of regime change. Instead, a microanalysis of political elites that was sometimes close to rational choice or game theories and that assumed a relative autonomy of the political became the flagship of the new approach to democratic transitions. More paradoxically perhaps, given the past production of some of its prominent contributors and their involvement in the politics associated with the dependency school, the *Transitions* volumes not only theorize the irreversibility of capitalistic relations of production, but also reflect and sometimes explicitly assert the impossibility of implementing even moderate Keynesian arrangements in the context of a powerful international economic orthodoxy. As such, they illustrate the transformation of a dissident and critical strand of political science, linked to the intellectual moment of the 1970s, into a normative theory of non-revolutionary change under capitalistic economic conditions.[1]

This transformation cannot be separated from a specific institutional context, and from the role of political science as a resource in the strategies of policy entrepreneurs. The collective endeavor that resulted in the *Transitions* studies started in 1979 as a project of the Latin American Program of the Woodrow Wilson International Center for Scholars. The program was established in 1977, and directed until 1983, by Abraham Lowenthal. A former officer of the Ford Foundation in Latin America, Lowenthal was "frustrated" by his work as Director of Studies at the Council of Foreign Relations, which diverted him from his interest in U.S.-Latin America relations. With the support of Albert Hirschman, Fernando Henrique Cardoso, and some Ford

Foundation officers, he submitted a proposal for a center of studies to the foundations community in Washington. The proposal attracted the interest of the director of the Wilson Center, who did not however have the budget for supporting the program. Lowenthal then secured the support of the Rockefeller foundation through Theodore Hesberg, chairman of the foundation board and president of Notre-Dame University, and the Ford Foundation, through his former colleague William Carmichael. Additional funds from the Rockefeller Brothers Fund provided sufficient funding for starting the Latin American Program on a three-year basis.[2]

As the program was established, a board of directors — called the "Academic Council" — was also set up and Hirschman agreed to chair it (the board comprised Fernando H. Cardoso, Guillermo O'Donnell, Ricardo Ffrench-Davis, Leslie Manigot, Olga Pelecer de Brody, Thomas Skidmore, Karen Spalding, and Philippe C. Schmitter). The creation of the board institutionalized the intellectual and political priorities of the academic currents it represented, and gave a distinctive profile to the Latin American program. The staffing of the board, reflecting a coalition of left-liberal and social-democratic sensitivities, oriented the program in a specific direction. It represented in a certain sense the aristocracy of an academic field, Latin American Studies, that was as a whole critical of U.S. foreign policy (with a few notable exceptions such as Robert Packenham or Howard Wiarda — who were not members of the Board). Many scholars on the board were also very close observers of and often participants in Latin American politics. They were chosen because they "were not primarily interested in scholarship for its own sake alone, but rather scholarship for its implications."[3]

At the same time, the program cultivated an image of professionalism which fitted its host institution. Created in 1968 as a component of the Smithsonian Institution, the Woodrow Wilson Center was a prestigious institution located at the intersection of academic and political circles. Its mandate stipulates that the Center serves "to unite the world of ideas to the world of policy by supporting pre-eminent scholarship and linking that scholarship to issues of concern to officials in Washington." The purpose of the Latin American Program was to conduct policy-relevant work that could inform "opinion leaders" on the prospects of U.S.–Latin American relations.

These specific traits explain the role of the Latin American Program in the 1980s and the significance of democratization studies. With Reagan's victory, such academic forums allowed the liberal establishment to mobilize scientific capital in its struggle against the conservative administration. Because of its hybrid character, the Latin American program was also a place where the "alternative" approach to hemispheric issues represented by critical Latin American Studies scholars could demonstrate its relevance to policymaking against the hard, "national-security" approach of many neoconservatives. As an alliance of activism and professionalism, the Program therefore provided a viewpoint on hemispheric matters contrasting the ideological approach of the Reagan administration, which subordinated democracy to the American crusade against Communism. In his foreword to the *Transitions* series, Abraham Lowenthal underscored this nondiscriminatory approach to democracy contrasting the use of strong political criteria by the State Department, when he wrote that the Program "sought diversity of many kinds . . . [and] awarded fellowships in the same semester to writers exiled because of their convictions from Argentina and from Cuba." (1986: viii) — a delicate neutrality echoing that of Amnesty International.

A very similar but more political initiative that somewhat overlapped with the Latin American program was the creation of the Inter-American Dialogue, an organization that would come to epitomize the liberal opposition to the Reagan administration policy in Latin America. The IAD started as a project of the Wilson Center Latin American program. The initial idea, developed by Lowenthal and Cardoso in 1982, was to organize a conference that would convey to Washington the concerns of Latin Americans with the poor state of U.S.-Latin America relations and the policies of the Reagan administration in the region. These concerns were not only limited to the nature and the direction of U.S. foreign policy, they included as well economic issues and the debt problem. The whole initiative was actually a war machine launched by the liberal establishment against the new policy course in Washington and the intransigent anti-Communism embodied by Jeane Kirkpatrick. In Lowenthal's words, it was meant "to provide a kind of forum for a critical look at what was going on." To give political credibility to the initiative, the conference was to be convened by Sol Linowitz, who had the necessary prestige and connections, and shared the general views represented by the Latin American Program and the same concern about the state of hemispheric relations.[4] Held in November 1982, the meeting was co-convened by Gabriel Plaza, former Secretary General of the Organization of America States. Using his connections, Sol Linowtiz secured the presence of Secretary of State George Shultz and Vice-President Bush who came at the end of the conference to hear summaries of the discussions, which contributed to give a certain political resonance to the meeting.

This political offensive had some impact because its critical outlook was buttressed by the liberal establishment and the reputation of its members.

The IAD inherited from this background a distinctive blend of elitism and reformism, clearly reflected in its membership: it included Sol Linowitz, Peter Bell, Jimmy Carter, Cyrus Vance, Raúl Alfonsín, Fernando Henrique Cardoso, Alejandro Foxley, Oscar Arias, Violeta Chamorro, Nicolá Ardito Barletta, Javier Pérez de Cuéllar, and Mario Vargas Llosa. It cultivated its difference vis-à-vis the more conservative approach of the State Department by playing the role of a learned and professional counter-power (Dezalay and Garth, 2002). The reputation and the influence of its members allowed the organization both to function as a mouthpiece for democratic demands and at the same time to enjoy professional credibility in Washington and in international organizations. This contributed to no small extent to building up hegemonic support for democratic changes in Latin America, insofar as they were led by a respectable and responsible counter-elite. In particular, the IAD articulated democratic activism and the demand for more open political systems with the need for orthodox economic management, notably through a policy of outreach toward financial and banking circles. The summary of the discussion on the debt problem after the first conference, for instance, was thus presented to the Secretary of State and the Vice President by Robert McNamara, who had just left the presidency of the World Bank. And its alternative elite was to become in the 1990s the governmental elite of Latin America (in fact, four presidents and a dozen ministers came out of the IAD).

Beyond the divergence of the policy agendas, it is therefore easy to catch a glimpse of the social proximity of the contenders — which is precisely what gave credibility to the policy alternative the IAD represented. Despite the ideological and political divide between a liberal foreign policy establishment in the opposition and a neoconservative cadre in power, these sophisticated feuds were nevertheless internal to a relatively homogeneous foreign policy elite. And such divisions were in a sense functional to the reproduction and the development of this elite. Liberal policy entrepreneurs such as Lowenthal filled the partial void left by the retreat of the administration into a policy that subordinated the hemispheric relations to the global theater of anticommunist operations. They were able to muster considerable financial and social resources, which allowed them to tap the academic community in order to build up intellectual agendas (something much more difficult for the administration). The creation of the IAD itself served the purpose of institutionalizing these resources, creating a stable organization that occupied a strategic position as gatekeeper to high-level discussions of certain international issues. The Rockefeller Foundation and, to a smaller extent, the Ford Foundation, both of which had already supported the creation of the Latin American Program at the Woodrow Wilson Center, provided the funds necessary for the organization of the second conference. To the extent that the Wilson Center did not issue policy statements, the publication of the conference report corresponded to the creation of an ad hoc entity, the Inter-American Dialogue, in the name of which the report was published.

A Farewell to Arms: From a Critique of the State to a Science of Elite Reformism

In this context, the contribution of the political scientists of the Woodrow Wilson Center was crucial. On the one hand, it stemmed from a genuine commitment to democracy in Latin America. The *Transitions* project was primarily aiming at exploring the nature of the different paths to democracy with a view to producing effective policy recommendations. On the other hand, it generated a formula for democratization that was fully compatible with the new foreign policy and the Washington consensus in economics.

From the outset, the project benefited from the active support of prominent voices in the Academic Council of the Program, such as Albert Hirschman or Fernando Henrique Cardoso (who contributed a chapter to the final publication).[5] The list of contributors to the project included other South American social scientists, such as Manuel Antonio Garretón or Marcelo Cavarozzi, who represented a progressive sociological tradition. Most of their North American counterparts can also be regarded as the academic faction of a social-democratic left, some of them with a long experience of Latin America. At the same time, the final product was characterized by rather moderate prescriptive conclusions.

This ambivalence is also identifiable in the language that runs throughout the four volumes. As Adam Przeworski retrospectively noticed, in spite of the emphasis placed on the strategies pursued by the political elites, the discourse was couched in "the dominant vocabulary of the time," that is "the macrolanguage of classes, their alliances, and 'pacts of domination' " (1991: 97). In his essay on Brazilian business circles and democratization, Cardoso thus speaks of "bourgeois hegemony" (1986: 137); O'Donnell and Schmitter evoke — in order, however, to suspend it immediately — the perspective of a socialization of the means of production (1986). In his own contribution, Przeworski punctuates the text with references that clearly belong to the standard leftist academic baggage: Marx, Gramsci, Balibar, Poulantzas . . .

This leftist legacy should not obscure the major transformation that was taking place and that was reflected in the various contributions to these volumes. For the project also symbolized the closure of a whole political era centered on the radicalism of the 1970s and, more specifically, the end of the politics associated with the dependency movement in the South. This evolution appeared clearly in relation to the question of the state and of the analytical tools adequate to address it. The new analysis of the state was no longer systemic, nor were the political remedies suggested, since the economic structures were, on the whole, left out. Instead, the Woodrow Wilson project gave its support to a more humble intellectual and political agenda, which assumed the relative autonomy of the state and focused on the power games between the different factions of the ruling elite as the principle behind regime change.

At the same time, this led to the rediscovery of a reformism that had been discredited since the early 1970s. As an editor of the project, who had defended in the past "a form of self-managing socialism in the image of Yugoslavia" (Lehmann 1990: 53) as a solution for the ills of Latin America, O'Donnell perfectly illustrates this intellectual and political shift. In the introduction to the volume on Latin America, he makes explicit the authors' "normative bias" according to which "political democracy" is "desirable per se, even after recognizing the significant tradeoffs that its installation and eventual consolidation can entail in terms of more effective, and more rapid, opportunities for reducing social and economic inequities" (O'Donnell 1986: 10). This concession, he argues, is reinforced by the "empirical generalization" that "there is not, nor is there likely to be in the foreseeable future, a *via revolucionaria* open for countries that have reached some minimal degree of social complexity and, concomitantly, of expansion of capitalist social relations" (ibid.). Far from being a peculiarity of O'Donnell's contribution, these claims constitute a recurrent leitmotiv of the entire project. The concluding volume emphasizes that such claims are shared by all the contributors — a surprising feature in a collective work written by scholars who had distinguished themselves by their political activism. As a reviewer put it concisely, the message delivered was "bad news for the socialist left" (Bermeo 1990: 364).

How should these theoretical and political choices be accounted for? The *Transitions* volumes consistently present them as a pragmatic adjustment to the actual conditions in Latin America. The argument is all the more convincing since the democratic credentials, often impeccable, of the contributors, buttress it. Lowenthal, in the foreword, states that the project is motivated by "a frank bias for democracy, for the restoration in Latin America of the fundamental rights of political participation" (1986: vii). In the last volume of the series, O'Donnell and Schmitter assert their normative commitment to political democracy, which is "per se a desirable goal" (1986: 3). As a reviewer later put it, this approach started by "recognizing the conflict between old theory and new facts" (Remmer 1991: 483).

Indeed the various chapters stress a genuine commitment to democratic change that seems to suggest a moderate political course as the best strategic option. The new thinking can be summed up as follows: if the process of industrialization and modernization did not necessarily lead to democracy, as the political sociologists of the 1950s thought, and if, conversely, dependent development did not necessarily confine countries to authoritarianism, as O'Donnell and other dependency theorists had suggested in the 1970s, then democracy had to be "not *the* polity of a particular stage in the development of capitalism, but a conjunctural outcome," following Goran Therborn's formulation (ibid.). That is, it was not the product of evolutionary transformations, but only of specific, transitory, and reversible configurations of political forces. This view was intrinsically an activist view, implying that democracy was indeed an outcome relatively independent of structural factors, and so always within reach — provided that there was sufficient political will among the relevant political actors. There were no valid reasons, in other words, for postponing democracy.

This fundamental step entailed several consequences, both practical and theoretical. For the political practice of the *Transitions* authors, it implied that the struggle for democracy fundamentally meant waging a battle against a structuralist legacy that, suddenly, was seen as an obstacle to political action rather than a useful theory historically linked to 'progressive' political practices. Remembering his participation in the project, Adam Przeworski recalls that he was struck to realize that the work of Barrington Moore "was not even mentioned during the first meeting of the O'Donnell-Schmitter democratization project in 1979" (1991: 96 fn.). Notwithstanding his surprise, Przeworski certainly offers the best example of this evolution toward a less sociological approach to politics. In retrospect he insisted that "while explanations in terms of structural conditions are satisfying ex post, they are useless ex ante" (Przeworski 1991: 97). An analysis of democratization as a matter of strategic choices made by different faction of the ruling elite was therefore chosen, as we have already seen, "on pure grounds of utility" (ibid.: 50). One reason for this was that "many participants . . . were protagonists in the struggles for democracy and needed to understand the consequence of alternative courses of action" (ibid.: 97). The contributors therefore emphasized the role of political agency in processes that were conceptualized as inherently uncertain and underdetermined.

As O'Donnell and Schmitter explain in the concluding volume of the series, theirs was an "effort to capture the extraordinary uncertainty of the transition" since, they argued, democratization processes fall within the category of "large-scale transformations which occur when there are insufficient structural or behavioral parameters to guide and predict the outcome" (1986: 3). In such contexts where impersonal historical forces, macro-structures, or laws of development have no explanatory power, the principle of change ultimately lies with the political actors and their strategic choices. Although most of the *Transitions* authors came from a tradition of structuralist analysis, they gradually adopted theories of *action* — alternatively inspired by rational choice, game theory, or methodological individualism — behind the façade provided by the "macrolanguage of classes." The authors thus emphasize "the high degree of indeterminacy embedded in situations where unexpected events (*fortuna*), insufficient information, hurried and audacious choices, confusion about motives and interests, plasticity, and even indefinition of political identities, as well as the talents of specific individuals (*virtù*), are frequently decisive in determining the outcomes" (ibid., 5).

It is inappropriate to see this evolution as a "conversion" of former structuralists to a new dominant paradigm emphasizing agency (as, for instance, argued by Santiso [1996: 57]). What is striking, instead, is the continuity with some of the themes previously developed through a structural, class-based analysis of the state — an analysis associated with the dependency moment, and especially with some writings of O'Donnell. Lehmann has rightly observed that in this kind of analysis, "subjectivity . . . turns out to be central to what started out as an apparently structural dynamic" (1990: 57). Indeed, one of O'Donnell's major contributions had been a structural class analysis of the coalitions commanding the heights of the bureaucratic-authoritarian states. As an alliance between the upper, transnationalized bourgeoisie, some of its more national factions, a technobureaucracy and the military (which can be in turn subdivided into different groups), the bureaucratic-authoritarian state found its cohesive force in the "fear from below," which cemented the alliance between the otherwise divergent interests of these social groups. With the repression of the popular sector, the dismantling of its organizations and "normalization," this fear gradually subsided while, conversely, tensions emerged within the ruling coalition as the fear gave precedence to the conflicting interests of its different factions. It is in these internal struggles that new political possibilities are opened up, the outcomes of which depend on the political skills and maneuvering ability of the "most enlightened actors of this system of domination [i.e. the BA state]."

In his contribution to the *Transitions* volumes, Robert Kaufman (1986) provides a similar analysis, in which it is difficult to ignore the influence of O'Donnell's authoritative model. Kaufman locates the causes of the decomposition of the "exclusionary" coalitions in power within the internationalization of Latin American economies and in the resulting pressures to comply with international economic prescriptions. In this perspective, the increasing role of foreign private investment, foreign technology, and exports tends to produce conflicts between the oligopolistic sectors benefiting from the import-substitution economy and the liberal technocrats who champion the new economic orthodoxy (Kaufman 1986: 85–89). O'Donnell had already suggested that, as a result of these transformations, "negotiation is constantly taking place over how much heterodoxy the liberal *técnicos* will have to concede in order to be allowed to maintain control of the main levers of economic policy" (1988: 193). While the sectors that had benefited from the previous economic conditions (and had often initially supported the bureaucratic-authoritarian state) become alienated, the pressure for monetary orthodoxy prevents redistributive arrangements that would "buy" their support. As a result, the BA state collapses under the weight of its internal contradictions, thus paving the way for a transition to democracy. But this outcome, in turn, is dependent upon the skills of the political actors involved.

While a structuralism rooted in a theory of the state still permeated by the Marxist accents of the 1970s serves as an explanation of the collapse of authoritarian rule, the transition to democracy, properly speaking, is determined in the last instance by voluntarism and the subjective dispositions of those sectors of the political elite that seek alliances outside the regime itself. It is the product of "statecraft" and "political entrepreneurship" (P. H. Smith 1991: 618). Democratization thus appears as the controlled enlargement of palace wars to society at large.

Imperium Honoratiorum

By focusing on democratic agents within authoritarian coalitions, political scientists located within the state the principle of its own transformation. It was hence possible to analyze political change as a process internal to the ruling elite and relatively unconstrained by the structural patterns of state-society relations. The theory of the capitalistic state of the 1970s that the same authors had in part elaborated thus completed its transformation into a description of possible "games" between the different fractions of the ruling elite and the probable outcomes in terms of political regime. The logic of political change became that of a "complicated minuet of political maneuvering" (P. H. Smith 1991: 618), mostly confined to presidential palaces. Far from entailing a project of social transformation, democratization was reduced to a matter of tactical calculations involving such actors as "the leader and his palace guard," the "soft-liners" and the "hard-liners" (O'Donnell and Schmitter 1986: 40), with the reformers trying to reach out to social elites in order to strengthen their positions.

This theory of democratization as an outcome of palace wars also entailed political consequences for the nature of the subsequent regimes, and many contributors translated these into straightforward political prescriptions. Kaufman states in great detail the argument for political moderation and for the containment of social demands. He argues that while pressures for economic orthodoxy generate tensions and conflicts between the different factions of the ruling coalition, their social impact might provoke popular uprisings that would only contribute to trigger reflexes of unity among the rulers — and thus strengthen a weakened authoritarian coalition. Hence, the safest coalition for democratic reforms is one that controls its supporters and channels mobilization toward moderate goals that do not threaten the benefits that the dominant classes derived from the authoritarian arrangement. In particular, the authors rule out the viability of any "socialist" alternative (Kaufman 1986: 100; O'Donnell and Schmitter 1986: 12–14).[6] "It seems crucial," as O'Donnell and Schmitter explain, "that . . . a compromise among class interests somehow be forged to reassure the bourgeoisie that its property rights will not be jeopardized for the foreseeable future" (1986: 46–47). But the need to reassure social groups prone to backing authoritarian solutions when their interests are threatened also leads the authors to express doubts about the chances of a social-democratic alternative. Kaufman thus argues that the necessary support of the Communist party for a social-democratic coalition runs the risk of alienating "established elites" (1986: 104). Using surprisingly orthodox and somewhat simplistic arguments, Przeworski even suggests that while a Keynesian economic project seems the best alternative, since it combines "private property, redistribution of income, and a strong state" (1986: 62) and might therefore satisfy everyone, it is vulnerable to economic crises (more precisely, to fiscal crises due to its allegedly inflationary nature).

Because transitions to democracy must contain redistributive demands, the main contribution of social-democratic forces to the process of democratization is "as opposition" (Kaufman 1986: 104) and preferably an opposition controlling its supporters, since a successful transition to democracy seems to require "docility and patience on the part of organized workers" (Przeworski: 1991, 63). Przeworski's evolution is highly emblematic of this entire political and intellectual shift: he combined very early on a critical reflection on the "transition to socialism" with the orthodox and academically legitimate instruments of rational choice (Przeworski: 1980). The result was, as Clyde Barrow suggests, that for the working class "it is 'more rational' to negotiate tangible concessions from capital in exchange for leaving production relations intact" (Barrow 1993: 61). In the last analysis, the preference of these authors falls with "center-right," "pro-business" alliances, "parallel in some important respects to the sociopolitical coalitions that initially backed bureaucratic-authoritarian rule" (Kaufman 1986: 105). In a position to muster important resources (financial support, media access, economic influence), this political elite is also the least likely to upset foreign economic interests. In short, "the formation of durable polyarchies requires, at least in their formative periods, accommodation with the still powerful political and economic forces on which the old authoritarian order was based: not only the military establishment but also the transnational business sector" (Kaufman 1986: 100). A lot of the new democrats, it may be expected, will be retooled autocrats.

With a "reluctant, but unmistakable" preference for political moderation (Bermeo 1990: 362), the political scientists of the *Transitions* project became the scientific promoters of a gradual, nonrevolutionary, pro-business, economically orthodox conception of social and political change, which left intact — when it did not strengthen it — the power of established socioeconomic and political elites. Well aware that such democratization serves "to ratify (if not to reify) prevailing social and economic inequalities" (O'Donnell and Schmitter 1986: 70), and in spite of their "normative references" lying much more to the left, they endorsed a limited formula of democratization, fundamentally confined to elite settlements and palace intrigues. At the same time, the role played by some of the contributors in the democratization process in their home countries, as well as the explicit social-democratic persuasions of their North American colleagues, contributed to no small extent to give political credibility to their prescriptions, which could not fail to appear as unbiased evidence — not in spite of, but precisely because of the reservations they expressed. As Nancy Bermeo rightly observed in her review of the four *Transitions* volumes, "the novelty of *Tentative Conclusions* [the fourth volume] lies as much in who is doing the talking as in what is being said" (1990: 363). Indeed, the paradox of the whole project is that it led scholars on the left to endorse and give a theoretical foundation to the project that the U.S. foreign policy establishment had been pursuing since the early post-war era: promoting democratic elites that would be moderate, respectful of capitalistic interests, and pro-American. The only difference, perhaps, was that the forms of democratic legality were taken more seriously and were certainly more valued by political scientists who had also been democratic activists.

The processes of political liberalization and democratization analyzed in the *Transitions* series therefore unfolded for the benefit of the social groups who have always been the conveyors of this hegemonic project and in which the liberal establishment recognized peers sharing the same responsible and elitist view of public affairs. O'Donnell and Schmitter are lucid when they argue that such processes of liberalization are most likely to empower "notables," that is, "respected, prominent individuals who are seen as representative of propertied classes, elite institutions, and/or territorial constituencies and, hence, capable of influencing their subsequent collective behavior" (1986: 40). In his analysis of the types of domination, Weber had already mentioned the ascent to power of these notables that he calls *honoratiores* in the context of democratic rule. His discussion was concerned with the way direct democracy dissolves into a rule by notables, when economic differentiation puts administration in the hands of those who can take time and have the leisure to occupy political offices. But his description of the *honoratiores* applies also to the notables who become democrats and preserve their power by effecting transitions to democracy with a certain timeliness. Because they are "able to live *for* politics without living *from* politics" (Weber 1978: 290), the paradox of these notables is perhaps to transform their economic interests into the moral guarantee of their disinterested embracing of politics. Such " 'economic' *honoratiores*" are entitled to participate in social administration and rule "as an honorific duty which derives from their economic position" (ibid.: 950–51). In the political pacts taken under consideration by the "transitologists," the social and economic power of these notables is used as a bargaining resource and the guarantee of a loyal, nonthreatening political opposition.

The formula for a successful transition to democracy elaborated at the Wilson Center was one that ultimately did not affect the social distribution of power, and therefore safeguarded the influence of the notables. With the support of some of these notables, political democracy emerged as an alternative to social democracy, in a way that echoed the strategy of the young Tancredi in Tomasi di Lampedusa's novel *Il gattopardo (The Leopard)*, when he realizes that the preservation of the old prerogatives requires that their holders be involved in the revolution: *"Se non ci siamo noi, quelli ti combinano la repubblica. Se vogliamo che tutto rimanga come è, bisogna che tutto cambi."*[7] Both conservative and open to change, this strategy followed by the most enlightened actors of the authoritarian system closely matches the secular efforts of the U.S. liberal establishment to create what Dezalay and Garth have called an "international of notables," and of which the Inter-American Dialogue is a blatant example. Paradoxically, this rule by the notables, this *imperium honoratiorum*, was to be theorized and in a sense justified by the activist scholars who, at the Wilson Center, made the transformation of a critical analysis of the state into a strategic expertise for reformers and "responsible" democrats.

A Strategic Position in the Scientific Field

There are several ways to explain this transformation of a critical area of political science into a dominant research program — virtually into a political doctrine. We have seen how the institutional context, the militant past of these scholars, their intellectual formation, the use of their scientific production as a symbolic resource in the battles opposing the liberal establishment and the neoconservative incumbents, as well as factors internal to the discipline of political science such as the opportunity to "avenge" area studies and in particular Latin American studies against the hitherto dominant comparative study of modernization, have influenced and determined this peculiar evolution. From a more political point of view, there was also the hope placed in those that O'Donnell had called the "most enlightened actors" of the authoritarian system, namely technocrats trained abroad and attempting an enlargement of political participation in order to implement economic orthodoxy. I now turn to the scientific, institutional and policy-related effects of this evolution.

Besides serving a political strategy, the conception of democratization as a process limited to the political sphere which emerges in the *Transitions* series also served a strategy of scientific credibility. By excluding the economy and the social distribution of power from the process of democratization, the political scientists of the Wilson Center basically reactivated an "empirical" definition of democracy in purely "procedural" terms. They linked up, in other words, with the Schumpeterian tradition and the notion of "polyarchy" that Robert Dahl had elaborated as concept distinct from that of "democracy," which was according to him subject to utopian interpretations. Lehmann, for instance, notes that by the early 1980s, these critics of the authoritarian state "were beginning to read Hobbes and Locke, to listen again to North American liberals like Robert Dahl" (1990: 58–59). This return to the mainstream tradition in political science finally brought the analysis of authoritarianism and democracy into line with the canons of "operationalization" and "falsifiability" — while it was precisely these criteria that were used to denounce the nonscientific character of dependency theory, for instance. On the other hand, the study of the strategic choices made by the political elites, the analysis of combinatory games among its contending factions, the question of preference formation in contexts of uncertainty (or, as economists would have it, of imperfect information), the use of notions such as "transaction costs" and "incentives" as heuristic devices, allowed this nascent subfield of political science to emulate the formal qualities — but also the professional legitimacy — of economics. The subsequent production of somebody like Adam Przeworski, who moved from a solid structuralism to an engagement with rational choice theory, is emblematic of this second aspect. In a different vein, the evolution of Robert Kaufman toward what was to become the new international political economy is another significant example.

While the development of democratization studies into a dominant curriculum, recognized and institutionalized in the major U.S. universities, was certainly made possible by this methodological transformation, it also benefited from the aura of democratic militancy and activism that surrounded its founding fathers. In other words, the development of this field within political science was to a large extent the result of its strategic position, which made possible the conciliation of opposite resources — "progressive" activism, scientific and academic legitimacy, political networks, militant networks, a strong international dimension, and credibility in the eyes of the exponents of economic orthodoxy.

In this regard, the critical reception of the *Transitions* volumes is highly revealing, because it makes very salient the strategic position of its contributors, brokering between opposed political universes. They could indeed put forward both their involvement with the democratic struggles of the continent, while at the same time using this political legitimacy to assert a "realistic" acceptance of economic orthodoxy.[8] Nothing illustrates this better than the critical reviews of the *Transitions* volumes, which have alternatively located this work at opposite poles of the political spectrum. For critics moving from a conservative position, the Woodrow Wilson project is regarded suspiciously as a direct product of the dependency school, exhibiting not only the persistence of a paradigm deemed to be refuted by the trend toward democracy in Latin America, but also the pursuit of a socialist political agenda masquerading as academic work. In a long review essay on the *Transitions* volumes, Daniel Levine thus explains that "dependency theory in general, and the *Transitions* series in particular, rest on a notion of critical theory which in the matter at hand leads analysis to reach beyond political democracy (with its characteristic cautions, compromises, and accommodations) to something better — presumably involving dramatically expanded popular participation in the context of some form of socialism" (1988: 379). Notwithstanding the fact that some of the authors were at the same time distancing themselves from their former role in the elaboration of dependency theory and reevaluating "formal" democracy, Levine argued that the distinction between mere liberalization and a broader notion of democratization encompassing societal relations and the economy, inherited from dependency, led the contributors to "undervalue the appeal of liberal democracy" (ibid.: 378). The series therefore smacked of "the development of an anti-authoritarian project embracing the totality of social life" (ibid.: 386) that had dangerous leftist overtones. Such a critique renders well the gap between the neoconservative conception of democracy as an ideology (a conception according to which democracy is made by democrats and is a matter of belief and persuasion) and the more disillusioned theory of democracy elaborated by those activist-scholars associated with the anti-authoritarian left.

But such distances are also the result of the viewpoint adopted. If the legacy of dependency theory and leftist anti-authoritarian struggles is underscored by conservative critiques, it is on the contrary the abandonment of any impulse toward structural reform that motivates the critique of the *Transitions* series coming from the left, in particular the one formulated by exponents of dependency theory. In their co-edited volume (which includes contributions by Gunder Frank and Amin), Gills, Rocamora and Wilson (1993) have summed up this argument, according to which the emerging field of democratization studies serves the elaboration of a model of "low-intensity" democracy. Relocating the "transitions to democracy" of the late twentieth century in a broader international context, they argue that these processes, which overlapped with the restructuring of the international econ-

omy and changes in U.S. foreign policy, are the corollary of economic liberalization and internationalization, and have mostly "ossified political and
economic structures from an authoritarian past" (ibid.: 3). Limited to the
political system, democratization, as it is theorized by the authors of *Transitions from Authoritarian Rule*, works in parallel with economic adjustment.
At the same time, this process secures the economic order outside the reach
of structural reforms. Paul Cammack (1997) developed a very similar critique which identified in this work the strict limitation of the scope of democratization to the political system, and the implicit endorsement, through
the prescription of a moderation of the claims to economic entitlements, of
the economic orthodoxy that gained momentum during the same decade
(1997: 216–21).

As Nancy Bermeo has judiciously observed, "if a call for moderation,
gradualism, and compromise came from Jeane Kirkpatrick or any other
scholar associated with the American right, it would be dismissed by all but
a small sector of the comparative politics community. Coming from
O'Donnell and Schmitter, this tactical message is much more surprising"
(1990: 362–63). What Bermeo captures in her observation is that the team
of political scientists affiliated with the Latin American Program of the
Woodrow Wilson Center was indeed in a position to combine symbolic
attributes, both scientific and political, that could not otherwise be easily
combined. As suggested by the above overview of the critiques they received,
they could exhibit both an activism in favor of emancipatory struggles, and
in the same breath an acceptance, albeit reluctant, of the prerogatives of the
ruling and propertied classes. Some of them had been exiles, radicals, or
leftists, but they worked with the support of the liberal establishment, and
elaborated a political formula for change within the overall framework of
the dominant international economic order.

This brings us back to the questions I raised at the beginning of this
chapter, regarding the ambivalence of the ready-made ideological oppositions that divide the field of foreign policy as well as the scientific field.
Their virulence too often masks an overlapping consensus and compatible
policy goals. The fact that the Latin American Program of the Woodrow
Wilson Center, the Inter-American Dialogue, and the critical scholarship
on transitions to democracy that they sponsored worked as a war-machine
against the Kirkpatrick approach to Latin America only contributes to obscure the relative compatibility of the discourses and expectations. This compatibility regarded in the first place the socialist alternative: with the authority granted by academia and political experience, the political scientists

of the Woodrow Wilson Center ruled out as bad strategy what the neocon-servatives ruled out as a moral and ideological evil. Despite this far from insignificant difference, the theoretical production flowing from the Center appeared more as an acceptable substitute than as an alternative to the Reagan administration policy. By promoting scientifically a moderate, pro-fessional and nonthreatening conception of democratization, perfectly in line with the traditional goals of the foreign policy establishment, it served, for the liberal elite, the double purpose of challenging the Kirkpatrick doc-trine while, fundamentally, entailing the same effects and asserting its cred-ibility as a doctrine of government.

"Dictatorships and Double Standards": The Neoconservative Doctrine

A Democrat in the Truman tradition, staunchly anticommunist and ill at ease with the left-wing reformers of the Democratic Party, Jeane Kirkpatrick combined an academic and a political career. Born in Oklahoma in 1927, she received an MA from Columbia in 1950, where she studied under Franz Neumann, and a PhD from the same university in 1968. Her involvement in Democratic Party politics (facilitated by her husband Evron Kirkpatrick, for many years executive director of the American Political Science Associ-ation and a close friend of Hubert Humphrey) led her to oppose McGovern and, after his nomination, to contribute to the foundation in 1972 of the Coalition for a Democratic Majority.[9] This opposition to the "New Politics" and the reformists within the party extended naturally to foreign policy is-sues, which constituted the neoconservatives' distinctive turf. Later in the decade, Kirkpatrick joined the Committee on the Present Danger, a group created by Paul Nitze, a former head of the Policy Planning Staff at State under Truman, in order to oppose arms control negotiations and the SALT II treaty. With its membership somewhat overlapping with that of the Coa-lition for a Democratic Majority, the Committee was another rallying point of the emerging neoconservative movement.

Kirkpatrick's experience illustrates how these neoconservative forums worked during the 1970s as ideological and political training ground for "a conservative policy elite that could claim that it was capable of governing" (J. A. Smith 1991: 203). Scholarly publications served the purpose of ac-cumulating credibility and of displacing the political struggle at the most general level of ideas, worldviews, and moral choices. The article that earned

Kirkpatrick her reputation as a major neoconservative foreign policy thinker was published in the November 1979 issue of *Commentary*. Allegedly, this piece caught the attention of the presidential candidate Reagan, who first appointed her foreign-policy adviser during his campaign and, later, his ambassador to the U.N. (Gerson 1991: xiv). If at first glance "Dictatorships and Double Standards" reads like a simple, if harsh, indictment of the international record of the Carter administration, it actually includes a critique of the whole paradigm of modernization, both as an academic theory, a philosophy of history, and a liberal reformist foreign policy. In that sense, the article is a direct attack on the intellectual and political creeds of the liberal foreign policy establishment.

The political substance of the article is well known. The Carter administration, Kirkpatrick argued, "actively collaborated in the replacement of moderate autocrats friendly to American interests with less friendly autocrats of extremist persuasion" (1979a: 34), by seeking to promote democratic regimes in such countries. According to her, campaigns for human rights waged without discrimination often led the administration to weaken right-wing dictatorships allied to the United States, and thus to embolden their "Soviet-sponsored" internal opponents. The result was the toppling of traditional authoritarian regimes which were capable of evolving incrementally toward more open forms of rule, by totalitarian regimes which were by essence monolithic and quasi-eternal. What was needed, instead, was "a morally and strategically acceptable, and politically realistic, program for dealing with non-democratic governments who are threatened by Soviet-sponsored subversion" (ibid.).

But far from being confined to the political, Kirkpatrick's critique extends to the theoretical aspects of the liberal worldview. The shortcomings of the Democratic administration are thus analyzed as the political symptom of the influence exerted by the paradigm and the ideology of modernization: "the foreign policy of the Carter administration is guided by a relatively full-blown philosophy of history which includes . . . a theory of social change, or, as it is currently called, a doctrine of modernization" (ibid.: 38–39). At the root of the ingenuous assumption that "one can easily locate and impose democratic alternatives to incumbent autocracies" is the view, pervasive in the early sociology of modernization, that modern, differentiated and pluralistic social systems constitute the natural direction of historical development, and that this process can be assisted.

If the scientific ideology of the liberal foreign policy establishment that justified in the past such initiatives as the Alliance for Progress or Title IX, had been somewhat shaken by the Vietnam war and South American developments, it was nevertheless reformulated under a slightly different form by a "globalist" tendency within the Carter administration. Recast as what was not yet called "globalization," modernization was seen as a process of technological change leading to the "technetronic era" announced by Brzezinski (1970). And to the extent that social development, under the impact of new technologies, was convergent and went toward an interdependent "world community," cosmopolitism, multilateralism, and more broadly the search for a world order transcending ideological divides flowed directly from this new modernization theory.[10] In many respects, trilateralism was also a direct manifestation of this search for a world order putting institutional flesh on the bones of globalization, a project pursued by political forces seeking to project U.S. policy beyond the realist paradigm in international politics.

Kirkpatrick's discussion of the limits of modernization theory as a model for social change, therefore, was an extension within the social sciences of a political struggle against the liberal establishment. Because it included an evolutionary and deterministic view of the historical process as one of convergent modernization and integration into a world community, modernization theory was ultimately seen as the cause of American decline:

> Although the modernization paradigm has proved a sometimes useful as well as influential tool in social science, it has become the object of searching critiques that have challenged one after another of its central assumptions. Its shortcomings as an analytical tool pale, however, when compared to its inadequacies as a framework for thinking about foreign policy, where its principal effects are to encourage the view that events are manifestations of deep historical forces which cannot be controlled and that the best any government can do is to serve as a "midwife" to history, helping events to move where they are already headed (ibid.: 39).

As a result, the reassertion of American power should involve the critique of structuralism in the social sciences, since this tradition rationalized and justified the effacement of American hegemony. To the extent that modernization theory had been also conceived as a deliberate attempt at building a progressive, future-oriented alternative to Marxism, it shared indeed some of its main features. Shmuel Eisenstadt, for instance, correctly observed that "the vision of the historical process which was connected to all these developments [i.e. the sociology of modernization in the 1950s] was very much in line with the classical evolutionary one. . . . Above all, they share some crucial assumptions about the nature of the transition between different *stages* of social development — a concept which was central to evolutionary and Marxist sociology alike. . . . [and they] assumed that the transition from one stage to another involved a radical break with the past and concomitant change in all spheres" (Eisenstadt, 1985: 12).

It was therefore easy for Kirkpatrick to suggest that the politics of appeasement and self-contrition pursued by the new foreign policy establishment could be directly traced back, via the modernization doctrine, to the influence of Marxism: "the motives and intentions of real persons are no more relevant to the modernization paradigm than they are to the Marxist view of history. Viewed from this level of abstraction, it is the 'forces' rather than the people that count" (Kirkpatrick 1979a: 40).

Having shown the relation between the structural-deterministic model of social change included in modernization theory, the policy of human rights and democratization pursued by the government and the cosmopolitical project of world order embodied by some of its most liberal fractions, Kirkpatrick went on to suggest that, given their capacity to evolve progressively towards democracy, "the best chance for democratic change in authoritarian states facing armed challenges lay in active American support for their government" (Ehrman 1995: 121). In the last instance, the line she adopted was a selective interpretation of the literature on political development. Democracy, she argued, was the product of a complex process of evolution, that required a certain number of preconditions: economic (such as those listed by Lipset[11]), but also cultural (such as those listed by Almond and Verba). But the *tour de force* of the article was to reinterpret these enabling factors, as the difficult outcomes of gradual and complex societal evolutions that could not and should not be hastened. Imbued with a historical pessimism inherited from theologian Reinhold Niebuhr and typical of neoconservative thinking, "Dictatorships and Double Standards" denounced the ingenuity of the progressive, future-oriented, deterministic conception of political change implied in the discourse of modernization, and especially the view that democratic pluralism is the universal "happy end" of the process of modernization. Instead, it emphasized the complexity and open-ended character of political evolution. Democratic government did not only require specific structural preconditions: it was also, and perhaps in the first place, a matter of "skilled" and "talented" leadership (1979: 37).

Often remembered for its justification of U.S. support for right-wing dictatorships, "Dictatorship and Double Standards" is less known for its critique of structuralism and modernization sociology. Starting as an indictment of the administration's record, it carried the critique straight into political science, outlining an entire theoretical continent as the ideological basis and scientific rationalization of the kind of liberal politics represented by the Carter administration. In her attack on the new foreign policy establishment and its scientific ideologies, however, Kirkpatrick followed a strategy entailing the same components as the one followed at the same time by the militant scholars of the Wilson Center in their search for a democratization formula: the rejection of structural theories of social change on the grounds that they led to political paralysis, and the assertion of agency, under the form of political leadership, as what determines in the last instance the possibility of democratization.

Of course, these strategies served opposite aims: In the case of Kirkpatrick, a certain form of decisionism related to the reassertion of America's hegemonic role; in the case of the contributors to *Transitions from Authoritarian Rule*, the critique of a modernization paradigm that was closely associated with authoritarianism in Latin America (in complete opposition to Kirkpatrick's interpretation). But beyond these differences, they entailed a very similar attack on established forms of political sociology with their emphasis on modernization and structural analysis. At the same time, Kirkpatrick's article outlined the limits of U.S. tolerance of social change in its imperial provinces. Democratization would be permissible to the extent that it did not involve any leftward turn or deviation from pro-American positions. In producing a theory of democratization that secured the power of "notables" and contained the influence of the revolutionary left, the Wilson Center scholars elaborated a formula that satisfied these criteria.[12] The main difference, as Nancy Bermeo has suggested, was indeed in who was doing the talking.

Democracy and the "Washington Consensus"

Political science and policy research thus became the battleground for contending intellectual and political agendas. At the same time, however, the contending factions converged around a common indictment of modernization as a barrier to political action. Forged as weapons in the political battles over U.S. foreign policy that were waged through scientific proxies, these strategies turned out to be mutually reinforcing in some of their out-

comes. The symbolic conflicts that opposed neoconservative policy professionals and critical scholars fighting for democracy are perfect examples of
"turf battles" in which the asperity of the conflict often conceals the proximity between the contenders and the agendas. Behind their divergences
and counter-positions, these political antagonists actually had in common a
subordinated position vis-à-vis the liberal foreign policy establishment. Taking advantage of its fragmentation in the wake of the Vietnam war, they
understandably sought to precipitate the crisis of the dominant liberal paradigms that buttressed its power in order to redefine their own positions.
Obviously, they proceeded on the basis of very different readings of the
situation and with very different aims. The neoconservatives attacked an
ideology that, in spite of its anticommunist function during most of the Cold
War,[13] had gone awry under Carter. In their eyes, modernization had become identified with a cosmopolitanism involving appeasement with the
Soviet Union and tolerance of liberation movements in the Third World.
This was also an opportunity to assert their capacity to govern as the only
legitimate heirs of the Cold War establishment.

Conversely, progressive political scientists sympathizing with the anti-
authoritarian struggles in Latin America saw some of Carter's policies a continuation of Cold War internationalism and U.S. imperialism via other
means.[14] As a result, their view of the Carter administration was equally
critical. For the former, modernization theory was in the last instance a
Marxist strand of theory, while for the latter, it was, with its application under
the form of "developmentalism," the cause of authoritarian experiments. In
both cases, the broader framework provided by structuralism as the dominant
episteme of political sociology was rejected as politically sterile or dangerous.
All the contenders had therefore an objective interest in the development
of a scientific research program that would replace the existing paradigms
with a theory of agency focusing on leadership, political reform and, as we
shall see, sound economic management.

But these antagonisms were also battles about the redefinition of the
symbolic capital that could be invested in the market of policy expertise.
Modernization theory was an ideology based on the negation of ideology
and of social conflictuality, which explains its predisposition to provide scientific credentials for policy expertise. By distinguishing between a scientific
order of knowledge, based on objective truth criteria, allowing for rational
and efficient problem-solving, and a political order, biased by calculations
and subjectivity, it entailed the promise of a technical overcoming of social
conflict. The critique of modernization theory must therefore be understood

in the context of a struggle over the nature of legitimate expertise. This critique was fundamentally related to *a democratic critique of the technocratic ideal of politics and of the government of the experts*, carried out from different angles.[15]

From the point of view of committed political scientists, the faith in modernization had directly evolved into (and legitimated) the rule of technocrats in Latin-American bureaucratic-authoritarian states. It was reflected in the alliance between the military and the economists, a technobureaucracy showing disdain for the "irrational" character of politics (Lehmann 1990: 52). For the neoconservative policy elite, on the other hand, the critique of this paradigm was the critique of a type of expertise that was historically associated with big government and liberal reformism — a liberal reformism, moreover, that symbolized in their eyes the "totalitarian temptation," flowing from "an excessive faith in reason, equality, democracy, social engineering" (Kirkpatrick 1979b) and leading government, as the argument goes, to decide for the people. Beyond this, it fuelled the growth a "new class" made of academics and other professionals that colonized the government and undermined American democracy. These normative critiques were all the more effective since they were made at a moment when the capacity of liberal-technocratic expertise to deliver public goods was called into question, and hampered by an inflationist context (Aaron 1978).

The critique of the liberal dogma of modernization was a critique of the exclusion of politics from policy expertise. By calling into question the separation between advocacy and technical rationality, the different counterelites of the 1980s sought to remove the main obstacle to their legitimate participation as experts in the field of state power. Against the technocratic model of expertise, they sought to impose a *political expertise* which did not ignore values, advocacy, conflictuality and militancy. On the contrary, this new form of expertise primarily entailed an understanding of political strategies, calculus, interest formation, and change, or ideological orientations as fundamental determinants of policy outcomes. Rather than an archaism bound to be superseded by rational and scientific policymaking, political conflict was viewed as the natural element of policymaking and therefore should be of central concern to policy experts. Under this emerging regime of expertise, their first-hand knowledge of political conflict suddenly became a valuable resource that they could use to renegotiate their positions.

To a large extent, the social sciences of the 1950s and the modernization paradigm were based on a deliberate attempt at limiting, overcoming or repressing social conflict. Long repressed in the unconscious of the discipline, political conflict thus returned to the center stage in the 1980s. After almost three decades in which the behavioral persuasion dominated, and following the delegitimation of the liberal ideology which underpinned it as a consequence of Vietnam, political scientists were eager to rehabilitate "substantive" concerns as legitimate objects of research (Ricci 1984). The new concern with political conflict and democracy was also a valuable resource on an expanding international market for a new type of policy expertise. In the early 1980s, the *Transitions from Authoritarian Rule* volumes perfectly illustrate the completion of this shift and the success of the strategies pursued by the critics of the modernization paradigm. From a science having as its object the evolution of societal structures,[16] the study of democratization had successfully become a science of political conflicts within the state apparatus. Born as a reaction to a liberal worldview which ignored power relations and political conflictuality and which, by the same token, had ended up reproducing asymmetric power and relations of dependence, this critical approach relied on an analysis of the state that most of the "transitologists" had acquired during their long formative Marxist or dependency period. The analysis of conflicts within ruling blocs that would become a distinctive feature of the "transitions to democracy" approach can be directly traced back to a structural analysis of the state as the coalition of potentially divergent class interests.

This critical knowledge of the state rapidly became a major asset on the international market for political virtue that these political scientists contributed to building and professionalizing. Acquired in the struggle against authoritarianism and imperialism, it evolved into a recognized expertise serving a new form of hegemonic internationalism. Three significant developments illustrate this conversion of a critical knowledge of the state into a dominant policy expertise: the evolution of this knowledge in the direction of a critical analysis of structural economic reforms through the new international political economy; the political functions of "transitology" in the 1980s, and the transformation of dependency theory through the political career of actors like Fernando Henrique Cardoso. Despite their differences, they have in common the recycling of a critical legacy into the circuits of power in the 1980s.

One of the byproducts of this transformation has been the work of a group of political scientists who got involved in the study of the political economy of structural adjustment, among them Stephan Haggard, Barbara Stallings, Joan Nelson, Miles Kahler, and John Williamson. Some who took part in the *Transitions* project, like Robert Kaufman or John Sheahan, linked the issue of democratization to structural adjustment policies. Keeping some distance from their former colleagues — "transitologists" who had "largely eschewed economic variables" (Haggard and Kaufman 1992: 319) — these self-appointed political economists showed that the politics of adjustment provoked shifts in the balance of power within the ruling elites.

In his early contribution to the Woodrow Wilson project on transitions, Robert Kaufman had argued that the internationalization of Latin American economies (the greater reliance on private foreign capital, imported technology, and the role of exports) had produced pressure for economic orthodoxy, especially in phases of economic crisis. Internally, this pressure was relayed by technocrats, usually economists trained abroad and sensitive to the signals emitted by international actors with whom they often shared a similar social or educational background. As a result, the need for "orthodox" economic reform tends to create conflicts between the oligopolistic sector of the bourgeoisie and the technocrats, thus splitting the ruling coalition. By looking at what happens to reform projects within the institutions of the state, these political scientists specialized in economic reform. Against the classical technocratic model of the policy process, they conceptualized the outcomes of economic policies as dependent upon the preferences of politicians, the nature of the conflicts opposing different groups of stakeholders, the nature of the resources they can invest in these conflicts and, especially, the transformation of economic policies in the course of these struggles. In this perspective, when they are implemented locally, in a specific context, the universal economic policies which form the Washington consensus modify the original social contract linking different parts of society, and therefore need to be politically managed and negotiated. This approach became a very useful instrument of policy reform as it was developed at a moment when the results of structural adjustment programs were coming up short. Very quickly, it found its way into the World Bank where it contributed to raise a concern with the issues of "governance."[17]

By working out the political causes for the success or the failure of structural adjustment programs, these political economists contributed to bring the issue of the political regime and of regime change within the scope of international financial institutions. This research program on political regimes and on the political economy of the state thus complemented economics as a hegemonic form of global policy expertise. By the end of the 1990s, the emphasis on political institutions and their internal dynamics as fundamental determinants of economic reform that they had developed had indeed become official thinking within the Bank (see Picciotto 1995; World

Bank 1997). The leftist critique of liberalism in the 1970s, which resulted in an analysis of conflicts within the state apparatus, was ultimately reinvested in the 1980s in the construction of a new orthodoxy and aggregated to the "Washington consensus."

"Transitology," the other major offshoot of this transformation of political science and policy expertise, has played a very similar role in the reconversion of a critical knowledge of the state into a dominant paradigm. This new approach to sociopolitical change became institutionalized in major academic institutions under the form of specialized curricula or research centers. By combining contrasting promises — that of emancipation and that of stability and order — it was sufficiently articulated and flexible to provide a common ideological umbrella for different political sensitivities and to generate political consensus. A fundamental feature of this prescriptive academic production was indeed the fact that it mobilized an entire tradition of Marxist or class-based analysis of the state directly inherited from the dependency school in a theory that accepted as the most plausible post-authoritarian outcome a "democracy of notables" leaving the actual distribution of resources intact, and by the same token preserving the power of "propertied classes, elite institutions" (O'Donnell and Schmitter 1986: 40). In other words, it entailed the promise of a democratization that dissipated the fears of Cold Warriors and anticommunist ideologues, expressed by Kirkpatrick, of seeing right-wing dictatorships replaced by "armed intellectuals citing Marx" (Kikpatrick 1979a: 45). In the "transitions from authoritarian rule" envisaged by the Wilson Center political scientists, the radicals had to be contained while the right had to be "helped" to do well (O'Donnell and Schmitter 1986: 62). Democratization became all the more acceptable in Washington since the alternative to incumbent dictators was not Kirkpatrick's armed intellectuals citing Marx but, increasingly, well-connected intellectuals citing Dahl and exhibiting irreproachable U.S. credentials.

The transformation of the former into the latter is symbolically illustrated by the career of Fernando Henrique Cardoso. One of the leading theorists of dependent development, Cardoso progressively distanced himself from the stronger versions of dependency theory which posited the structural incapacity of dependent capitalism to overcome the detrimental terms of foreign trade, tackle the unemployment and underemployment generated by the combination of industrialization and importation of labor-saving technologies, and achieve any significant level of redistributive justice (these approaches were for instance those of Ruy Mauro Marini, André Gunder Frank, or Theotônio dos Santos.) Instead, he considered phases of economic growth as an opportunity for "associated capitalism" to generate genuine development and for governments to implement social policies (rather than structural reforms) that would remedy the contradictions of this process (Dos Santos 1998).

It is not surprising that this theoretical revision matches a social-democratic turn, which sees Cardoso playing a leading role in the founding of the Brazilian Social Democratic Party in 1987–88. This role put him at the center of the process of revision that transformed social-democratic theory and practice worldwide in the late 1980s-early 1990s, a revision characterized in the first place by a positive reassessment of market capitalism. "The first post-Marxist of them all," (Lehmann 1990: 73) the sociologist-turned-Senator could contribute all the more easily to the elaboration of a moderate formula of democratization since he came from the *Partido do Movimento Democrático Brasileiro* which had always been deeply suspicious of *basismo*.

The combination of democratic credentials with strong international networks built through the CEBRAP, the Inter-American Dialogue or the Institute for International Economics gave Cardoso the political credibility on the international scene that motivated his appointment as Minister of Foreign Affairs and shortly afterward, in May 1993, as Minister of Finance in the government of Itamar Franco, in the midst of a stabilization plan. This background "undoubtedly strengthened his, and Brazil's profile in the world's key financial centres, especially among the commercial banks bent upon recouping payments arrears" (Cunningham 1999: 78). During his stay in office and, subsequently, his terms as President, Cardoso came to embody a conservative "dependent reformism" (Dos Santos 1998: 60) based on the policies associated with the Washington consensus, as even sympathetic critics have not failed to notice (i.e. Cunningham 1999). It is paradoxically this critic of dependent capitalism who would put an end to the fixed exchange rate in 1993 and, at the end of his first term as president, had to devalue the Real and abide by IMF conditionality.

Such examples bear witness to the structural transformation of the position of critical knowledge in the emerging configuration of global power, where the exercise of hegemony has successfully assimilated the paradigms historically linked to resistance to hegemony, emancipatory struggles and democratization. To be sure, this transformation was facilitated by external factors. If the new political science of democracy provided a scientific justification for the efforts of foreign policy activists to build a "campaign" for democracy through such initiatives as the National Endowment for Democracy, it is because these activists actively sought the involvement of academic communities. Shortly after the creation of the NED, its first president, Allen Weinstein, moved to the Robert Maynard Hutchins Center for the Study of Democratic Institutions.[18] Under his tenure, the Center published a book (Goldman and Douglas 1988) in which political consultants involved in the Democracy Program that led to the creation of the NED or in other cold war institutions, and academics with a record in the administration, inaugurated a *genre* that would soon become popular, located between the academic essay and the practitioner's manual. The publication shows very well how the use of social sciences was a component of a broader strategy to launch a global "campaign for democracy." One of the contributions in particular, sheds some light on the very conscious use of "critical" theories as both a weapon and a source of legitimacy for this campaign. Written by Raymond Gastil, a political scientist whose claim to fame is being responsible for the famous "Freedom Country Scores" that the conservative think tank Freedom House produces every year, this piece of work suggests that critical knowledge is functional to the democratic crusade that was initiated in the 1980s. Resuming the tradition of the "State Department socialism" of the 1950s, Gastil made the case for what he called a function of "proximate criticism": "that is, that the ideas most likely to promote democratic change in the minds of Soviet citizens are those not too far from the assumptions of the socialist world they know. . . . This implies that our ideological offensive should begin with emphasis on the many historical and contemporary Marxist critiques of the Soviet Union and descriptions of successful socialist aspects of the West" (Gastil 1988: 42). In policy research, politics or the social sciences, the promotion of the non-Communist left was still one of the major strategies for exporting Americanism. In the case of Latin America, nobody was better prepared to fulfill this function than the post-Marxist, ex-dependencistas, social democratic scholars who moved from the anti-imperialist, anti-authoritarian struggles of the 1970s to the theorization of liberal democracy in the 1980s.

5   International Relations Theory and the Emancipatory Narrative of Human Rights Networks

"L'existence idéale, idéelle, spirituelle des 'idées' [relève] exclusivement d'une idéologie de l' 'idée' et de l'idéologie."

— Louis Althusser "Idéologie et appareils idéologiques d'Etat" in *Positions* (Paris: Editions Sociales, 1976), p. 118.

The New Idealism in the Social Sciences and International Relations

The much-celebrated triumph of democracy at the end of the twentieth century is often presented as the victory of an idea. The spread of democracy was not the result of economic development or increased social differentiation, as suggested by the old paradigm of modernization theory, but rather a diffuse process driven by beliefs, values, and ideas. The intangible "power of ideas" had toppled the material arrangements of established powers. In the late 1980s, with significant timeliness, a consultant for the State and the Defense Departments revived the old theme of the "end of ideology" that dominated debates among social scientists in the 1950s and announced once again the end of ideological conflict. The "end of history," indeed, was nothing else than the end of the historical nature of future conflicts. This time, however, the reason was not material progress and social reform, but the triumph of the ideology of liberal capitalist democracy. Fukuyama's 1992 bestseller perfectly captured the pervasive equation of democracy with an *ideology*.

The social sciences have been at the center of this transformation in the representations of social change. The effacement of materialist conceptions of history and social change has certainly played an important role. Explanations of social phenomena drawing upon a hard, objectivist ontology have been banned from a scientific discourse that massively turned away from the earthly realm of social practices toward the sky of ideas, in what psychoanalysts would call a process of sublimation. Few established research programs or methodological approaches seem to have been spared by this powerful trend: historical macro-sociology, structuralism, political economy, modernization, and dependency theories have taken the road of a post-Marxism that was increasingly "post" and not very Marxist. Instead, there has been a resurgence of theories articulated around communicative processes, symbolic and linguistic interactionism, cognitive "framing" of issues, epistemic bases of political change that cannot be simply imputed to the linguistic turn in the social sciences. Across disciplines, the standard notions of causality have been revised in favor of "ideas" that have taken the place of material forces as the primary components of social phenomena.

Among the social scientific disciplines, international relations theory has probably made visible these developments more than other scholarly and policy discourses. The classical paradigms that had defined this discipline in relation to the Cold War were suddenly challenged. A younger generation of scholars sought to shift the discipline's center of gravity away from the material order of security and power, toward the intangible order of communicative action and meaningful exchange. To the extent that bipolar conflict was no longer the structuring force of the international scene, the problems inherent to a new world order were primarily interpreted as problems of *social* integration or collective action between a plurality of actors that were not all state institutions. The concept of the "transnational" was thus one of the most visible manifestations of this effort to reach beyond the nation-state system, in a perspective of global integration, indicating a return to the cosmopolitical tradition and its concern with the *civitas maxima*.[1]

This pull toward social theory gave some scientific legitimacy to this new approach and opened it to external intellectual influences, sometimes allowing for fruitful exchange. At the same time, the preoccupation of these scholars with non-state actors, such as international lobbies, NGOs, social movements, or wider networks cutting across institutional boundaries gave them a political legitimacy. They imported into a discipline historically structured around the viewpoint of the state the concerns of actors that often opposed it. This siding with the ruled as opposed to the rulers also explains the elective affinity between this research program and the case-studies of human rights, the "rights of the ruled"[2] — although environmental norms or gender movements have also received their share of attention.

But the triumphal entry of international civil networks into international relations theory has also served methodological purposes. Against the traditional emphasis on material interests and resources, these new approaches have stressed ideas, norms, and beliefs as important factors determining identity and interest formation. As opposed to the old world of states based on a material conception of power, the new world of "transnational" relations is fundamentally a world of communicative processes and ideas. To the instrumental rationality that underpinned the realist models of international relations, the new approaches opposed a communicative rationality entailing the ideal of a free speech situation. A primordial linguistic intersubjectivity is the element in which identities are constantly negotiated and redefined, rather than materially given. From that perspective, "transnational" relations involve a conception of power essentially as the "power of ideas." (e.g. Risse, Ropp, Sikkink 1999). Symbolic power, however, is certainly a more appropriate description for this modality of power. Borrowed from Pierre Bourdieu, the notion of symbolic power designates the power to impose divisions, distinctions, and hierarchies as *legitimate*. "Symbolic power," as Bourdieu writes succinctly, "is a power of creating things with words" (Bourdieu 1990: 136). More precisely, it is the power to make domination seem legitimate. It is a power that adds its effect to power relations and consolidates them. As we shall see, the international champions of the "power of ideas" — NGOs, transnational issue networks, activists, moral entrepreneurs — most often do not represent some kind of counter-power but are a crucial element in the definition of today's hegemonic forms of power relations.

By distinguishing sharply between instrumental and communicative action, or between interests and "principled ideas" (Risse-Kappen 1995: 8), the new theories of international and transnational relations have reintroduced in the study of international relations the old sophomoric distinction between morals and politics. By the same token, they have generally tended to present non-state actors as moral actors, or rather as the agents of the moralization of international life. Representing the "power of ideas," international networks of activists have been implicitly recast in the role of bearers of specific universals, whether the abstract universal of human rights or the concrete universal of the environment — in a sort of Hegelianism of the third sector where the "power of ideas" realizes itself through the historical process of globalization. The result has been a normative bias in favor of these transnational movements throughout the literature under review. From human, indigenous or women's rights to environmental protection, the new activists involved in the establishment of global prescriptions have become the subjects of a scientific narrative where globalization is primarily an emancipatory process, and democratization is one of its most salient facets. Rather than the outcome of complex political, social and economic developments, democratization has been increasingly construed as a process of "diffusion" or "contagion" (Whitehead 1996) of ideas and normative references conveyed by "transnational advocacy networks" actively exploiting expanded communication opportunities across political and symbolic borders (Keck and Sikkink 1998).

This chapter focuses on these social scientific accounts of activism, and in particular, on the conceptual categories that have been mobilized in order to "explain" the constitution and the effectiveness of international human rights networks. I argue that the idealism underlying the theories grouped under the misleading label of "social constructivism"[3] contributes to the production of an instrumental account of the formation and operation of activist networks, in the sense that this account works to their benefit and furthers their interests. In explaining the emergence of new forms of global activism by their adherence to the "principled ideas" they profess, recent IR theories have implicitly, but consistently, suggested that these global advocacy networks were moral and disinterested actors — having no other identity than that of granting normativity to the global norms they claim to defend.[4] By the same token, this scholarship has developed in a very anti-sociological way, in spite of its self-assigned label. The real, material, social genealogy of these global activisms is almost systematically absent from available studies, which do not ask which social contexts, which rewards and incentives generate the "interest in disinterestedness" (Bourdieu 1997: 148) that characterizes the dedication to universal values. In a similar fashion, there is no interrogation on which local strategies are possibly served by these global struggles around universals. This blind spot is all the more paradoxical in that the new transnational activists are also identified as "norms entrepreneurs" (Sikkink 1999), a metaphor that is suggestive of the mechanisms of competition for the symbolic profits and clientelist relations that structure the international arena of the militant production of norms.

In view of these side-effects, flowing from the fundamental methodological choices operated by political scientists, it is therefore legitimate to ask whether such social scientific discourses do not belong to the very strategies through which activist networks construe the public image of their disinterestedness. This is further justifiable by the fact that, in many cases, scholars writing on human rights activism or other advocacy coalitions are extremely close to the networks they analyze (Dezalay and Garth 1998b). The result is the smuggling into scientific discourse of the public justifications that the participants in these networks put forward in their strategic practices. This conversion of description into justification clearly locates these IR theories and their producers within the wider networks they write about: by providing scientific rationalization, expertise on normative technologies (what works and what does not) and justification, these scholars definitely contribute to the production and reproduction of the new global activisms.

I now analyze in greater detail this academic construction of a progressive narrative of emancipation and democratization which revolves around the figure of the international NGO. I pay special attention to the "case-study" of U.S. human rights foreign policy as an illustration of the "power of ideas" and I compare it to some of the findings presented in Chapter 2. While they tend to associate transnational activism with subordinated groups of actors, these theorists construe transnational activism as an ambiguous category that is also prone to functioning as hegemony. Nothing illustrates this ambiguity better than the genealogy of the concept of "issue networks" which is often used to designate these global activisms. It has been imported into international relations theory from the analysis of the policymaking process in Washington, thus extending to global processes the specific model of U.S. politics. By the same token, it also extends to global policymaking processes the models, the templates, the resources validated by the hegemonic power. This genealogy is the object of the second part of the chapter. It leads to a critique of the relationship that exists between this new idealism and international militant networks. Because they provide a strategic expertise that is also a resource for activist networks, scholars fulfill a functional role within the strategy of such networks.

The Social Construction of Social Constructivism

Within the discipline of international relations theory, the recent focus on transnational activism has been motivated by a dissatisfaction with conventional realist approaches and their objectivist epistemology based on material power, interests, resources, or systemic mechanisms (Goldstein and Keohane 1993: 4–5). Under the heading of "social constructivism," scholars who did not identify with the classical realist tradition of the discipline, centered around concepts of national security and recently revived as "neo-realism," introduced within the discipline a concern for the role of non-state actors in the production of international norms and international legality.

Tellingly, in their offensive they revived some of the scholarly debates of the late 1960s and 1970s which had accompanied the policy of *détente* and contributed to producing the category of the "transnational" (e.g. Nye and Keohane 1971). Published in 1995, the programmatic volume of this new approach was suggestively entitled *Bringing Transnational Relations Back In*. It explicitly acknowledged the theoretical lineage with the liberal approaches in fashion in the post-Vietnam foreign policy discourse (Risse-Kappen 1995: xi). But while the learned debates among international relations theorists in the 1970s focused on technology and the economy as transnational forces,[5] the revival of the transnational in the 1990s moved from a technical to an *activist* paradigm centered on new subjects, the international NGO or the transnational issue network, and on their role in the production of norms, with a special emphasis on human rights.[6]

In order to understand the main features of this new scholarly discourse on transnational activism — in favor of democracy and human rights, endowed with academic authority and, by definition, associated with progressive and emancipatory practices — it is important to understand how the logic of its production overlaps with struggles and stakes internal to the academic field of international relations. The investment in research on international NGOs and transnational relations served the strategic needs of the "young Turks" of international relations theory who, by calling into question the state-centered representations of international politics, sought to oppose the old guard of "security" scholars in the propitious context of the end of the cold war. The surge of nongovernmental actors in world politics, and more specifically of activist organizations, was primarily used to justify the critique of the dominant scholarship (Wapner 1995). Keck and Sikkink, for instance, typically argue that "world politics at the end of the twentieth century involves, alongside states, many non-state actors who interact with each other, with states, and with international organizations," and that "scholars have been slow to recognize either the rationality or the significance of activists networks" (1998b: 89).

In this perspective, the special attention paid to human rights NGOs had a crucial tactical value. Audie Klotz, Rosemary Foot, Thomas Risse, Kathryn Sikkink: most of the principal exponents of "social constructivism" have also written on human rights networks. In privileging this issue among others, the "social constructivists" were able to link up to these highly symbolic resources and to use them in order to strengthen their position within the field. But they could also use the emancipatory repertoire associated with such networks. Human rights movements, indeed, are promptly described as "forces for empowering the abused, making the voices of the weak heard, and reminding those with more resources and more enviable records of protection of their obligations to common humanity" (Foot 2000: 254). By a sort of analogy, therefore, the struggle of these new IR scholars against state-centered theories of the international system ran parallel to the struggle of human rights activists against the state. By importing the front lines of global struggles around universal stakes into their field, they were able to secure symbolic gains and political legitimacy. Highlighting the role of NGOs and transnational activists in international arenas also amounted, for these scholars, to becoming spokespersons for subordinated groups of activists whose existence "prevailing theories failed to remark" (Keck and Sikkink 1998: xi), in a scholarly discipline traditionally at the service of state power. They could thus establish their professional and scientific practice as alternative and progressive. At the same time, however, the success of this strategy rapidly conferred a "dominant" status to this scholarly discourse.

As Dezalay and Garth have argued (2002), it is important to stress the capacity of this new emancipatory paradigm, centered on NGOs and human rights, to constitute a new orthodoxy and to function in a hegemonic rather than a counter-hegemonic fashion. After all, the scholarly pioneers of "transnational" relations themselves had already in the 1970s pointed out the complementarity between transnational actors and national states and the compatibility of their interests.[7] The evolution of the "social constructivist" approach bears out this intuition. Not only has "social constructivism" become a rapid-growth sector of international relations theory and generated a voluminous literature, but also the awareness that "transnational human rights networks" exert nothing less than a constituent power in the establishment of international legal standards and that activism is therefore becoming a crucial hegemonic resource is by now common wisdom in major international and national state institutions.

The U.S. State Department, for instance, underscores the complementarity between its policies and transnational networks. With the nomination of Harold Hongju Koh as Assistant Secretary of State at the Bureau of Democracy, Human Rights, and Labor, the Clinton administration appointed a "social constructivist" of sorts. Koh was indeed a representative of the new literature on norms and international relations that has developed at the intersection of law and political science (e.g. Koh 1997). Written under his auspices, the 1999 Country Reports on Human Rights Practices offers a striking example of the complementarity between national foreign policy and transnational networks, suggested by Keohane and Nye almost thirty years earlier. It also echoes the learned debates in international relations theory and adopts the main concepts of social constructivism. Starting with the observation that globalization comprises "three universal 'languages:' money, the Internet, and democracy and human rights," the report identified in "transnational human rights networks" the vectors of an "overlooked" third globalization (U. S. Department of State 2000: 1). Accompanying the expansion of financial markets and the diffusion of new technologies, these networks evolve "out of communities of like-minded individuals who gather around shared interests and values." Fully aware of their importance and of their spanning across the public-private divide, "the United States is committed to the long-term project of helping such networks develop into an international civil society, an effective partnership of governments, international agencies, multinational corporations, and . . . NGO's that will support democracy worldwide and promote the standards embodied in the Universal Declaration of Human Rights" (ibid.) From the point of view of these hegemonic institutions, therefore, transnational issue networks immediately appear as a specific modality which is *internal* to the exercise of their power.

This transformation of an "alternative" and progressive paradigm into an instrument of transnational government and a specific mode of domination (symbolic power) bears witness to the polyvalence of social constructivism as a scientific and prescriptive discourse. The construction of this new orthodoxy, however, should also be seen in the light of the strategies pursued by the NGOs — which incidentally explain why the transformation of a critical, alternative discourse into a quasi-official doctrine met with no criticism from NGOs. This process, whereby "dominated" political scientists become the speakers for other "dominated" groups in order to modify their own position, and, ultimately, attain a "dominant" status, can also serve the strategic purposes of human rights activists and other norms entrepreneurs.

If they play an important role in the production of international legality and morality, the power of NGOs and transnational issue networks is not formalized and recognized. As Antonio Cassese observes, NGOs have not yet "acquired full international subjectivity" in the juridical sense (Cassese 1990: 174) in spite of their tremendous development and their role in the design and enforcement of international standards in such fields as human rights or environmental awareness. That networks and NGOs become legitimate units of analysis and even major categories in a field such as political science (and in particular international relations theory, which has so far been a "science of the state") therefore takes on special importance. In introducing NGOs and international activist movements into the field of in-

ternational relations and in producing and imposing unifying concepts —
especially the concept of network — "social constructivists" partake in the
collective construction of subjectivity for these organizations that assert their
expertise internationally. The professional strategies of these scholars and
the quest for strategic positions and recognition by international institutions
pursued by the networks they study are, therefore, mutually reinforcing. This
scientific contribution is all the more important in that the scholarly description of these networks often construes them as agents of emancipation
and, to use Cassese's expression, the "mouthpiece of world conscience."

Because it has contributed to the production of this new universal subject
as the friendly, moral and emancipatory face of globalization, striving to
"unify the world" through human rights, to quote Cassese again, it is important to consider political science as a discourse open to and convergent
with the strategies of these militant networks. This appears clearly when one
considers the epistemological choices that have been made in order to construe these networks as moral subjects.

The Epistemological Production of Global Moral Actors

The mode of organization of activist organizations defending human
rights or other global causes and their normative purposes have led political
scientists to characterize them as transnational "issue" or "advocacy networks." In doing so, they have sought to distinguish them sharply from other
types of collective actors whose behavior could be accounted for in terms of
institutional identities, externally given interests, material resources, or "opportunity structures." Such notions could be dispensed with or relativized,
while instead ethical concern and commitment were taken as the primary
factors explaining collective action and even collective identity. One of the
distinctive traits of social constructivism is indeed that the ideas commanding commitment gain both ontological and explanatory primacy over the
material interests and the social identities that they contribute to defining.
Thus, for Risse, Ropp and Sikkink (1999: 7), "social constructivists emphasize that ideas and communicative processes define, in the first place, which
material factors are perceived as relevant and how they influence understandings of interests, preferences and political decisions. . . . In other words,

material factors and conditions matter through cognitive and communicative processes."

The endorsement of specific values or, in the IR jargon, of a set of "principled ideas," count as an *explanation* of collective action. For Margaret
Keck and Kathryn Sikkink, who are among the main proponents of this
approach, advocacy networks are thus "organized to promote causes, principled ideas, and norms, and they often involve individuals advocating policy
changes that cannot be easily linked to a rationalist understanding of their
'interests.' " (1998: 8–9). Their formation is "motivated by values rather than
by material concerns of professional norms" (ibid.: 2).

Susan Burgerman makes a very similar claim when she writes that, in
such cases, "the motivation for collective action is not directly related to
material interests" but to the "intellectual or moral commitment to a
cause" (1998: 908). The argument is reiterated throughout the literature
on transnational issue / advocacy networks, and it entails a very important
consequence for the scientific explanation of social facts: political or moral
causes (and by extension, ideas) are endowed with *causal force*, to the extent
that they can account for the emergence of collective action.[8] In other
words, if "ideas matter," it is because they have the same kind of reality
as a material object which causes the movement of another by colliding
with it.

It is worth dwelling further on this articulation between ideas and social
phenomena since, for the proponents of these approaches, nothing less than
"the causal relationship between material and ideational factors is at stake"
(Risse, Ropp and Sikkink 1999: 6). Actually, in arguing that the formation
of issue networks is "motivated" by ideas, these political scientists implicitly
conflate two kinds of explanations that have been kept distinct in the social
sciences. On the one hand, by suggesting that ideas or values *motivate* the
formation of advocacy networks, they rely on a form of naturalist explanation
of social phenomena whereby explaining an action is equivalent to locating
it as the outcome of a causal process. On the other hand, by emphasizing
that this causal power of ideas as related to their "high value content" (Keck
and Sikkink 1998: 2), their intrinsic "persuasiveness" (e.g. Yee 1996: 89–92)
or, in other words, a cogency derived from their social meaning, scholars
also turn to an anti-naturalist conception of explanation as a *redescription* of
its subjective rationale.[9]

In his overview of social constructivist approaches, Yee provides a perfect illustration of this methodological ambiguity when he writes that "Meaning-oriented behavioralist explanations of the causal link between ideas and policies . . . 'must be accompanied by a *causal story* indicating that mechanisms through which observed correlations evolved.' In ideational analysis, these mechanisms stem significantly from institutions and from the ideas themselves" (Yee 1996: 85). Therefore, what causally explains the emergence of networks of human rights activists or other "norms entrepreneurs" are not the social predispositions and calculations of their members or wider structural factors, but the intrinsic cogency of human rights or other values that they may endorse. Note that, by the same token, the public meaning or the generally accepted "point" of human rights activism, in order to function as a cause, is conflated with the motivations of the individuals involved in such practices. Ideas become motivations *per se*, without any reference being made to the specific investments and calculations which they make possible. As a result, the cognitive pretension to being able to account for the social constitution of these collective international actors is, in theory, entirely satisfied by the ideas or values they endorse.

What are the immediate consequences of this "resurgent idealism" (Wendt 1999: 92) for political science? In the first place, it implicitly posits the autonomous existence of ideas, *sub specie aeternitatis*, independently from their realization in social practices. Practices are even considered to be the causal outcomes of the cogency of ideas. Typically, in the jargon of political science, ideas would thus be taken as "independent variables." Even when the possibility of an inquiry into their social production is mentioned, it is immediately eluded: "We do not seek to explain the sources of these ideas; we focus on their effects" (Goldstein and Keohane 1993: 7). Whether for collective action or public policies, the ideal produces, and therefore explains, the social.[10]

Second, by conflating the motivations leading specific actors to coalesce into networks dedicated to a cause on the one hand, and that cause itself on the other, it realizes a methodological *tour de force* which blurs the boundary between the rationality of an action and the publicly stated reason for that action, or rather, its justification. Indeed, it should be emphasized that there is, in this type of approach, a complete overlap between the scientific explanation of collective action (its formation is motivated by salient ideas) and the self-description provided by the actors (who emphasize their commitment to a cause). The self-description of strategic actors is thus directly and unreflexively translated into the scientific vernacular.

The Academic Saga of Human Rights and U.S. Foreign Policy

These salient epistemological aspects entail important consequences for the way democracy and human rights activism is understood, as the new approaches to transnational activist networks in international relations are most often theories of democratizing agents and of the diffusion of democratic norms. In particular, these aspects matter for the historical account of the rise of human rights and democracy policies in the United States that is often found in the literature under scrutiny.

In deciphering a new logic of action in the practice of transnational issue networks, where interests and social or political strategies have almost no place, political scientists have produced idealist narratives of the diffusion and enforcement of norms that are constitutive of democratic government. Given the premises on which these theories were built, this narrative has also equated the surge of non-state actors with a moralization of international politics. Driven by values and ideals, the practice of these actors has been by and large identified as a form of progressive, emancipatory politics that contributes to the extension of basic freedoms, rights, and entitlements. This view results from the type of case studies usually encountered in this literature (human rights occupy the first place) as much as from the initial assumptions guiding the theory. To the extent that advocacy networks are characterized by the centrality of "principled ideas" in their formation and that such ideas are defined as "normative ideas that specify criteria for distinguishing right from wrong and just from unjust" (Goldstein and Keohane 1993: 9) — i.e. moral criteria — then the process whereby these ideas become norms (i.e., inform the practice of a given collectivity) is indeed a process of moralization.

This moral repertoire is recurrent in the literature. Wapner, for instance, mentions that this work on ideas allows such actors to have a significant impact on "international morality" (1995: 317). Burgerman asserts that they are "mobilized around moral issues" and that, because they are motivated by ideas rather than interests, they ensure the maintenance of "moral regimes [that] are not self-enforcing, are not amenable to strategies based on reciprocity, and offer no intrinsic material incentives for cooperative behavior"(1998: 906–7). It is even argued that such transnational networks of activists, because they contribute to shifting "the balance of power . . . in favor of the dispossessed," represent a novel form of "progressive action at the global level." They thus qualify as "candidates for counter-hegemonic globalization" (Evans 2000: 231). Imperceptibly, the description of such networks as principled actors has become a political characterization that emphasizes their progressivism.

From this characterization, it flows almost "naturally" that such networks have moralized U.S. foreign policy and positively influenced governments or international bodies. According to "social constructivists," the capacity of "ideas" to persistently inform foreign policies, even beyond the initial impetus of policy advocates, issue networks, or other kinds of related activists is explained by the causal virtue of ideas themselves. By becoming "encased" or "embedded" in institutions, the life expectancy of ideas is expanded and, by the same token, the practice of institutional agents is constrained by these ideas.[11] At this level the epistemological foundations of these theories directly impinge upon the logic driving the *historical* account they give of U.S. human rights and pro-democracy policy in the 1980s — which seems, throughout the literature, to be the classical case study (not least, because it seems to be often recycled). In order to understand the precise social functions of this scientific discourse, it is therefore interesting to compare these narratives to the reconstruction of these policies presented in the previous chapters.

The U.S. case is also exemplary because it allows one to draw easily an opposition between benevolent liberal networks committed to the extension of human rights and a cynical, realist, conservative, and aggressive administration — and to illustrate the success of the former. The U.S. case lends itself perfectly to a demonstration of "the power of ideas" to influence agents that are not committed to principles, but are nevertheless constrained by their rhetorical adoption or instrumental use of such "principled ideas." The adoption of legislation and the implementation of a human rights policy under Carter is considered the turning point at which the idea of human rights somehow sinks into the institutional environment and the foreign policy administration to such an extent that the Reagan administration was later unable to uproot it and had to adopt it gradually. In order to sustain the claim that a merely instrumental adoption of a rhetoric of principles implies a behavior that displays a minimum of consistency with it, Risse et al. have argued that this had been the case of the Reagan administration:

> When the principled position in favor of democracy was first adopted by the Reagan administration, most interpreted it as a vehicle for an aggressive foreign policy against leftist regimes, such as the USSR,

Nicaragua, and Cuba. (This would be consistent with the instrumental use of a principled idea.) But because democracy as a principled idea had achieved consensus among political elites and the general public in the United States, the Reagan administration found itself obliged to a minimal consistency in its foreign policy, and thus eventually actively encouraged democracy in authoritarian regimes which the Republicans viewed as loyal allies, such as Chile and Uruguay. (Risse, Ropp and Sikkink 1999, 10)

An earlier account of the same period by Kathryn Sikkink rings very similar bells:

When Ronald Reagan assumed the presidency in 1981, human rights activists predicted that U.S. human rights policy would disappear. . . . [After the Senate announced that it would not tolerate the dismantling of Carter's human rights policy] the Reagan administration next attempted what amounted to a covert dismantling of the human rights policy. The administration accepted and endorsed the policy in principle while subverting its meaning in practice. . . . Within a year of taking office, however, the Reagan team changed their human rights policy. A leaked copy of the memo calling for the change indicates that they shifted their stance because they had become aware of broad support for human rights policies among members of the Congress, the American public, and the Western allies. Once adopted, the new policy in support of democracy demanded a minimal inner consistency. Reagan administration officials who used the human rights and democracy banner in their crusade against Nicaragua felt obliged occasionally to protect themselves against charges of bias by also criticizing human rights abuses by some right-wing regimes, such as those in Chile and Uruguay. (Sikkink 1993: 154–55)

In both cases, it is suggested that the establishment of a human rights policy in the United States was due to liberal policy activists who managed to turn their cause into an official policy under Carter. This policy withstood a change in administrations because it had become entrenched in the foreign policy establishment and its institutions, and, more broadly, in the political system as a whole. What is also implied thereby is a sort of neutrality of the idea of human rights, in the sense that both the concept and the practices attached to it are not fundamentally contingent upon the actors who implement them: the idea of human rights somehow "took hold" of the Reagan administration and forced it into policies it did not really envisage maintaining. Because there can be no purely instrumental uses of a principled idea, as both passages suggest, the moral nature of human rights eventually polices the practices explicitly seeking to derive their legitimacy from this idea.

In a way, in their interpretation of this episode, IR scholars project onto historical reality the same opposition that divides the field of international relations theory into idealism and realism. This historical account is more the product of a preexisting, abstract explanatory framework, based on an idealist conception of social change, than the fruit of an investigation informed by a truly historical content. In fact, what these idealist theories of activism and foreign policy cannot grasp is precisely the historical nature of the moral discourses and legal doctrines they are concerned with. In reifying "ideas," they do not see that ideas are fundamentally "contested concepts" (Connolly 1983) the meaning of which is the stake of political struggles between contending groups of actors.

This is even more the case with human rights, which do not have all the attributes of other jurisdictional domains (such as normative consistency, clarity, or secondary norms of applicability). Human rights and democracy have emerged as positive and diversified constitutional realities before even becoming international legal provisions. They are therefore the contextualized objects of contending interpretations and understandings. Their meaning does not exist independently from the practices and discourses about human rights and democracy. As a consequence, it does not make sense to say that the Reagan administration "subverted the meaning" of human rights: as we have seen, it actively produced its own human rights doctrine which deeply and durably transformed the understanding of these rights and their implications for American foreign policy.

In particular the successful amputation of social and economic rights from the generic conception of human rights can be safely attributed to the Reagan administration. The transformation of human rights into an *ideology* that could be actively exported through institutions such as the National Endowment for Democracy promotion is also the result of a contest over the meaning of the human rights doctrine. Far from being constrained to adopt a policy promoted by others, the Reagan administration was no less militant in promoting human rights and democracy than the networks of progressive activists allegedly transforming the outlook and logic of international relations today. Actually, it was its own political cadre who, in the first place, understood the "power of ideas" and successfully put it into practice.

The account of the genesis of human rights and democracy policies in the 1980s that may be found in the international relations literature is also flawed on a number of historical if not factual instances. Sikkink argues, for example, that one of the factors explaining the absence of a human rights policy until 1973 (when most of the legislation regarding human rights was passed) was the obstacle constituted by the cold warrior mentality (1993: 145). Rosemary Foot, in her study of human rights in China, also imputes to "cold warriors" the U.S. reluctance to advance the cause of human rights during the 1960s (2000: 32). My analysis of the NED and of the transformation of the democratic crusade of the Cold War into "democracy promotion" shows that it was actually a small but influential network of cold warriors who promoted the adoption of a human rights policy — albeit in a highly specific form — under Reagan. Another bias of "social constructivist" accounts of U.S. foreign policy, due in particular to the tendency to view human rights activism as a generically progressive phenomenon, is the linkage that Sikkink establishes between human rights and civil rights activism, and the Carter human rights policy: the civil rights movements, she argues, "contributed more than ideas: a generation of activists trained in its rigor turned their organizational skills to promoting equal rights in the international arena" (1993: 163). While Carter's assistant Secretary of State for humanitarian affairs, Patricia Derian, and some of Andrew Young's aides at the United Nations came from the civil rights movement, many moderate civil rights activists close to the AFL-CIO when the union was at the front line of the cold war later became conservatives and contributed to Reagan's human rights and democracy policy. Activists such as Carl Gershman, Joshua Muravchik or Bayard Rustin, but also many other prominent "democracy experts" come from the civil rights movement and became active Reaganites.

In virtue of its epistemological basis, social constructivism has thus produced a narrative of normative progress that enhances the prestige of the transnational issue networks it deals with. At the expense of historical complexity, this narrative works to their symbolic benefit and fits their strategies. Precisely because it fulfills strategic functions, this emancipatory narrative on human rights cannot be taken for granted. In particular, the strategy of these networks is to emphasize the struggles that oppose them to national governments or exponents of *Realpolitik*. This tends to conceal a lot of what they actually share with such "opponents" in terms of educational background, career, social position or professional skills. A deeper, structural, complicity is shared by such groups which develop by opposing each other.

The Champions of Global Civic Virtue

To gain a better understanding of these norm entrepreneurs, who today embody a progressive and global activism, and of the functional role of political science in the construction of their identity, it is important to emphasize the ambiguity of these new global actors. While they appear as moral agents, as a mouthpiece for those whose rights are abused by sovereign power, as speakers for the ruled and the dominated, they are also fully integrated into the global apparatus of power, be it in international institutions or national governments. Today, most if not all of the hegemonic institutions of the post–cold war world, from the State Department to the World Bank, abide by the new orthodoxy of human rights and democracy, and have shifted to a "grass-roots," "bottom-up" and nongovernmental paradigm of political power. NGOs and activist networks have actively taken part in the construction of this new dominant orthodoxy. Nothing illustrates better this intrinsic ambivalence than the concept of "issue networks," commonly used by political science scholars to describe these actors. Its genealogy shows how today's conception of human rights activism follows the model of the professional "policy entrepreneurs" of the 1970s. In other words, no real distinction is made between activist movements for democracy and human rights and Washington policy consultants. Far from being counter-hegemonic, as some have suggested, these networks tend to internationalize the Washington model of policy entrepreneurship and to institute it as the universal format for emancipatory struggles. What is internationalized by the same token is a market that valorizes the same managerial skills and resources, in particular the strategic expertise offered by political scientists.

The notion of "issue networks" appears to have been used for the first time in Washington policy consultant Hugh Heclo's contribution to a 1978 publication by the American Enterprise Institute for Public Policy Research, *The New American Political System* (King 1978), which was concerned with the transformation of American politics. Entitled "Issue Networks and the Executive Establishment," it is an attempt at explaining how the sheer mass of government activity was expanding over the 1970s without, however, leading to the growth of the administrative bureaucracy. The answer, Heclo, argues, lies in both the widening participation of informal and loosely organized groups in public policy and in the parallel development of specialized policy expertise outside of government, or what Heclo calls "specialized subcultures composed of highly knowledgeable policy-watchers" (Heclo 1978: 99). The rise of these new actors, highly proficient in specific policy areas and participating in the policy process without occupying formal positions in it produces a phenomenon of "government by remote control" (ibid.: 92).

The architecture of these groups of informed participants, Heclo writes, is not that of the traditional and easily identifiable "iron triangles" linking interest groups, Congress members, and executive bureaus. Rather, these new "webs of influence" comprise large numbers of participants who are usually professionals, experts, or committed individuals socializing through shared concerns and interests in the same issues. Their members also exhibit a "growing skill base." It is these emerging webs, transforming Washington politics, that Heclo decides to call "issue networks." From the very outset, the notion exhibits all the characteristics that one finds in subsequent writings that use the same concept for describing very different, international phenomena — writings that do not seem to have significantly altered or enriched the concept. Issue networks are composed of individuals who are "issue-skilled," reputed for their specialized expertise. The primary cement of an issue network is the knowledge base shared by the participants. In that sense, issue networks often overlap with "epistemic communities."[12] But these participants are also "more than mere technical experts": they have explicit normative positions; they are "policy activists." In the words of contemporary theorizing on the same topic, one would say that they are based not only on causal, but also on principled, knowledge. The emphasis on symbolic, rather than material, stakes is also salient in this first definition of issue networks. Heclo writes indeed that "any direct material interest is often secondary to intellectual or emotional commitment"(ibid.: 102). Contemporary IR theories have merely retrieved this definition without making substantial modifications.

The basic features of the concept of issue networks are all present in Heclo's seminal writing. In fact, his text is frequently cited in the current literature on activism. What is surprising, however, is the discrepancy between the collective actors that are designated today as "issue networks" and those that Heclo captured in the late 1970s. Heclo's theorizing does not concern the surge of transnational groups promoting human rights or democracy, but rather a structural transformation taking place in the microcosm of Washington politics, somewhat independently from the substantive or normative contents of the issues around which networks emerge. This transformation in the first place regards the changed composition of the policy elite due to the increased relevance of technical knowledge: traditional circles of policy insiders and other kinds of establishments were challenged by the rise of specialized expertise. Based on a well-delimited empirical ground, Heclo's account relates the importance of cognitive resources in the policy process to specific social groups: the notion of "issue networks" actually captures the growing importance of "academia, think tanks, and people with specialized credentials" (ibid.: 112).

Second, these new political actors have not replaced traditional elites, but instead constitute an additional layer of political complexity. This process has not only generated political oppositions. It has also transformed the general outlook of policy debates toward a more adversarial style, to the extent that "the overlay of networks and issue politics not only confronts but also seeps down into the formerly well-established politics of particular policies and programs" (ibid.: 105). That is, after the liberal technocratic faith of the 1950s, the rise of issue networks has subordinated the policy sciences to a confrontational logic, where technical skills and scientific knowledge serve activist purposes.

Wagner and Wittrock, in their analysis of the political use of social science knowledge, also notice that, following the unraveling of the liberal consensus, social scientists "then turned away from the state as their addressee," (1987: 21–22) looking instead for alternative agents of social change. Social movements, but also what Blumenthal has called the "conservative counterestablishment" (1986), will be these new addressees. These forces will contribute to the emergence of a real "market of ideas" that will realize the fusion between militancy and expertise. The technocratic takeover of the policy process, denounced in an earlier period by conservative voices, actually turned out to be a take-over led by policy activists determined to shape the fabric of public policy (Blumenthal 1986).

It is part of the rhetoric and the strategy of transnational issue networks to use the symbolic resource of "making the voices of the weak heard" (Foot 2000: 254). But, as has been suggested, the development of transnational issue networks is also the expansion of a dominant model of policy expertise which emerged in Washington in the 1970s. Deliberately ignored in the literature on the topic, this hegemonic function of transnational issue networks imposes the logic of a "market of ideas" upon the struggles for rights and entitlements. By the same token, it contributes to the policing of these struggles which, in order to be successful, have to mobilize dominant types of expertise and to be professionalized through the mediation of lawyers, political scientists, media specialists, or public relations experts. The traditional forms of activism have thus been transformed, and new "repertoires" of political action have emerged, more elitist and based on the militant mobilization of cognitive and interpersonal skills. The quantity of academic writings on the topic is in itself an indicator of the increased codification of these practices. From this viewpoint, the ambiguity of today's global activisms becomes more obvious, since the extension of emancipatory battles corresponds with the extension of a dominant model of collective action and the exportation of hegemonic expertise.

This last point regarding the internationalization of hegemonic kinds of knowledge and expertise in the wake of activist struggles for rights is an invitation to pay attention to the role of academics in the production and expansion of this new industry of human rights and democracy. Lawyers, obviously, but also political scientists produce an expertise that is increasingly invested in these transnational struggles through issue networks. They provide these new international actors not only with instruments, but also, as I have suggested, with legitimacy. Linking up with struggles which are highly rewarding in symbolic terms allows scholars, in turn, to fight on a more local turf by using these external resources: thus, the opposition of social constructivists with realists or neorealists, that of "transitologists" against modernization sociology or, more generically, that of political scientists against economists, are local conflicts waged by the proxy of more universal symbols.

In writing about issue or advocacy networks, epistemic communities, and the power of ideas to influence policies, political scientists therefore have been theorizing practices in which they were increasingly involved. Human rights and democracy have been the twin issues around which a major transformation of policy research and advocacy took place in the 1980s: increasingly placing emphasis on values and ideals as compared to technical problem-solving, this transformation has permitted the valorization of political commitment *cum* intellectual skills beyond the campus perimeter. An activist ethos acquired in the movements of the 1960s and 1970s became progressively functional to a new articulation between foreign policy goals and their transnational implementation. At the same time, the administrative and entrepreneurial skills which came to be associated with the conduct of academic research (e.g. Jacoby 1987) were qualities easily reusable in the wider context of value-oriented, principled expertise. The role of social and political scientists in the constitution of the techno-scientific skill base of issue networks is the concrete historical and social background against which the development of a scientific discourse on transnational activism and the idealist theories of policy change associated with it must be matched. From this perspective, it becomes possible to read the concepts and the logic informing theories about the political consequences of ideas as abstract redescriptions of an emerging academic activism. By substituting the logic of ideas with the logic of social practices, however, these theories also misrepresent their real object. An anonymous "power of ideas" is thus substituted for the socially determined power of professional idea brokers and committed academics. The methodological choice of taking ideas as "independent variables" further contributes to this misrepresentation by making it difficult to assign them to specific, socially located actors.

Notions such as "issue networks" or methodological assumptions such as "ideas matter" point to a migration of concepts from the early ideology of professional policy advocacy into contemporary political science. The idealist epistemology that characterizes "social constructivism" is also a scientific translation of the idealism that accompanied the emergence of a market for policy advocacy. The "power of ideas" was a crucial marketing argument for policy professionals busy valorizing their skills. It was also a political slogan closely associated with the neoconservative resurgence and its offensive in the field of intellectual opinion-making and policy advice. *Ideas Have Consequences* was the title of a classic book of American conservatism by Richard Weaver (1948) long before being adopted as a methodological assumption by "social constructivists." If the neoconservative movement has contributed so significantly to the emergence of a "market" and a "battleground of ideas" in the 1970s, it is because it represented a strong reaction to liberal pragmatism and its technocratic implications. It represented a return to the tradition of philosophical idealism, with its emphasis on the historical existence of ideas and moral values (J.A. Smith 1991: 22–23). The idea that ideas matter was the necessary correlate of this political activism that sought political influence from outside governmental institutions and turned scientific or pseudo-scientific influence into political currency.

As I have pointed out, the adoption of these concepts by IR theorists and political scientists has not entailed any major transformation of their meaning or properties. In that sense, the uncritical acceptance of these terms in scientific discourse is indeed the sign of a "scientific ideology." What has changed, however, is their universe of application. Initially referring to the growth of policy research brokerage and professionalized advocacy networks in Washington, the concept has become a model for the international scene and for a new policy expertise embodied by NGOs and transnational activist networks. It indicates the globalization of a hegemonic policy model and its adoption by those who often seem to oppose hegemonic policy agendas. In that sense, the dominant use of "issue networks" and related concepts only confirms the analysis presented in the previous chapter. The next one shows how these moral actors have come to play a central role in the definition of a normative form of "governance" centered around democracy and neoliberal economics.

6 Financing the Construction of "Market Democracies":

The World Bank and the Global Supervision of "Good Governance"

A History Made of Reversals

The scientific and activist discourse on the power of ideas and of transnational issue networks has found a significant outlet in the political science literature on the World Bank. Whether it concerns the relations between the Bank and NGOs (Hodson 1997; Fox and Brown 1998), the role of development "ideas" or environmental groups in changing its policies (Finnemore 1997), or the place of minorities or women in its projects (Hodge and Magenheim 1994), much of the focus has been on the emergence of emancipatory values and "universals" (human rights, environmental protection) in the practice of the Bank. These reformist prescriptions have often percolated into the language of the institution itself. In a sense, nothing could illustrate better the power of "principled ideas" than their capacity to become "institutionalized" in an organization that, at least initially, was concerned with the most material interests of all: money and interest rates.

By the same token, however, this literature has contributed to making the Bank a virtuous institution that increasingly shared with its former critics the same normative language of rights, empowerment, and participation. This perfectly fitted the strategy of the Bank, eager as it was to demonstrate its concern with ideas and principles. The 1999 World Bank Report, for instance, presented the institution as a "Bank of knowledge," while collaboration with NGOs has been systematically emphasized since late 1980s.[1] Today, the institution once confined to the technical task of providing infrastructures and international safety nets in the Bretton Woods system has placed its financial instruments at the service of political virtue, from the adoption of "participatory methodologies" to the promotion of "good governance," the fight against corruption, or the protection of indigenous minorities. By promoting "participatory development," for instance, the World Bank promoted "the process by which people, especially disadvantaged people, influence decisions that affect them. The disadvantaged are not only the absolute poor, but also those who are handicapped by a lack of wealth or education or because of their ethnicity or gender" (World Bank 1992: 27).

How did a bank evolve into a producer of transnational norms, concerned with democratic rights and emancipation? This transformation may not be so surprising if we accept that rights and money are two similar means of communication and administration to the extent that they are both binding instruments (Luhmann 1981). However, this evolution was far from being obvious. Not only did the Bank's mandate prohibit any intervention in political affairs, but to the extent that it had its own view of politics, the World Bank initially had an almost explicit preference for authoritarian states, deemed to be more efficient in the implementation of structural adjustment plans because less sensitive to social demands. In Chile, Pinochet's neoliberal economists known as the "Chicago Boys" were probably the best example of what the World Bank considered to be sound economic and political management. By the 1990s, however, the Bank became a defender of human rights and democracy, promoting the participation of subordinate groups to policymaking. It has made the alleviation of poverty an issue that can be solved only by implementing progressive economic *and political* reform; it works hand in hand with NGOs and, increasingly, finances them.

After being on the cutting edge of the neoliberal policies of structural economic reform in the 1980s, the Bank has rediscovered the virtues of social participation and collective institutions. The role of the state and in particular its capacity to intervene in the economy were positively reassessed. A 1992 report on *Governance and Development* thus argued that "even in societies that are highly market-oriented, only governments can provide two sorts of public goods: rules to make markets work efficiently and corrective interventions where there are market failures" (World Bank 1992: 6). Throughout the decade, this lesser emphasis on market mechanisms and the focus on norms, institutions and others immaterial public goods led toward an increasingly vocal critique of the market ideology of the 1980s. In 1998, Joseph Stiglitz, who then was still chief economist, even declared the "end of the Washington consensus" and the need to go "beyond . . . the neoliberal model" (Stiglitz 1998).

This chapter explores this reversal and resituates it in a longer-term ge-

nealogy of development doctrines. In fact, the entire history of the World
Bank has been made of such reversals. The World Bank was for a long time
an institution primarily concerned with economic development in the traditional sense. Developing countries were believed to need pump-priming
and massive investments, mainly in the form of public infrastructures, in
order to achieve growth and economic takeoff. The operations of the Bank
were matching the dominant paradigms of development and modernization
theory, and focused on industrialization, import-substitution, and infrastructures. Ranging from the provision of productive assets to the building of
country-wide infrastructures, its projects were designed and implemented by
a army of modernizing bureaucrats: technical engineers, agronomists, planners, and Keynesian development economists who staffed the various Bank
departments. This "bricks-and-mortar" approach to development was em-
blematically illustrated by such grandiose projects as Indian dams and power
plants, which became the source of institutional pride as much as of external
criticism. Under the two presidencies of Robert McNamara, the institution
that started to lend money cautiously in 1946 multiplied its volume of operation several times, notably through concessional grants, engaged in economic development research, disseminated its opinions and advice, thus
completing its transformation into a full-fledged aid agency. Interviewed by
Michael Schechter, McNamara himself declared, "I had always regarded
the World Bank as something more than a Bank, a Development Agency"
(Schechter 1988: 363).

Since then, the Bank has undergone major structural and ideological
transformations. The most salient and most discussed is certainly the adoption in the 1980s of an increasingly neoliberal agenda and its active promotion through policy-based lending articulated around structural adjustment programs. The break with McNamara's idea of the Bank as a
development agency was made very explicit. In a 1995 news conference,
Mark Malloch Brown, then director for external affairs at the Bank, made
that clear: "We're a bank. We're not an aid agency" (Kapur, Lewis, and Webb
1997: 374). The rise of the Washington consensus (Williamson 1993) has
indeed changed the priorities and orientations of the Bank. Its aggressive
pro-market stance, its push for economic liberalization, and the elimination
of state monopolies signaled a major change on these issues, since the Bank
was basically undoing what it had been doing for decades.

This paradigm shift can be reduced neither to the mere exportation of
Reaganomics, nor to a pragmatic revision of the Bank's strategy on the basis
of external events such as the outbreak of the debt crisis in 1982. In 1981,

Carter appointed a new president who had Republican sympathies and the approval of the Reagan team, Alden Winship (Tom) Clausen. Clausen certainly contributed to bringing the Bank closer to the Reagan administration. But this new course was also the result of internal transformations, of new power relations within the Bank between its various departments and ideological components, and of the changing skill base of its staff. The new agenda reflected the recruitment of a new generation of economists endorsing neoclassical orthodoxy in their discipline and sharing a similar educational background. To the technical, managerial, and planning capacities of the Bank officer of the 1960s and 1970s, the 1980s opposed private sector commitment and concerns for financial and political cost-efficiency. Previously marginalized, the "closet conservatives" of the McNamara era finally had their revenge when they reached positions from which they could call the tune. As to the dramatic effects of this shift in the developing world, they have been extensively documented and are well-known: in 1988, the publication of the United Nations report *Adjustment with a Human Face* exposed the perverse effects of structural adjustment on social welfare and poverty and initiated a debate still going on today.

The narrowly economicist and monetarist Washington consensus of the 1980s has been followed by a rediscovery of political institutions as *arenas* where demands are formulated and rights are claimed. According to the official narrative, there was first a rededication to poverty alleviation issues after 1986, under the aegis of Barber Conable, following its toning down during the Clausen years (Kapur, Lewis, and Webb 1997: 357–60). Then, environmental and gender issues became explicit concerns of the Bank, culminating in the establishment of the Environment Department in 1987. Moving into the 1990s, the World Bank sought to rationalize these developments into a single coherent and marketable agenda, encapsulated in the notion of "good governance." Always a prescriptive institution, the Bank became a normative agency, involved in the promotion of political participation, transparency, accountability or the rule of law. The Bank even grounded the notion of governance in human rights tenets, at least in background papers if not publicly. This bold step into the realm of transnational norms and emancipatory movements meant that the Bank would deal not only with macroeconomic fundamentals, but also with the whole political and legal order. The promotion of economic liberalization was successfully converted into a struggle for democratization.

For many detractors, this emancipatory turn is another cosmetic operation meant to respond to mounting criticisms and to increased scrutiny of its activities by various organizations and especially environmental pressure groups (George and Sabelli 1994). But for others, and notably for many Western NGOs or respectable "issue networks" seeking to reform the Bank, this turn bears witness to their positive influence on this institution. Cosmetic or not, therefore, this new development discourse cannot be insignificant: it involves and even generates "interest groups" within and outside the Bank, and becomes the staging point of local struggles for nongovernmental activists or scholarly entrepreneurs who see in these changes an opportunity to redefine their stakes in the formulation of development policies.

I argue here that the fight for democratic political systems was tightly connected to the imposition of neoliberal economic orthodoxy. The World Bank has been one of the major operators of this new universal model of governance. To a large extent, this model is also the construct of new producers and exporters of development policies. After the bankers and the economists of earlier periods, the dominant development coalition now includes NGOs, activist networks, and political scientists. Previously subordinated, these actors actively used their symbolic or scientific capital to enter a dominant coalition. We have examined how a whole line of critical political science used the class-based analysis of the state associated with dependency theory to produce a political economy of economic reform that could be reinvested in the marketplace for global expertise. By strengthening the most reformist components within the Bank and by contributing to the legitimacy of institutional economics, these "Washington political economists" (Dezalay and Garth 1998a: 5) quickly imposed their doctrine as a new orthodoxy. Solicited to help "getting the politics right" before "getting the prices right," social scientists enjoyed a long sought professional revenge on their colleagues from economics, who switched freely from their academic offices to international bureaucracies, all expenses paid, where they had managed to consolidate their hold over the production of developmental prescriptions. The notion of "governance" was loose enough to accommodate diverging normative interpretations of "development."

The success of the learned advocates of democracy overlapped with the success of NGOs in becoming official partners of the Bank (World Bank 1996; 1997) and in bringing up the themes of participation and empowerment, of human rights and environmental protection. The production of "social constructivist" theories of transnational issue networks gave even more legitimacy to these spokespersons for all the dominated groups and the good causes. At about the same time, traditional development NGOs had become increasingly professionalized and had shifted their concern with long-term development toward a focus on short-term impact, visibility, and public relations campaigns. Their new strategies also relied more on policy knowledge, learned arguments, and research brokerage (Hours 1998: 88–91). These mutually reinforcing trends contributed to "polic[ing] the boundaries of professionalism" in development institutions (Cooper and Packard 1997: 5). On the one hand, more encompassing legal, political and participatory approaches to development increased the value of noneconomic knowledge within the World Bank. A 1991 World Bank discussion paper, for instance, recommended giving more importance to social scientific approaches in the design and assessment of development projects (Cernea 1991). On the other hand, this new focus on norms went hand in hand with a more activist approach to development, based on participation by disadvantaged groups and the defense of basic rights. Yet, as we shall see, this "emancipatory turn" was entirely subordinated to the logic of economic adjustment and neoliberal state reform.

Bankers, Bureaucrats, and Economists at the Bank

Located at the crossroads of academia (it borrows, processes, and applies economic theories), the U.S. administration (it cannot separate its operations from the foreign policy of its main backer) and financial banking (it invests money raised on the financial markets), the World Bank is a complex institution that reflects the dynamics of these different seats of power. To a large extent, its identity is shaped by the interplay between these different institutional environments. Their respective influence, the constraints they place on the Bank, and their representation within it are contributing factors in determining its policies.

The World Bank as we know it today developed its distinctive features only in the 1960s and 1970s. Earlier, its role had been a bone of contention among its founders. On the one hand, John Maynard Keynes, Dexter White, and the New Deal administrators surrounding them thought it would allow for the stabilization of international trade and, hence, for the intervention of the welfare state in the national economy required for reorienting massive wartime production and ensuring a smooth transition to a peacetime economy. On the other hand, financial bankers were concerned that such a state bureaucracy, entitled to make sovereign loans, might weaken the position of Wall Street on the international financial scene, recently boosted by the flight of European capital. The result was a fragile compromise: while the

Bank's member states would control the flows of capital, the institution would be handled and managed by representatives of the banking world (this rule has known only two exceptions: McNamara and Conable.) This compromise was weak because the rationale behind the establishment of a postwar free-trade system underpinned by the Bretton Woods safety nets reflected primarily a concern with security and stability. Wilsonian liberal internationalism and U.S. national interests converged in the notion of "economic security" (Pollard 1985). The cold war quickly determined a political use of trade and lending that privileged foreign policy over concerns with the financial soundness and bankability of projects. The initial compromise between the administrators and the bankers was thus disrupted in favor of the former, and located the World Bank in the field of state institutions. As Dezalay and Garth observe, "such a political context does not lend itself to a strategy of autonomization" (1998a: 15) and tended to confine the Bank to a subordinate position in Washington.

Yet, the Bank started to increase its autonomy in the 1950s. Although it remained a bureaucratic institution under state supervision, the World Bank had to build up its autonomy on the financial markets. In its attempts to augment its funds by selling bonds, the Bank had "to win financial trust, beginning with that of U.S. investors, and to do so despite its odd character as an international, public sector institution" (Kapur, Lewis, and Webb 1997: 77). The professional background of its presidents allowed them to maintain relations with Wall Street that proved instrumental to the purpose. With a capacity to finance itself independently, continued growth, substantial profits, and lessened budget constraints, the Bank diversified its activities, recruited personnel, and developed its own institutional identity. Until then, the Bank had been run by well-connected former bankers and government officials, "an exclusive, merit-ridden, prudent, quite civil, and cerebral club" in which engineers and economists occupied the lowest ranks and were subordinated to gentlemen representing Wall Street or the foreign policy establishment (ibid.: 1174).

When George Woods hired him to recruit economists, Irving Friedman was surprised to find that very few members of the staff "were willing to be regarded as economists [since] an economist in the Bank was the death of a career." The expansion of the Bank in the following decade contributed to modify its professional standards and to shape a distinctive *esprit de corps*, reflecting the ascent of economists within the institution. The increase of available funds allowed Eugene Black to create the Economic Development Institute in 1956 with the support of the Ford and Rockefeller Foundations.

The EDI provided a first platform from which economic research could be done at the Bank, although it did not yet have the "the nexus with academic and research development-studies departments and institutes that would become so common in the 1970s and 1980s" (Kapur, Lewis, and Webb 1997: 1172).

The rise of the economists started under the presidency of George Woods, at which time the Bank felt the need to raise its "hemline of bankability" in order to invest its surpluses. What has been labeled the "decade of economics" at the Bank started indeed when the institution had to widen its range of activities and consider new forms of lending (for education, for instance), while reassuring a financially conservative constituency of bond-subscribers such as Chase National Bank or First Boston Corporation, in which old friends had a say.[2] These reassurances had to be couched in the language of sound economic analysis, and economists were hired to prepare the Bank's financial expansion by calculating the "economic rates of return" of the new projects envisaged — an exercise that contrasted with previous estimates of country "resource needs," a term that did not easily convince bankers. Macroeconomics thus became an important feature of the professional approach to development, and it was given prominence in the newly reconstituted central Economic Department whose activities were independent of the regional bureaus.

While recruiting numerous economists, George Woods also launched the Young Professionals Program in 1966, which brought to Washington an international crop of graduates, most often trained in economics (Schechter 1988: 355; Kapur, Lewis, and Webb 1997: 1176). McNamara, who sought relentlessly to expand the size and the activities of the Bank, continued this practice; he managed to boost the professional staff from 757 in 1968 to 2,552 in 1981 (ibid.: 1181). The dominance of economists became more visible with the development of research functions within the Bank. During these two decades of expansion, the discipline of economics also acted as a powerful factor of integration, homogenizing an international workforce around a common professional standard. Economists were finally at home within the Bank.[3]

The rise of economists also reflected the changing role of academic knowledge in policymaking. The triumph of the policy advisory experts in the Kennedy administration signaled the interweaving between "epistemic communities" and the federal administration. Kennedy's "action intellectuals," drawn from the Ivy League, enjoyed a discrete presence at all levels of the administration and a certain public visibility. Economists certainly benefited most from the adoption of Keynesian policies by the reformist administrations of the 1960s. Indeed, the hegemonic diffusion of Keynesian ideas in the policy process "determined the main kinds of expertise (training in macroeconomics) and the sort of analysis (aggregate economic analysis) that would be given most weight in public policy debates" (J. A. Smith 1991, 109).[4]

Keynesianism also ensured the convergence between national and international reform programs. To the extent that it defined a development strategy that involved state intervention and planning, it perfectly fitted the spontaneous ideology of state economists in the U.S. administration and development economists in the World Bank. The strength of Keynesian ideas also reflected their dominant position in the academic institutions producing most of the policy elite, in particular Harvard (Hall 1989). Development economics directly grew on the fertile soil of Keynesianism, of which they were an "ideational ramification," since Keynesianism drew "a sharp distinction" between virtuous economies and economies where resources were underemployed (Hirschman 1989: 358). At the World Bank, the McNamara years (1968–1981) certainly offer the most spectacular illustration of the growth of development economics. In this field, the amount of research done at the Bank and its outreach capacity soon made the institution an "arbiter of development norms and development meanings" (Finnemore 1997: 219).

The Debt Crisis and the Washington Consensus

Which factors led from the "Keynesian" consensus of the 1960s and 1970s to the so-called "Washington consensus" of the 1980s? The swift decline of development economics and the adoption of a neoliberal agenda internationalizing the monetarist and deregulatory policies implemented in the United States and the United Kingdom determined a major transformation in the discourse and practice of development that can be considered as a real "counterrevolution" (Toye 1987). It took place in the economic context created by the oil shocks and the impact of the debt crisis on lending institutions (Bromley 1995). In the United States, the repercussions of these events in the international economy combined with domestic stagflation to undermine the Keynesian paradigm of economic growth and development. Neoclassical economists, who until then had occupied subordinate positions in the political and academic hierarchies, took the opportunity to join a political offensive against Keynesianism and assert their methodologies as a new professional norm (Ascher 1996). A neoliberal conception of economic policy based on the withdrawal of the state from the management of social services and infrastructures and a greater reliance on market forces was imposed as a dominant policy standard. This new consensus was then internationalized through the channel of international financial institutions such as the World Bank and the IMF. Because they had capacity to enforce globally these new political and economic standards, control over the political line and the policy expertise produced and exported by these institutions was a major area of bitter conflicts between advocates of neoliberal policies and other actors of development policies.

The term "Washington consensus" evokes the idea of a "discourse coalition." That is, a system of interactions and alliances among scholars and policymakers which, when it is successful, can lead to a reconfiguration of policy issues, representations of society, and social scientific discourse (Wagner and Wittrock 1987: 44). The Washington consensus was the result of the convergence between the interests and the strategies of a new generation of economists, usually associated with the Chicago school; a Republican and neoconservative administration that led an economic and ideological attack on development aid, and major commercial banks which had started to operate on the development 'market' in the previous decade.

Throughout the 1970s, McNamara's Bank had remained a relatively insulated institution, eager of its autonomy. The former president of the Ford Motor Company and Secretary of Defense brought a managerial style to the Bank and understood the political and strategic implications of modernization. He was thus able to transform the Bank into a global operator and presided over a spectacular expansion of its activities. From 1968 to 1981, the lending volume rose from $1 to $13 billion, staff increased fourfold, and the administrative budget was multiplied by a factor of 3.5. In the same period, it is estimated that McNamara and his treasurer Eugene Rotberg were able to raise $100 billion on financial markets for expanding the activities of the Bank. This expansion enabled the Bank to lessen its dependency on Wall Street, as McNamara and Rotberg managed to penetrate European and Japanese financial markets as well.

With the arrival of a neoconservative team at the White House, however, the World Bank found itself at odds with its supervising administration at a critical moment. The victory of Reagan, the departure of McNamara in 1981, and the outbreak of the debt crisis in 1982 created a situation which was propitious to an internal reorganization and a redefinition of its mission.

The awareness of the critical level of Third World indebtedness, fuelled by the recycling of petrodollars through commercial lending during the 1970s, led the new administration to call into question the expansionist strategy of the Bank. The institution at 1818 H Street was increasingly viewed as a spending-prone bureaucracy substituting itself for the market. These grievances were further relayed by Wall Street circles, which had lost some of their influence on the Bank since it had managed to issue its bonds on the European and Japanese financial markets. As the 1980s began, the discrepancy between the Bank and the U.S. administration was such that the new Under-Secretary of Treasury, Beryl Sprinkel, commissioned a report in order to determine whether or not the World Bank exhibited "socialistic" tendencies (Kapur, Lewis, and Webb: 1997, 338).

Outside the administration, a fringe of the right traditionally opposed to foreign aid used very similar arguments against the World Bank. As late as 1987 — after six years of neoliberal cultural revolution within the Bank — James Bovard, an analyst of the Cato Institute who regularly criticized foreign aid in the *New York Times* and the *Wall Street Journal*, asserted that the World Bank was "run like a Soviet factory, concerned only with meeting its quantitative production goals" (Bovard: 1987). And in spite of Reagan's approval of his nomination as president of the Bank and his zeal in chanting the virtues of liberalization, Alden Clausen's relations with the administration would prove extremely difficult during his whole mandate.

With the end of a long political cycle of reformist administrations that provided a basis of support for the Bank's policies, the coalition sustaining its developmental project was shattered. So was its ideology of managerial modernization. The weakened position of the institution in the early 1980s made possible a drastic normalization under the aegis of Clausen. The alignment of the Bank's mission with the priorities of the government was sealed with the design of "structural adjustment programs" which became the hallmark of its activities throughout the 1980s. This new form of lending signaled a move away from project loans toward financial support for macroeconomic policy programs. It also signaled a departure from the previous focus on poverty reduction. These supply-side policy prescriptions usually included such components as balance-deficit reduction, contraction of public spending, lifting of trade barriers, privatization of state-owned companies, and export-oriented policies.

The adoption and the subsequent rise of structural adjustment lending, however, did not pay mere lip service to the "marketplace magic" rhetoric of the Reagan administration. Nor were they the result of academic discussions about what works better in development aid. The sustained commitment of the World Bank on these matters points to the formation of an alliance of different actors who held stakes in these policies and who largely contributed to establishing this new policy discourse on the ruins of the previous creeds. Besides the U.S. administration, this alliance involved two other groups intertwined with the World Bank: U.S. commercial banks, and neoliberal economists.

In spite of its imprint on the management style of the World Bank, the influence of the financial world on the Bank had declined in the 1960s and the 1970s, as Woods and McNamara were expanding the market on which the Bank borrowed funds from North America to Europe and Asia. By the same token, they also extended the community of bond-owners far beyond Wall Street, thus diminishing the influence of the financial establishment on the Bank. After the first oil shock, however, commercial banks came to play an increasingly important role in development lending. With the oil surpluses piling up in huge deposits in North American commercial banks, they started looking at developing countries as potential clients in position to absorb sums that would be difficult to invest traditionally in the private sector. The prospects were all the more bright, given that the Third World was indeed in need of investment and that, as Citibank president Walter Wriston famously declared, a state can never go bankrupt. It was relatively easy to convince the new clients since the availability of petrodollars deposited in North America or in European offshore banks (the so-called "Euromarket") resulted in extremely attractive interest rates. In 1976 and 1977, for instance, the Euroloans even offered lower interest rates than the IBRD (World Bank) loans. Moreover, while World Bank loans were systematically attached to specific projects or, exceptionally, programs, commercial loans offered far less constraints since they were not attached to conditionalities of any sort: all that mattered to the creditors was not even the repayment of the principal, but the capacity to service the interests in the long term. For developing countries, the incentives to borrow were not only financial but also political. Commercial loans presented an opportunity to reassert sovereignty over the options of national development and escape the discipline of the international aid regime (Wood 1986).

The combination of these factors led to a lending frenzy and helped to turn development lending into a market for bankers. The World Bank's outspoken optimism about the future and its downplaying of the rising debt problem were not really conducive to caution (in spring 1982, a couple of months before the country defaulted, a World Bank report on Mexico, though noting the critical size of its debt, asserted that the country's prospects called for increased lending). Citibank, Chase Manhattan, and Manufacturers Hanover Trust were the most audacious banking institutions to venture into massive loans to third world countries, and some of them turned to the World Bank's know-how to develop their own portfolios, using country-risk analysis techniques originally developed by Bank analysts. In 1974, for instance, Citibank hired Irving Friedman from the World Bank with a view to developing this new field of activities. The boom of this development market was also self-sustaining, insofar as debt servicing called for renewed borrowing. As long as the system kept going, so did lending volumes; and large banks were syndicating smaller ones on this profitable business, with the encouragement of the World Bank. In this context, one can better understand what stood behind the criticisms of the World Bank that were voiced by the financial community and the Reagan administration in the early 1980s: this multilateral institution was not so much a red-tape bureaucracy as an intergovernmental competitor on a market that American commercial banks could presumably entirely take care of, for their own profit.

The lending machinery collapsed in August 1982, when Mexico declared that it would default on its debt servicing. This event had massive consequences for the banking sector. Citibank suffered from an exposure on the Latin American continent amounting to twice its net corporate assets, and Mexico alone owed it $3.3 billion (two-thirds of these assets) (Caufield 1996, 132). Other banks were in similar situations, and the prospect of bankruptcy became very real when Argentina and Brazil threatened similar defaults shortly after Mexico. With American majors on the verge of a severe crisis, the government stepped in and quickly relaxed several banking laws and regulations in order to prevent the consequences of earnings revision, while encouraging commercial banks to keep lending in order not to write off their outstanding loans.

On the other hand, the enforcement of the banks' contracts came to be ensured by the IMF and the World Bank. They offered loans to the heavily indebted countries, tied to renewed commercial lending that was used to serve the interest of the debt. For the World Bank, not only were its own loans and credibility jeopardized, but it was also placed under external and systemic pressures to increase its loans for the sake of maintaining the debt-servicing capacity of its clients. Indeed, both the appeals of the U.S. government "to relieve the pressure on the IMF and American commercial banks" (Mosley, Harrigan, and Toye 1991: 302–303) and the internal need to lend rather than withhold money in order to cover borrowing operations (ibid.,

46) account for the strategy adopted by the Bank — whose creed, after all, had always been lending.

If these pressures found a certain resonance within the Bank, it is also because its president, Clausen, was particularly sensitive to the issue. Before his appointment in 1981, he had spent thirty years at the San-Francisco based Bank of America, the largest commercial bank in the country, of which he became CEO in 1970. Under his leadership, Bank of America developed a substantial portfolio of foreign loans during the 1970s (Kraske 1996: 214). He was thus perfectly attuned to the preoccupations of his fellow bankers, and ready to help. His strong Republican credentials, on the other hand, made him receptive to the concerns of a government siding with the banking sector. The debt crisis thus led to a redefinition of the role of the World Bank, and accounts for the most salient features of the structural adjustment programs. The adoption of this type of lending, traditionally made by the IMF, stresses the move from development aid to the prevention of financial crises. Clausen excluded poverty alleviation from the Bank's agenda and prioritized new forms of lending meant to allow developing countries to keep up payments to their private creditors.

The first rationale for structural adjustment was to devise a format of operations that could funnel much more funds than traditional project lending.[5] As a Bank officer interviewed by Catherine Caufield put it, "Project loans are million-dollar pipelines. That's not enough anymore. We need billion-dollar pipelines now" (Caufield 1996: 140). "Program" lending would offer this opportunity and allow the Bank to convert the short- and medium-term private debt into long-term debt centralized by the World Bank. Concretely, it simply meant that the Bank was paying debt interest to commercial banks and increasing its credits. While preventing a crisis that would probably have led to several bankruptcies among American majors (Woods 1986: 286–87), it was trying to secure conditions of continuous debt servicing in heavily indebted countries — thus acting no longer as a development agency but as a trustee of financial investors. Far from being a mere technical innovation designed to cope with a rapidly changing international context (Hürni 1980: 119–20), the core components of structural adjustment programs reflected the endorsement by the World Bank and the IMF of the concerns of commercial banks. The prescriptions aiming at reducing public spending and downsizing the public sector were thus meant to liberate surpluses that would pay debt interest, while large-scale privatization programs allowed many banks to swap debt for equities over these tradable assets.

From Development Economics to Neoclassical Economics

The rapprochement between the World Bank, commercial bankers, and the Reagan administration fostered the emergence of a strong coalition of interests behind the structural adjustment agenda. The policies it included, however, needed to be legitimated within the framework of a development project. Structural adjustment could not be justified on the grounds that it was good for Citibank. On the other hand, the central tenets of structural adjustment were at odds with the major theories in development economics which, from the works of Paul Rosenstein-Rodan to those of Hollis Chenery, had played a role in the formation of the Bank's economic thinking and reliance on administered modernization (Adler 1972). As it was embodied and practiced at the World Bank, economics could not provide this legitimation. The context of the debt crisis thus directly impinged upon the status of existing economic knowledge within the Bank and opened a struggle between different and competing definitions of policy-relevant economics.

These changes did not lessen the role of economics in shaping development discourse. However, they signaled a change in the composition of the scientific clienteles of the World Bank and the rise of neoclassical economics as the new authoritative knowledge about development. Eager to regain the confidence of the Reagan administration and to bring the Bank in line with its new priorities, Clausen chose Anne Krueger as Vice-President, Head of the Economics Research Staff — which, interestingly, replaced the Development Policy Staff — to replace Hollis Chenery. An academic exponent of neoclassical economics and rent-seeking theory close to the neoconservatives, Anne Krueger undertook a swift homogenization of her team around the tenets of Chicago economics. Out of the thirty-seven executive officers in her department, only eight were retained in their former positions. These high-level changes also reflected the transformation of economics as an academic discipline and in particular the generalization of the methodological standards associated with the Chicago School. A large-scale recruiter of economists and a massive consumer of academic research, the World Bank was exposed to these changes (de Vries 1996: 240; Stern and Ferreira 1997: 547). In turn, imposing their line in international financial institutions was a major stake in the struggle between neoliberal economists and their opponents. The World Bank and the IMF could indeed be used as conduits for internationalizing and enforcing the new economic doctrines and their policy prescriptions. In fact, the international diffusion of economic doctrines cannot be dissociated from the hegemonic political projects in which they are included, and development aid has always been a large part of such projects (Hirschman 1989: 348, 352, 358).

In order to understand the success of the new economic orthodoxy, it is important to pay attention to its social construction. In the social sciences as in religious matters, an "orthodoxy" always overlaps with an attempt at defining the battle lines that are drawn between true and false knowledge. Labels such as "orthodoxy" or "heterodoxy" are thus resources used in social struggles for recognition and distinctiveness (Delaunay 1996, 143). The main problem when analyzing the social construction of an "orthodoxy" in economics, therefore, is not to explain in which ways it represents a superior kind of knowledge with respect to competing paradigms, but instead to explain how this perception is successfully imposed and translated into institutional benefits, among which is the power to set professional standards and methodological norms in a given discipline. This entirely depends on "the capacity of a social group to secure control over the mode of theoretical production and over the social reproduction of its exponents as a distinctive category (disciples)" (Gerbier 1996: 198).

As far as the control over theory was concerned, the rise of Chicago economics as the dominant force within the discipline was directly related to a very intense investment in the mathematization of economics. Confined for a long time to marginal academic positions and almost excluded from politics, neoclassical economists sought to distinguish themselves from the dominant Keynesians by turning to "pure economics" and "pure theory," while their predecessors were meddling with politics, administration and planning. In contrast, the massive use of mathematical formalization was seen as a guarantee that they were employing the standards of the scientific method, notwithstanding the nature of the problem treated. Pure economics could be applied universally. Very revealing in this respect is a remark by Gary Becker — who got his PhD at Chicago in 1955 before teaching in that university — about the influence of Milton Friedman on his own work.: "he revitalized my interest in economics and made me see that you can attack social problems with economics. *I did not have to move out of economics to deal with relevant problems*" (Becker 1990: 29 — emphasis mine). This methodological distinctiveness also corresponded to social distinctions. Initially, the mathematization of economics at Chicago overlapped with a strategy compensating for the lack of "social capital" of economists who often came from a poor or immigrant background and occupied subordinate social and academic positions compared to the gentlemen-economists from Harvard and elsewhere (Dezalay and Garth 1998a: 4–8). To a large extent, therefore, the opposition between neoclassical and Keynesian economics overlapped with a competition between dominated and dominant elites.

Obviously, development economics was directly affected by these changes, both as a theory and as a field of activities the exponents of which had frequently been involved in various international agencies in their capacity as experts. As a theory, development economics suffered from its direct Keynesian descent. As Albert Hirschman has noted: "Keynesian doctrine drew a sharp distinction between the economic mechanisms ruling in a fully employed economy and those applying in an economy where manpower, capital, and other resources are underemployed. This intellectual posture made it respectable to construct yet another special economics, this one applying to 'underdeveloped areas' " (Hirschman 1989, 358–59).

Given this epistemic exceptionalism with respect to mainstream or high economic theory, development economics became a privileged candidate for neoclassical methodological normalization. It was soon marginalized (Treillet 1996: 157). Before turning into an ideological confrontation between promoters of free markets and monetarist policies on the one hand, and advocates of state-led industrialization or trickle down investment strategies on the other, neoclassical economics thus asserted its "orthodox" character over development economics principally by setting the methodological standards for the whole discipline and becoming the "only professionally legitimate approach for development economists" (Ascher 1996: 314). The result was either a neoclassical colonization of development theory or its complete removal from the academic and policy research scenes. Paul Krugman thus observes that "high development theorists were having a hard time expressing their ideas in the kind of tightly specified models that were becoming the unique language of discourse of economic analysis" (1994: 40).

Economic historian William Ascher has shown that, in the case of the World Bank research community, a "diluted" form of neoclassical economics had already been introduced in the 1970s through the adoption of increasingly quantitative and marginalist methodologies, especially in project evaluation, that were changing the treatment of traditional, structuralist issues. This trend in the Bank's economic work was also certainly fostered by the increasing need for mathematical precision and McNamara's legendary fascination with exact numbers.[6] In any case, before the major upheavals of the 1980s, which took on strong ideological overtones, the neoclassical penetration in this development institution was well on its way, "masquerading as methodological improvement" (Ascher 1996: 324). Moreover, the hegemonic institutionalization of Chicago economics in academia matched more or less the period of recruitment expansion of the Bank which brought in young graduates trained in the new orthodoxy, thus facilitating the whole process of homogenization.

In his entertaining ethnological account of the economists' profession written in the early 1970s, Axel Leijonhufvud grasped the main internal demarcations within the discipline, as well as the hierarchy of specializations that reflected the rise of neoclassical economics. He also seems to have grasped the coming disgrace of development economics:

> The priestly caste (the Math-Econ), for example, is a higher "field" than either Micro or Macro, while the Develops just as definitely rank lower. . . . The low rank of the Develops is due to the fact that this caste, in recent times, has not strictly enforced the taboos against association with the Polscis, Sociogs and other tribes. (Leijonhufvud 1973)

These divisions were imported to the World Bank in the 1980s and enforced by Anne Krueger. The personnel department, for instance, complained about the implementation of a surveillance system classifying the Bank's economists according to their different schools of economic thought, and favoring the "loyalists" (Kapur, Lewis, and Webb: 1997, 1194). The methodological supremacy of neoclassical economics, already rampant in the Bank, was thus matched by its institutionalization. A highly targeted recruitment policy and a greater reliance on fixed-term contracts for economic research allowed the enforcement of the new intellectual discipline. The newcomers tended to consider development economists as not only "deficient in appropriate technical economics skills," but also "wedded to the 'statist' ways of the past" (ibid.: 1193). With the traditional theory and practice of development thoroughly delegitimated and defeated, nothing could prevent the World Bank from adhering to the neoliberal agenda of the early 1980s, emphasizing monetarist macroeconomic policies and microeconomic price mechanisms as the universal panacea for economic problems, including underdevelopment. Increasingly, policy conditions were attached to structural adjustment loans, often including, for example, the compression of spending on social services, the privatization of public assets, or the reduction of the size of the public sectors. In advocating lending for sustaining macroeconomic policy changes, World Bank economists also endorsed the policy preferences of the financial community and the government under the scientific form of economic theory.

The "wisdom of the day" therefore lay "among the economically influential bits of Washington, meaning the US government and the international financial institutions" (Williamson 1993: 1329). The Washington consensus was thus the result of the converging financial, political and professional interests of different stakeholders in development institutions. By playing a major role in the shaping and the internationalization of the Washington consensus, the World Bank regained and even reinforced a structural power that it had lost during the 1970s, when development had become every commercial banker's business. With the debt crisis and the consequent waning of private lending, the Bank became, along with the IMF, the lender of last resort. Often leading consortiums of public or private creditors, increasingly involved in "policy dialogue" with borrowing countries, the World Bank developed the notion of "conditionality" in its lending practices. The benefits of loans were attached to specific policy prescriptions that recipient countries had to implement. These prescriptions were in line with the main tenets of the Washington consensus, and involved such items as the downsizing of the public sector, privatization, budgetary cuts, the broadening of the tax base, or financial liberalization. The exportation of the Washington consensus was further relayed by the strong ties between Bank staff and the officials from the borrowing countries' economic ministries, many of whom had transited at one point or another through a position at 1818 H Street and had used their international credentials to further their domestic career. The successful international diffusion of the Washington consensus made it look like "the outcome of worldwide intellectual trends" (Williamson 1993: 1329).

Changing Patterns of Policy Legitimation

The evolving pattern of interaction between policy and research also must be taken into account. Geared toward planning and social engineering, the early period of development assistance was in line with the linkage between social sciences and policymaking that emerged in the wake of the Second World War. During the war social scientists had become quite involved in governmental agencies and planning activity. This involvement, in turn, had established a long-lasting model of scientific investment in the administration of social affairs, which changed the traditional processes of policymaking while it led to an unprecedented growth for the social sciences, driven by political demands and the expansion of the welfare state system.

This situation reinforced the belief that government could successfully intervene in social affairs, provided that it was supplied with all the relevant data and knowledgeable advice (Fischer 1990: 93). Social issues could be properly addressed if policymaking was rationalized and based on sound technical expertise, to be delivered by social scientists. The 1950s and 1960s produced many scientific endeavors that led to high expectations regarding the contribution of the social sciences to development and well-being: the theory of the policy sciences (e.g. Lerner and Lasswell 1951) and its perspective of a scientific rationalization of the policy process; modernization theory and its various ramifications; the thesis of the "end of ideology" and of the overcoming of class conflict by a social reformism and a rational policy process informed by value-free, objective social sciences; the idea of a "knowledgeable society" (Lane 1966), both democratic and stable, guided by objective truth criteria and scientific politics. All these modern technocratic utopias promised to raise "the chances for non-ideological consensus built on social-scientific expertise" (Wagner and Wollman 1986: 28).

Development economics was closely related to this context. At the World Bank, the 1960s saw the rise of a development technocracy, a trend that was reflected in the growth of the most technical departments, such as the Agriculture division, which had become the largest department of the Bank by the mid-1970s. The increasing capacity of the Bank in data collection, a growing use of statistical instruments, cross-country comparisons, economic surveys, complex estimates of needs and rates of return produced a more knowledge-intensive research on development and constituted the scientific basis for the policy prescriptions of the time (Adler 1972: 33–34). Combined with increasing resources, this confidence in technical rationality culminated in the optimism of McNamara's managerial vision of development:

> We do not want simply to say that rising unemployment is a "bad thing," and something must be done about it. We want to know its scale, its causes, its impact and the range of policies and options which are open to governments, international agencies and the private sector to deal with it.
>
> We do not want simply to sense that the "green revolution" requires a comparable social revolution in the organization and education of the small farmer. We want to know what evidence or working models are available on methods of cooperative enterprise, of decentralized credit systems, of smaller-scale technology, and of price and market guarantees.
>
> We do not want simply to deplore over-rapid urbanization in the

primary cities. We want the most accurate and careful studies of internal migration, town-formation, decentralized urbanism and regional balance. (Address to the Board of Governors, Copenhagen, September 21, quoted in Mason and Ascher [1973: 476–77])

Throughout the 1970s, however, this optimism was gradually replaced by a certain skepticism, and ultimately by a growing disillusionment with the technocratic methodology for liberal reform and modernization. The emphasis shifted onto the complexity of social phenomena, if not on the undecidability of "objectivity" criteria for policy formulation. There was a growing awareness that "any particular set of facts will be consistent with a variety of theories and . . . [that] it may be impossible or excessively costly to acquire the data that would permit analysts to reject false theories." (Aaron 1978: 105). This situation of epistemic uncertainty considerably undermined the idea of a shared objective knowledge, and therefore the scientific legitimation of policy choices. This new epistemic pessimism linked up with an emerging critique of technocracy and a new form of policy advocacy. It also fitted perfectly the strategy of neoliberal economists and neoconservative politicians launching a political offensive against the liberal establishment from their positions in newly created think tanks, foundations and policy research centers (J. A. Smith 1991; Blumenthal 1986). Writing in 1978, a scholar characterized this turn as "a conscious return to prescription after many arid years searching for a non-existent, value-free haven" (Sharpe 1978: 68).

It is in this context that neoliberal economic policies and their legitimation by neoclassical economics were articulated. They represented a form of policy knowledge that did not aim at making state policies more effective but, on the contrary, at curtailing them. The reaction against the liberal establishment was also a reaction against a certain use of the social sciences strengthening the intervention of the government into the economy. Moreover, the anti-state ideology of neoliberalism and the formal simplicity of neoclassical economic hypotheses made them policy products that perfectly suited the model of expertise that was offered by think tanks and political foundations. After the technocratic style of expertise of the 1960s, the policy expertise produced in the think tanks of the counter-establishment, such as the Heritage Foundation or the American Enterprise Institute, was characterized by a more adversarial style, and a greater focus on the persuasiveness of the message itself. Specifically tailored for different media — books, newspaper, or television interviews — the production of policy advice was submitted to more constraining and competitive rules.

In many ways, the "marketplace of ideas" was a real market, driven by the competition for corporate funding, media coverage, and public and political attention. In the field of economics, these trends are illustrated by the rise of the so-called "Brookings economists." While not necessarily related to this venerable think tank, these professional policy advocates were usually "skilled Ph.D.'s willing and able to explain issues to journalists in under an hour and in a language preciously close to English" (Weinstein 1992: 74). Capable of reprocessing academic research into usable, readable, and understandable proposals for politicians, opinion-makers, or the media, the success of these "instant experts" was buttressed by their proficiency with marketing techniques and the simplicity of their message. The ideology of the market cannot be dissociated from a market for ideological products.

In the domain of development research, this calling into question of social scientific reformism and modernization took the form of the neoliberal resurgence seeking to dispense with "development economics" and to break with a "statist" and "bureaucratic" policy of development. In the 1980s, neoclassical economists within the Bank used the claim to methodological superiority in order to strengthen underlying — but sometimes explicit — political purposes, notably the advocacy of the market as a more efficient provider of public goods, the ideal of a minimal state, confined to the functions of law and order, and the assumption of public choice and rent-seeking as the best possible economic theory of the state. The practice of development research was entirely subordinated to these assumptions or commitments, and this evolution became more pronounced in the late 1980s and early 1990s. In his report for the Bretton Woods Commission on the World Bank's research, Wapenhans thus came to the conclusion that the Bank's research agenda "is directed by the need to substantiate politically inspired shifts in policy direction" (World Bank 1992).

The suppression of Economics Research as an independent vice-presidency in 1987 made the Bank more dependent upon external research and upon an academic environment that had changed considerably as a result of methodological standardization in the field of economics. With the normalization of development research with respect to the dominant paradigm of economics, a number of external policy research institutions started to get involved in development policy analysis. While this was a traditional activity for the Brookings Institution, newly created and more conservative organizations, such as the Heritage Foundation, started to publish on development issues in the 1980s and contributed to the ideological construction of the "Washington consensus."

"Good Governance" as the Structural Adjustment of Political Regimes

Yet, this hegemonic political project sustained by the U.S. administration, the financial sector, neoliberal economists, and a vibrant policy research industry was rapidly discredited by the World Bank itself, which had contributed to its construction, ensured its international diffusion, and enforced its prescriptions. The shift from the narrowly macroeconomic and financial concerns of the Washington consensus to the emphasis on norms, the rule of law, rights, and entitlements characteristic of "good governance" has often been considered as indicating a new course for the Bank, inspired by a greater attention to social and political issues. After the ideological attacks on the state of the 1980s, it seemed to introduce a more balanced approach rediscovering the importance of political institutions in explaining economic and developmental outcomes. While a 1994 report of a conference organized by the Bretton Woods Commission still stated that "the Bank Group can do even more to speed the movement from state to market — and . . . will do more" (Bretton Woods Commission 1994: 44), the 1997 World Bank Development Report, entitled *The State in a Changing World*, enshrined this new approach and was based on the assumption that "markets and governments are complementary" (World Bank 1997: 4).

The new developmental activism inaugurated by the "good governance" agenda also had moral and legal components. It involved a fight against corruption, for the integrity of the public sector and the accountability of politicians; it involved a strong belief in the virtues of the "rule of law" as a remedy to the ills of "failed states" and underdevelopment. Not only the process of policymaking, but also the issue of the political regime was included within the scope of the new development agenda (Hyden 1992: 6– 8, 16ff). A vibrant "civil society," "transparent" institutions, and "participation" were needed in order to hold the rulers, politicians, and administrators accountable. As a result, this developmental activism was very easily equated with a pro-democracy policy fostering the emergence of liberal regimes, even though the Bank was very careful to cast these policies in a seemingly technical and apolitical way, imposed by its mandate (Goetz and O'Brien 1995; Shihata 1991). As early as 1989, the World Bank asserted that development required "a systematic effort to build a pluralistic institutional structure, a determination to respect the rule of law, and vigorous protection of the freedom of the press and human rights" (World Bank 1989: 61).

This evolution is considered as a break with a narrowly economic, and politically harmful, concern with structural adjustment. Keep in mind, however, that the structural adjustment program had an anti-democratic edge. In the 1980s, some World Bank economists, and most notably Deepak Lal, did not hide their preferences for "quasi authoritarian" regimes, supposed to be more efficient in implementing structural adjustment measures because they were relatively immune to social pressures (Lal 1987). Instead, the notion of "good governance," according to its main drafters, derives its core values from the Declaration of Human Rights. This shift, certainly, is not completely foreign to a wide-ranging policy of public relations launched by the Bank in the late 1980s, in order to improve an image tarnished by harsh criticisms. For the Bank, such a shift was presented as a natural evolution for an institution that is constantly "learning," as it repeats insistently, from its own mistakes and from those of its partners. This image of a humble organization, readily admitting its own mistakes, has been recently strengthened in some of its publications by statements that have the flavor of an auto-critique.[7]

This narrative of a "progressive," emancipatory, and democratic turn at the World Bank was directly related to the new role of NGOs in the developmental process. "Human rights advocates and champions of democracy," according to Caufield (1996: 196), "have been heartened by the prospect of the Bank's using its leverage to further their cause." And indeed, one cannot think of a better marketing argument for NGOs than using this as a demonstration of their power, and claiming a role in this positive transformation of development policies. The Bank's focus on "good governance," from that viewpoint, can be easily presented as the result of their successful mobilization. This new agenda, in fact, attracted much interest from NGOs, some of which actively took part in the production of governance-related policy prescriptions (e.g. Clayton 1994).

Many of the topics covered by the notion of governance clearly reflect the concerns of these non-state actors and can be considered as NGO turf. Beyond the emphasis placed on the role of political institutions, legal environments, popular participation, rights, and civil society, this notion sometimes conveyed an appealing emancipatory language. The political conditionalities of structural adjustment programs have been replaced with the much more symbolic "green conditionalities," "people's conditionalities," and "governance conditionalities" (Dias 1994). In many cases, it is argued that the World Bank changed its strategies after "the failure of its structural adjustment programmes to produce a definitive success on African mainland" (Lancaster 1993: 9; see also Ravenhill 1993: 22–23). This view also seems to be shared by some senior Bank officials or consultants, who mention a "negative experience in adjustment lending" (Frischtak 1994: 1). It is also suggested that the Bank has distanced itself from the promotion of state minimalism (Picciotto 1995: 1). The 1997 World Bank development report seemed to support this view when it set out to criticize a narrow-minded advocacy of a minimal state and suggested that in applying market-oriented strategies for development, "countries sometimes tended to overshoot the mark" (World Bank 1997: 24) — a surprising statement from an institution that had been reproaching third world countries for not committing themselves enough to structural adjustment ten years before.

At the same time, influential development economists combined a commitment to market reforms with a positive reassessment of the role of the state, contrasting with the previous advocacy of a minimal state. Paul Streeten, for instance, a leading development economist, defended the idea of "a strong state," not a strong state "with a limited agenda" confined "to ensuring that individuals . . . can pursue their own purposes with a minimum of frustration," but "a strong state, with an expanded agenda." (1993: 1281). This view, finally, came to be endorsed by the Bank's chief economist in an article co-authored with his colleague from the EBRD (Stern and Stiglitz 1997). This publicized revision of market extremism even received a political characterization by Robert Picciotto, Director General of the Operations Evaluation unit of the Bank, who claimed that the governance agenda was "equally distant from the failed interventionist doctrines of the left and the 'state minimalism' of the right" (Picciotto 1995: 1) and sought to "encompass, and transcend these orthodoxies." (ibid.: 17). This revisited image showed a milder Bank, less narrowly concerned with macroeconomic fundamentals, less ideological, and more concerned about widely accepted rights and values (those embedded in the notion of "good governance"). As a result, some observers went as far as to declare the "end of the Washington consensus."

The break with the goals pursued under structural adjustment programs is, however, far from obvious. A closer look at the evolution of World Bank thinking on the matter reveals more continuities than ruptures. Nevertheless, the Bank went through some delusions with structural adjustment. If many critiques have underlined the negative effects of these policies (e.g.

Chossudovsky 1997) the idea that something had gone wrong also made its way within the Bank, and some reports stressed, euphemistically, the underperformance of these policies. The reforms sought under structural adjustment — mostly concerning macroeconomic policies — were to be reached through the use of political conditionalities attached to the loans extended. In the words of senior Bank officers, this would allow them to "win access to the most senior policy makers, thereby permitting the Bank staff to accelerate reform and to influence its character . . . to buy a place at the policy table" (Berg and Batchelder 1985: 11, 27).

By the later 1980s, however, it was acknowledged that in most cases these goals had not been reached. The diagnosis of this failure pointed, as expected, at the state: in the neoliberal view, which was then dominant at the World Bank, rent-seeking and public choice theories implied that the state, like any other economic agent, was an interest maximizer. A contradiction was thus identified in a policy seeking to entrust recipient states with the task of privatizing parts of the public sector, contracting its size, or opening up national markets in which public or private companies linked in one way or another to the state apparatus would be exposed to international competition. In other words, less government through government was seen as the problem intrinsic to the way structural adjustment was pursued by the Bank. Not only did this line of thinking allow the blame to be placed on recipient states for poor results, but it paradoxically turned the failure of structural adjustment into a proof that its anti-state assumptions were well grounded.

For the Bank, therefore, what hindered structural adjustment was the whole process of policymaking, and the nature of the relations between the private sector, the state, and large segments of society. It is precisely this pattern of public-private interactions that was designated by the term of "governance," when it appeared for the first time in a 1989 report identifying the African crisis as one of "governance" (World Bank 1989: 60). The pursuit of structural adjustment required the reform of the whole political framework, and special attention to the institutional contexts in which policies are designed and to the channels through which they are implemented. It also called for attention to regulatory standards and legal systems, and to the specific patterns of interactions between social groups and political clienteles. The subsequent work on the definition of "governance" was characterized by a continuous expansion of the domains considered to be relevant to policy formulation and implementation — up to the point where the whole system of state-society relations was at stake (World Bank 1992, 1994).

From price mechanisms and trade and currency issues, the emphasis had shifted to institutions, law, interest groups, accountability, political freedoms, human rights.

In other words, "good governance" did not substantially modify the goals of the Washington consensus. Rather, it was meant to *improve* the performance of structural adjustment programs by reshaping the state in accordance with the main tenets of an ideology of economic globalization and free trade. The opening up toward NGOs, and new emphasis on democracy made these unpopular policies look more legitimate and progressive. The Washington consensus was not revised, but enlarged to include new constituencies and stakeholders.

In shifting the targets of the World Bank from economics to politics and society, the concept of "governance" also opened a space of inquiry, research, and experiment in the mechanisms of socioeconomic development which contrasted with the previous exclusive focus on economics. Occupying this space meant producing a knowledge that could not be confined within the boundaries of orthodox economics and that did not lend itself to mathematical formalization and reduction to numerical variables. It meant exploring the linkages between the administration and interest groups, the relative weight of informal structures of socialization and codified norms, the role of value systems in shaping political and economic behavior, the relation between the legal system and policy outcomes, the degree of publicity of the policy process — which in turn involves both the status of the media and the channels of popular participation, hence, political freedoms and rights and, ultimately, the nature of the political regime. In other words, turning development into a matter of "governance" involved investing in other disciplines than orthodox economics. Even though the concept of "governance" was fuzzy, vague and ill defined (Moore 1993a, 1993b; Petiteville 1998: 122; Williams and Young 1994), its success was due precisely to the fact that it allowed many different types of expertise to compete for the redefinition of the state and of its role (Dezalay and Garth 2002).

Previously subject to very low exchange rates on the market of international expertise, political science and political economy were now resources that could compete with economics. The transformation that we have traced in chapter 4 and the critical knowledge of the state produced by heterodox social scientists in the 1970s was brought to bear upon this new global agenda and became adaptable to its purpose. In a similar fashion, the new environmental, participatory and human rights standards that percolated through the language as well as the conditionalities of the World Bank provided NGOs with the opportunity to convert their experience and their symbolic capital into a recognized expertise. Both these developments contributed in turn to opening the market for global expertise to non-economists. This situation lent itself to active exploitation by the groups that so far had been confined to subordinated positions in this market, and could now compete more successfully.

NGOs, Issue Networks and Policy Brokerage

The successful entry of NGOs into the official development community in the late 1980s is the result of a paradoxical process. In a way, it is directly related to the success of neoliberal economists who in the late 1970s and early 1980s managed to secure a dominant position in national and international institutions by adopting an activist strategy combining scientific credentials with a very militant style of policy advocacy. By the same token, this strategy had legitimated a type of advocacy identical to the NGOs' "issue networks" and other types of "norm entrepreneurs." Beyond this symmetry, the retreat of the state from many areas of social services implemented through structural adjustment plans created opportunities for NGOs, who could claim to be the spokespersons for the losers of structural adjustment, development, or financial globalization. Their rapprochement with scholarly communities and their increased professionalization further contributed to delineate a strategy where advocacy, scientific credentials, and expertise, became indiscernible resources. The opposition of these groups to structural adjustment policies was successful only to the extent that it was based on the reproduction of the very strategies that had previously allowed neoliberals and exponents of structural adjustment to impose their policies and legitimate their practices. While it was often used for quite different ends, this mimetism influenced both their professional practices and their political orientations in ways that cannot be ignored.

NGOs, often equated by international institutions with a sort of amateurism, had long been isolated or confined in a subordinate position when they spoke for the losers of structural adjustment policies. With the emergence in the 1980s of humanitarian NGOs that focused on emergency situations (even capable, in some cases, of "declaring" emergencies, and better equipped to mobilize public opinion and attract funding), development NGOs working on longer term perspectives found themselves in a critical situation. While most declined in influence, others had to adapt themselves to a logic of competition and a market discipline if they were to survive, requiring in turn a considerable professionalization of their practices. Public relations, fund-raising, and management came to be primary concerns for staffs increasingly trained in those techniques. Today, the qualifications required for senior positions within NGOs reflect the evolution of those activists who have also become managers: trained in law, business administration, or finance, experienced, with a good capacity to "liaise" with political circles or the business community, their profile often does not substantially differ from those of corporate managers. This professionalization has paradoxically led NGOs to attract personnel increasingly similar to that of the multilateral or governmental institutions which they often challenge. In some fields, such as human rights, this trend has reached such a level that for many young graduates, an NGO position is the preliminary step in a career leading straight to responsibilities in intergovernmental institutions.

The emergence of the NGO issue at the World Bank that started around 1985–86 and the subsequent intensification of their relations and cooperation is related to this evolution. Far from stemming from their representativeness or membership size, the new power exhibited by a wide range of NGOs was linked to their increased capacity to challenge development policies in those very terms in which they were formulated, to make use of the same expertise, and to pursue sophisticated strategies of public relations. However, since this efficiency was dependent upon the adoption of the opponent's resources, argumentative repertoires, and patterns of policy legitimation, it led to a further rapprochement instead of a political confrontation.

Barber Conable, president of the Bank between 1986 and 1991, deserves credit for having understood the potential that NGOs represented for the World Bank. Unlike his predecessors, Conable was not a banker but a former Republican Congressman and an experienced politician, appointed at the head of the IBRD with the help of his friend James Baker, then Secretary of the Treasury. This background made him particularly sensitive to these new political clienteles lobbying Congress and voicing their concerns about or their opposition to the Bank's programs. The NGO phenomenon was rapidly identified as one of the most pressing issues that the Bank had to face. The department of External Affairs opted for a preventive cooptation involving mostly an exercise of "administrative relabeling" which saw projects suddenly involving gender, environmental, or participative dimensions without any substantial changes: "Sound ecology is good economics" was how Conable saw the whole issue.

In 1987, Conable revived a lethargic committee in charge of relations with NGOs that had existed since 1982, and appointed James Clark to supervise it the next year. Until then, Clark had been the head of the policy unit at Oxfam. Coming from the struggles against the Bank-sponsored Narmada Dam project in India in the early 1980s, Clark was also knowledgeable about the internal workings of the Bank, as he had been traveling twice a year to Washington in order to lobby the World Bank-NGO committee. He then realized that there were "allies" within the Bank, not only among the technical specialists closer to old-style development economics, sharing similar concerns about environmental or social issues and distrustful of neoliberal economists, but also on the board of governors, where some directors representing countries with a tradition of socially conscious foreign aid could be sensitive to NGO claims.

Clark's appointment also crowned a deliberate strategy of professionalization of NGO lobbying pursued by Oxfam, which had sought to "discipline" the strategies of the NGO sector. At the same time, Conable also increased the financial volume of operations which, directly or indirectly, were managed by NGOs or involved their participation in the project cycle. From 5 percent in 1988, the percentage of projects involving NGOs reached 37 percent in 1991, at the end of Conable's mandate. In 1997, it had reached 47 percent. Increasingly, various kinds of NGOs thus came to operate as subcontractors of the Bank, providing services, consultancy, or simply local knowledge. The simultaneous expansion of the consultancy market of the Bank — which extends more than $1 billion a year of contracts to external consultants (Caufield 1996: 248) — has helped fuel this form of interactions with a wide range of organizations easily classified as NGOs or emanations of "civil society." This only accelerated the convergence of their organizational culture. In turn, the social consequences of structural adjustment plans on public services, the environment, or disadvantaged groups opened many spaces in which NGOs could prosper and make symbolic investments that could then be converted into financial returns and entitlements to "participation" in project management or policymaking.

If NGOs have managed to be accredited as official stakeholders of development policies in their own right, it is also because they have built up in the last decade a very strong and efficient expertise. The opening of NGOs toward the academic world can be considered as one of the most significant transformations of nongovernmental activism in the last decade. For many NGOs, it was not only a matter of gaining scientific credentials that they sometimes lacked: building ties with scholars was also a way to constitute an expertise capital bound to be increased through service provision to aid donors and development banks or, even, other NGOs. Some organizations have since made major contributions to the development of a learned discourse on nongovernmental actors and governance.[8]

The opening toward academic communities was made, logically, in the direction of those development scholars who had shared with NGOs a similar subordinate position in the hierarchies of policy expertise, and in particular of political scientists concerned with democracy, human rights, and economic reform. The kind of knowledge they possessed could not be recognized in development policies as long as an exclusive focus on macroeconomic management assigned an intellectual monopoly over these policies to orthodox economists. This hierarchy of knowledges that lasted throughout the 1980s and underpinned the Washington consensus explains to a large extent the critical attitude of non-economist scholars working on development toward structural adjustment policies and the institutions implementing them, especially the World Bank. For these non-economists deprived of authority and legitimacy, NGOs often appeared as efficient "brokers" of their research, capable of diffusing its content to wide and diversified audiences, albeit in a simplified form. In turn, many NGOs were eager to beef up their professional profile by tapping scholars who could be easily represented as "civil society" or "participation" experts.

Toward the end of the 1980s, the overt admission of shortcomings in structural adjustment lending and the weakening of its justifications provided an opportunity for those dominated development actors such as NGOs and non-economists to impose their competencies and gain official recognition. The analysis of these shortcomings, the emphasis on institutional, political, cultural, and legal factors allowed many political scientists both to show the limits of a purely economic approach and to demonstrate the superiority of their knowledge by pointing to its potential contributions.

It is not mere chance that the learned clienteles which got closer to the Bank in the 1990s were in many cases its former critics. As we have seen in chapter 4, a critical knowledge of the state, linked to neo-Marxist methodologies, was instrumental in producing a critique of economic policies that, in the last instance, included the promise of more efficient implementation. It is indeed a critique of liberal economics — and of economists — that fueled the work of political scientists involved in an analysis of structural adjustment (euphemistically relabeled "economic reform") and in the production of a "political economy" that complemented a use of institutional economics within the Bank, which considered projects as "instruments of institutional reform" (Picciotto 1995). The agents of this successful conversion of a critical knowledge of the state into a dominant expertise (Haggard and Kaufman 1992, 1994; Haggard and Webb 1994; Nelson 1995) thus acquired influential reputations as reformist analysts of structural adjustment.

Similarly, the concept of governance resulted from the combination and the reprocessing of a certain number of academic traditions which informed the first formulation of the concept in the 1989 World Bank report on Sub-Saharan Africa (Williams and Young 1994: 91). As Latin Americanists contributed to the revival of political economy at the Bank, as we saw in chapter 4, Africanists invested in the construction of the notion of governance (Ake 1996; Hyden and Bratton 1992; Macgaffey 1990). By working on countries where weakly institutionalized state structures that were often inherited from a colonial past overlapped with informal but more effective patterns of politics, these political scientists produced a literature exploring the role of traditions and informal norms and rules as factors of social integration and the political functions of "civil society." The success of this research program was due in part to the fact that it broke with structuralism in a timely fashion (Hyden 1992: 8). But it was also the result of a very efficient scientific marketing, notably made by Goran Hyden, which connected this notion of governance to several "up and coming" topics in political science and economics. The emphasis on the "informal" resources of the polity and the economy was successfully translated in terms of a research on "social capital" (ibid.: 7). This operation assigned the concept of governance in a field which had been very successfully developed by neoliberal development entrepreneurs, around the "best-seller" of Hernando de Soto (1989), *The Other Path*, which advocated with populist overtones a contraction of the administration and the public sectors in order to release the "creative" energies of society, and which benefited from a very good reception within the World Bank. This strategy of competition with economics led Hyden to underline that "the study of governance is performance-oriented" in that it sought to determine the most efficient ways of "mobilizing and managing social capital." As a result, "it comes closer to the literature on business management" (Hyden 1992: 22).

These theories found a positive resonance within the Bank, where they served the strategies of a small constituency within the African Region bureau, involved in a positive reassessment of African traditions. This "cultural" reformulation of neoliberal policy prescriptions amounted to an attack on overstaffed and underperforming governments not on the basis of doctrinal economic considerations, but on the basis of the fact that "the underlying cultural premises of these institutions were alien to the vast majority of Africans" (Landell-Mills 1992: 543). Reified and idealized "African traditions" and "indigenous institutions" were thus pitted against an utterly foreign state, and seen as a new form of social capital that could be mobilized for economic reform. Poor development was caused by "a high degree of concentration of political power and the colonial inheritance" (World Bank 1992: 11). By addressing these causes of underdevelopment, good governance therefore overlapped with a project of postcolonial democracy. Because it combined an anticolonialist rationale and a cultural bias, this strategy was also perfectly adapted to be supported and adopted by NGOs and activists, who saw in the defense of "indigenous" traditions by the Bank the sign of a positive evolution to which they could not be completely foreign.

Using their scientific capital also to accumulate the kind of symbolic capital attached to emancipatory movements, transnational activism and the defense of indigenous cultures, these scholars successfully competed on the market for international expertise. The positions they built as the main ideologues of development in the 1990s were the result of these investments in learned productions that were both emancipatory and functional to hegemonic reforms — very similar to those made by the "Washington political economists" from which the governance scholars had initially sought to distinguish themselves. The concern for democratization would rapidly become a shared concern, with Michael Bratton linking the issue of governance to the firmly established literature on democratization (Bratton and van de Walle 1997). Involved in the production of expertise, it was somehow logical for some of these governance scholars — Pearl Robinson, Joel Barkan, Richard Joseph, Michael Bratton — to join the Research Council of the National Endowment for Democracy as democracy experts.

While the motto of structural adjustment was "get the prices right," the consolidation of a new development agenda around the notion of governance seems to have replaced it with "get the politics right," thus ratifying the official role of political scientists in the formulation of policies aiming both at economic development and more democratic politics. Meant to increase the "transparency" of institutions, strengthen the legal framework, or broaden the channels of "participation" in the political process, these projects could no longer be assessed in economic terms or through cost-benefits analyses. Instead, what was needed were indicators that could capture the degree of autonomy of "civil society" or the openness of political institutions, institutional and sociological studies of policymaking procedures, or, in other words, a kind of knowledge that social scientists could provide more easily than economists. Just as orthodox economists had made their entry at the Bank in the evaluation departments in the late 1970s, so did political scientists a decade later. The implications of the new agenda for the professional composition of Bank staff were actually identified. As early as 1991, a technical paper already suggested that non-economists should not be confined to assessment work, but involved in project design and implementation (Cernea 1991). The proposal was only a modest one, and made in a publication that cannot be considered as reflecting the Bank's position on the issue. However, it made its way to the status of official recruitment policy. In 1996, an official report called *Social Development and Results on the Ground* advocated a large-scale recruitment of those who are called "Nessies" in the Bank's jargon — which stands for "non economics specialists" but which is also an indicator of the patronizing way in which these newcomers were considered in an institution still dominated by economists. Initially critical and marginal, their expertise ends up being a full-fledged, well-established and exportable orthodoxy.

The "governance" agenda thus appears as the result of complex realignments in the development community, and of a diversification of the cognitive resources mobilized in development institutions. The internal tensions, or contradictions, of this agenda — in which human rights, democratic development, poverty alleviation, the environment, minorities empowerment, and ethnic cultures seem to combine harmoniously with privatization, commodification of services and social relations, and the opening to the global marketplace — reflects the success of a strategy which sought to reframe the expansion of capitalist social relations as a force of emancipation and empowerment.

Conclusion

In 1583, against the civic and Republican ideal defended earlier by Machiavelli, the Italian Jesuit secretary Giovanni Botero defined a new form of rationality related to the emergence of the modern state. This knowledge sought to codify "the appropriate means to build and to preserve and amplify a kingdom" (Botero 1997 [1583]: 7). The specificity of this knowledge was that it adopted and identified itself with the point of view of the state and of its administrative apparatus: it was aptly defined as *Reason of State* (*Ragion di Stato*). Modern political science was entirely built around this paradigm, as a science of the state. Ever since, the reason of state has never ceased to be identified with this state-centered rationality, and in particular with the absolute superiority of the state over the individuals which it comprises.

It is also against this form of transcendent sovereignty and against the unlimited pretension of its power that all modern democratic movements have arisen. The idea of universal human rights has sought to place a limit on the reason of state and to define a sanctuary which it could not trespass. Today, however, these traditional delimitations seem to be more evasive than ever and tend to fade away. Democracy and human rights are increasingly used in order to *extend* the power they were meant to limit. The promotion of democracy and human rights defines new forms of administration on a global scale and generates a new political science. When one listens to the contemporary political scientists who theorize the expansion of democracy and human rights, it is difficult not to hear something like a distant echo of Botero's Reason of State: when a scholar professing democracy defines a new domain of research into the "specific technical knowledge about the building and preserving of democratic institutions" (Goldman 1988: 116), it is difficult not to recognize, almost word for word, a variation on "the appropriate means to build and to preserve and amplify a kingdom." Like Botero before them, who was secretary to the archbishop of Milan Carlo Borromeo, the scholars producing a "science of democratization" are the learned secretaries of new forces of Counter-Reform: Freedom House, the National Endowment for Democracy, the World Bank and other institutions combining spiritual power and earthly interests. Like Botero before them, they give their advice to the powerful or teach to their heirs.

I have followed the different processes which led to this transformation, which involved two main dimensions. On the one hand, tracing the constitution of a new form of Reason of State has meant identifying trends within political science that contributed to produce a certain type of knowledge allowing for the active management of democratic transformations. In the same way as Botero had laid the basis for a science of the state (mercantilism) that reflected the emergence of the modern state, yesterday's modernization theories and today's democratization studies are the academic reflection of emerging technologies for the global administration of political regimes. Far from being a mere theory, detached from the field of democracy and human rights, political science has been entirely internal to it to the extent that it brought these issues within the scope of a technical policy knowledge for dealing with them.

On the other hand, I have sought to follow the historical and social development of the actors producing this knowledge and of the activists who invented the institutional forms of contemporary democracy promotion. In this respect, the legacy of the Cold War crusades and the role of U.S. policies against Communism in the internationalization of democratic activist networks underscores the *structural subordination of the field of human rights to the field of state power*. At the same time, however, the analysis of the democratic crusade of the 1950s (of which the Congress for Cultural Freedom was the model) or of the democracy promotion programs of the 1980s (in the case of the National Endowment for Democracy) illustrates a paradoxical continuity. These projects have become hegemonic because they systematically managed to integrate emancipatory and progressive forces in the construction of imperial policies. In the 1950s, the various currents of the Trotskyist and socialist Left with their trade union components were instrumental in giving a strategic depth to the Truman doctrine. In the 1980s, a liberal, anti-imperialist, and democratic Left, along with the human rights movement, provided the conceptual language, the ideological tools, as well as the fluid logistics for Reagan's imperial policy of democracy promotion. Whether the labor unions and the socialists yesterday, or NGOs and human rights activists today, these forces increasingly tend to provide the external envelope of a power reshaping polities, societies, and economies on a global scale according to the prescriptions of a new reason of State.

At the level of the individual actors of this transformation, this process has taken complex forms that cannot be reduced to co-optation or conversion. By establishing transnational networks or generating a critical knowledge of the state, they have often crafted tools that could be reversed and used in order to reassert another reason of state, a global administrative rationality that traded upon dominant forms of expertise and policy knowledge, cloaked in emancipatory languages. This transformation of practices articulated to the critique of state power into global weapons stored in the arsenals of state power has not always gone unnoticed and has left some committed democratic activists bitter:

> There is great dissatisfaction among many who enthusiastically welcomed the end of authoritarian regimes; the democratic forces seem at times to weary or to lose their way. Many friends and *compañeros* of the antiauthoritarian struggles today occupy high positions in government or in party leadership. . . . In a sense, the authoritarian period was easier than the current situation. We knew then why and against whom we were fighting, in a solidarity stitched together as much from the critique of that domination as from the democratic wager which we were making. Now we must find an answer to the question of how to make a democratic critique of democracy. (O'Donnell 192, 17–18).

Taking stock from this last suggestion, this book had no other ambition than to contribute to this democratic critique of democracy.

Appendix

A List of "Democracy Experts": The Research Council of the International Forum for Democratic Studies

Lahouari Addi
Pauline Baker
Peter L. Berger
Janusz Bugajski
Gerald Curtis
Denise Dresser
Charles H. Fairbanks
Louis W. Goodman
Sung-joo Han
Joanathan Hartlyn
Saad Eddin Ibrahim
Terry Lynn Karl
John Lampe
Juan J. Linz
Kanan Makiya
Michael McFaul
Yasmeen Murshed
Guillermo O'Donnell
Thomas Pangle
Robert Putnam
Richard Rose
Philippe C. Schmitter
Richard L. Sklar
Vladimir Tismaneanu

Mutiah Alagappa
Shaul Bakhash
Nancy Bermeo
Yun-han Chu
Robert Dahl
John B. Dunlop
Mark Falcoff
E. Gyimah-Boadi
Robert L. Hardgrave
Steven Heydemann
Richard Joseph
János Kis
Liang Heng
Seymour M. Lipset
Vincent Maphai
Fatima Mernissi
Andrew J. Nathan
Martha Brill Olcott
Minxin Pei
Peter Reddaway
Chai'Anan Samudavanija
Stephen Sestanovich
Aleksander Smolar
Laurence Whitehead

Abdulahi An-Na'im
Joel D. Barkan
Michael Bratton
Michael Coppedge
Francis Deng
Donald Emerson
Steven Friedman
Stephan Haggard
Harry Harding
Donald L. Horowitz
Adrian Karatnycky
Atul Kohli
R. William Liddle
Abraham F. Lowenthal
José María Maravall
Leonardo Morlino
Joan M. Nelson
Oyeleye Oyediran
Adam Przeworski
Pearl T. Robinson
Robert A. Scalapino
Lilia Shevtsova
Stephen J. Stedman

Lisa Anderson
Samuel H. Barnes
Daniel Brumberg
Wayne Cornelius
Nikiforos Diamandouros
João Carlos Espada
Francis Fukuyama
Peter Hakim
Iliya Harik
Samuel P. Huntington
Ibrahim Karawan
Bolívar Lamounier
Arend Lijphart
Scott Mainwaring
Cynthia McClintock
Joshua Muravchik
Ghia Nodia
Ergun Özbudun
Vesna Pusić
Anibal Romero
Andreas Schedler
Masipula Sithole
Nathan Tarcov

Notes

Introduction

1. Most of these lines have been written before September 11 and the ensuing wars in Afghanistan and Iraq. Because the analyses presented here are mostly historical, I did not feel the need to alter them. For sure, the crisis and the global management of its aftermath by the Bush administration most definitely represent a regression within the overall logic of the constitution of a democratic cosmopolitical order. The military instrument has replaced issue networks as the main pillar in the construction of a new world order. I however believe this recent development is not politically sustainable in the long run. The tendencies it has slowed down, I also believe, are irreversible. The very attempt to cast the war in Iraq as a liberation war and a campaign in defense of democracy bears witness to this new reality. These events may have temporarily confined to the background the institutions and the projects analyzed here, but they have not made them obsolete.
2. On Transparency International, see Coeurdray (2003). A history of Freedom House — a cold war organization created by Eleanor Roosevelt — is still lacking. For some indications, see Korey (1999: 443–67).
3. In fact, the few available ethnographic or sociological studies of internationally recognized NGOs in developing countries tend to underline their social proximity or their overlapping with ruling families which also wield influence in the field of state power. See Pouligny (2003); for an analysis of the social background of humanitarian workers, see Dauvin and Siméant (2002).
4. For Weber's exposé of the rule of the *honoratiores*, see also Weber (1978: 950-51).
5. This index of corruption actually measures the perception of corruption by selected economic actors (consultants, expatriates, businessmen, etc). For an

overview of the methodology used in the construction of the index, see http://www.transparency.org/cpi/2003/dnld/framework.pdf

6. Michel Foucault has pointed out that while human rights had emerged as a weapon against all possible forms of domination and power, there was a risk of "reintroducing a dominant doctrine under the pretext of presenting a theory or politics of human rights" (1994: 349).

7. The use they make of the concept of "hegemony" is also questionable from a philological point of view, if only because what these authors usually mean by "hegemony" is the diffusion of the values, worldviews, and beliefs of the dominant classes to the subordinate groups — while Gramsci had actually developed the concept in the overall perspective of a victory of the working class.

8. In his recent autobiography, which offers many insights into the historical constitution of the human rights movement, Aryeh Neier also suggests that the instrumental endorsement of human rights by the Reagan administration strengthened the movement. He notes that in his own dealings with Elliot Abrams, the Assistant Secretary of State for Human Rights appointed by Reagan in 1982, he reckoned that his team should try "to work with him in the expectation that our concern for the intrinsic significance of human rights and his concern for its instrumental value might often lead us to find common ground in practice" (Neier 2003: 186).

9. For a concise but nevertheless systematic presentation of the concept of field and useful clarifications, see Bourdieu and Wacquant (1992).

10. The function of law and economics as disciplines of power and their hegemonic use in international relations have been analyzed by Dezalay and Garth (2002).

11. In this respect, the decision taken in Fall 2000 by the Council of the American Political Science Association to approve the creation of two new sections, respectively Comparative Democratization and Human Rights, is highly revealing of the role of academic disciplines in this process of institutionalization.

1. From Cold Warriors to Human Rights Activists

1. All these examples are taken from the 1998 report of the National Endowment for Democracy.

2. This interpretation is discussed at length in chapter 5.

3. Thus, Joshua Muravchik, a neoconservative writer associated with the American Entreprise Institute and the National Endowment for Democracy, can claim that human rights is the essence of Americanism and that "Any victory for freedom is a victory for America"(1986: 68). In an article published in *Commentary*, Samuel Huntington reformulated this old proposition in his inimitable pseudo-scientific style: "a significant correlation exists between the rise

and fall of American power in the world and the rise and fall of liberty and democracy" (1981: 38).

4. While their work is often very useful and offers valuable information, this is for instance the general direction in which the work of investigative journalists such as Holly Sklar and Chip Berlet proceeds, tracing links between institutions such as the National Endowment for Democracy and the CIA or other governmental agencies involved in the Cold War. See Sklar and Berlet (1991).

5. The National Endowment for Democracy, for instance, has been created under the supervision of personnel many of whom have links with the intelligence apparatus. Thus, Walter Raymond, from the CIA Operations Directorate, who had been in charge of pro-Contras public relations campaigns in the United States, moved from the CIA to the National Security Council in 1982 as Senior Director of Intelligence Programs and supervised the creation of the NED. John Richardson, former president of Radio Free Europe and subsequently director of Freedom House, became chair of the NED Board of Directors. On the relations between NED and CIA, see Muravchik (1992: 206), Wiarda (1990: 145–46), Sklar and Berlet (1992), Ciment and Ness (1999).

6. It is highly revealing that these activists had denounced at the same time real liberation movements in the Third World as "the armed component of totalitarianism," to quote the famous definition of Daniel Moynihan, a Democrat senator who once figured as one of the most efficient spokesman of the nascent neoconservative mood.

7. Originating in Italy in the 1920s and imported by the anti-Stalinist Left in the United States during the 1930s, the concept of totalitarianism became a pillar of U.S. foreign policy after 1947, at the same time as it became a significant academic topic. On the genealogy of the concept, see Gleason (1995); Traverso (2002).

8. On *Partisan Review*, see in particular Cooney (1986), and Bloom (1986).

9. David J. Dallin ed., *Concentration Camps in Russia*, "World Events" supplement, *The New Leader* 30, no. 13 (March 29, 1947). In his analysis of U.S. labor socialism, Joshua Muravchik writes that "Meany and Lovestone arranged publication of a map of Soviet concentration camps" (2002: 252). To my knowledge, this publication refers to the *New Leader* supplement on the subject.

10. Although he was an early fellow-traveler of the Trotskyists, James Burnham (1905–1987) does not belong to the mainstream of New York socialism: he was of the upper class while most of the New York intellectuals of the 1930s were of humble immigrant background. Catholic in a predominantly Jewish cultural and political environment, he was also among the first to break with Trotsky and to complete his odyssey toward conservatism. Before rallying the socialist ranks, he had developed a corporatist and almost spiritualistic form of anticapitalism, which probably reflected the influence of his educational background (a strict and rigorous neo-Thomist education), but also prefigured his

later political evolution. On Burnham see the special issue of the *National Review* 39, no. 17 (September 11, 1987), which contains several biographical articles.

11. An occasional contributor to the *Partisan Review*, Hannah Arendt would later build her theory of totalitarianism on this comparative perspective. See Arendt (1961).

12. Shachtman's distinction was motivated by a quarrel with more orthodox Trotskyist interpretations assuming that the USSR represented a form of "state capitalism." This theory itself derived from the assumption that, since fascist imperialism was the ultimate stage of capitalism before the advent of socialism, and since Russia was not yet socialist, then the Soviet Union was still in the capitalistic phase of its development. Shachtman argued that the Soviet state had actually destroyed all remnants of capitalist production and that "bureaucratic collectivism," as he labeled this new stage of historical development, constituted a distinctive form which was neither capitalist nor socialist.

13. All the observers recognize this continuity. Sidney Blumenthal ironically writes that "in many important respects, neoconservatism is the political culture of the Old Left preserved in aspic," and that "not the least of their assets is a conceptual method of thinking from which conservatives have shut themselves off: Marxism" (Blumenthal 1986: 123). But this continuity is also recognized by the main protagonists of this episode as well, most of whom emphasize the stability of the approach (ideologized, militant, keen on "political warfare") while the goals have considerably changed.

14. On Lovestone, see Morgan (1999).

15. In fact, this peculiar ideological configuration of the cold war was not foreign to the integration of the working class and of its organizations into the political system, that is, to the development of the Welfare State itself, in Europe as in the United States.

16. The notion of "State Department socialism" occasionally resurfaces in the history of the anti-Stalinist left. In the 1950s, for instance, the left wing of the Trotskyist movement opposing Max Shachtman's plan to merge with the Socialist Party was afraid of "going over to the political positions of what [they] called State Department socialism" (Wohlforth 1994: 38–39). In the 1980s, the nickname of "State Department socialists" would still stick to some social democrats converted to neoconservatism (Massing 1987).

17. Sidney Hook was a former City College student and a disciple of John Dewey. Theoretically, his ambition was to find a synthesis between Marxism and pragmatism. Hook was one of the first "New York Intellectuals" to move rightward, and he played an important role in the creation of the Congress for Cultural Freedom in 1950.

18. In a different fashion, the need to adopt a clear position on issues of socialism and democracy would lead to debates within the *New Leader*. In an exchange

with Sidney Hook which continued for several issues in a row, Max Eastman — a Trotskyist who also collaborated with *Partisan Review* — even picked up the argument recently made by the economist Friedrich Hayek in his *Road to Serfdom* (1945), namely that there was no middle ground between total economic planning and the preservation of freedom by submission to the impersonal forces of the market, and that even the smallest measure of economic planning inevitably led to totalitarianism, and used it to criticize Hook's plea for "democratic socialism." See Eastman (1945: 5).

19. In fact the strength of radical politics in 1930s New York is directly related to this social background. In a context of economic depression, which directly affected these poor and immigrant social strata, Marxism offered a powerful instrument for combining both a modernist critique of cultural and religious traditions, and a political critique of the capitalist host society. It provided, in other words, an alternative to the dilemma between assimilation and Judaism which most of these groups faced. On this aspect, see in particular Wald (1987), Cooney (1986: 10–18).

20. My purpose here is not to go over the history of the Congress for Cultural Freedom, as this institution has recently been the focus of very good scholarship, after an initial period in which the debates over its role were still clouded by the ideological contrasts between a revisionist historiography and an intelligentsia close to the organization itself. After the initial work of Christopher Lasch (1969) on the role of the CCF in the "cultural cold war," and Coleman's (1989) defense of the institution to which he himself belonged, Pierre Grémion (1995) and Frances Stonor Saunders (1999) have done, albeit with contrasting views, extensive research on the Congress. Very useful observations on the late evolution of the Congress, but also on the cultural dimension of the struggle for democracy and against Communism in Europe in the 1950s can be found in Volker Berghahn's biography of Shepard Stone (Berghahn 2001)

21. Frances Stonor Saunders (1999) describes the institutionalization of special programs aiming at fighting doctrines hostile to the American system on a "scientific" and "cultural" basis. See in particular pp. 146–56.

22. In fact, the tremendous institutional development of Soviet studies in the postwar era cannot be understood without keeping in mind this political background. Simple factual knowledge about the Soviet Union had immediately a political value. Massively funded by the government and by philanthropic foundations, Soviet studies drew heavily on the skills of many émigrés and scholars close to the worldview of the non-communist left. See Markwick (1996), Simpson (1998).

23. There is a vast literature on the strategic management of social scientific knowledge by the philanthropic foundations. See in particular the classical studies of Fischer (1993), and Arnove (1980); for a general overview, see Geiger (1988).

For an assessment of the foundations' role in the shaping of postwar U.S. foreign policy, see Parmar (1999, 2002).

24. Some aspects of the relation between scientific strategies and democratization policies are discussed in Volker Berghahn's biography of Shepard Stone (2001).

25. On the 1955 conference, see Grémion (1995), as well as the reports written by several participants (Bell 1960; Shils 1955; Lipset 1960).

26. In some respects, the end of ideology thesis is influenced by the late reception of the works of Max Weber in the United States (the first texts were translated by Talcott Parsons in 1930) and their impact on sociologists such as Lipset and Bell, who read the Weberian rationalization process and the disappearance of ultimate ends into postwar "abundant society" at the same time as they were abandoning their own ideological commitments.

27. This political evolution led to an endorsement of liberal democracy that was no longer merely *instrumental* but straightforwardly *normative*. At the very beginning of his text on the end of ideology, referring to his book *Political Man* as a whole, Lipset writes that "a basic premise of this book is that democracy is not only or even primarily a means through which different groups can attain their ends of seek the good society; it is the good society itself in operation" (1960: 403): that is, the normative commitment to the postwar liberal consensus comes first, and is the foundation upon which the social scientist operates.

28. Forty years after the "end of ideology" thesis, the reconstruction of U.S. hegemony on the basis of a notion of democracy and human rights was matched by a similar thesis asserting the end of ideological conflict, also elaborated by a State Department ideologue. Francis Fukuyama's "end of history," indeed, in many ways resembles this previous attempt at "naturalizing" the American model and declaring the clinical death of alternative worldviews. In particular, it represents a similar attempt at turning a political consensus into an abstract, quasi-metaphysical evidence. While the "end of ideology" reflected the liberal consensus of the 1950s, the "end of history" reflected the Washington consensus of the 1990s and the emergence of "market democracy" as the generic form of modern politics in a global age, offered as a model to all nations and actively exported by a whole range of specialized institutions. See Fukuyama (1992).

The "end of ideology" also captured the belief that the "abundant society" of the 1950s would remove the basis for social conflict. In fact, the notion of economic growth was then conceived as an instrument of absorption of conflict (Paggi 1989: 32–43). "Abundance" was directly opposed to the paradigm of "scarcity" on which the whole conservative opposition to the possibility of social reform had been based, from its origins in Social Darwinism and Malthusian theories. The subsiding of antagonistic strategies on the left in favor of a positive reassessment of political stability and social dialogue is a political consequence of the perception of the postwar U.S. economy. Contemporary ideologies of globalization, as the "end of history" thesis, use similar economic arguments to delegitimate global social antagonisms. The debate about genetically modified organisms, for instance, has seen promoters of market liberalization brandish fantastic promises of agricultural overabundance that would erase hunger and poverty, thus undercutting the causes of global social conflict.

29. Source: U.S. Department of Education, Biennial Survey.

30. For a comparison with ex-Communists, see Diggins (1975).

31. The memoirs of Charles H. Page, who taught at CCNY in the 1930s and until 1946, offer a detailed and vivid account of the intellectual atmosphere of that institution. See in particular chapter 3. See also Bloom (1986), especially pp. 34–42.

32. For the largely sociological and cultural analysis of the evolution of "upwardly mobile Jews," see Bloom (1986). For a more political approach, in part opposed to the socio-cultural one, see Wald (1987).

33. The experiences of Aryeh Neier, for instance, are in many ways comparable to that of many future neoconservatives: born in Berlin in 1933; his family runs away from Nazism, travels to England and arrives in the United States shortly after the war. Neier studies law. Politically, he feels close to Norman Thomas' Socialist Party (at a time when the party is infiltrated by Shachtman's troops); he enters the Students League for Industrial Democracy and becomes its president, before renaming it Students for a Democratic Society (SDS) in 1959. He opposes the Shachtmanites who operate within the League for Industrial Democracy. These affiliations clearly situate him in the anti-Stalinist left. Yet, his career at the helm of the American Civil Liberties Union, Human Rights Watch and, ultimately, George Soros' Open Society Institute demonstrate a constant dedication to liberalism that, in the 1980s, would led him to take position *against* the Reagan administration, as opposed to the neoconservatives. See Neier (2003, xx–xxi).

34. Isserman (1987: 192) ironically writes that "in the past, Shachtman had identified working-class interests with whatever the party he was involved with at the time said they were. Abandoning that delusion, he went to another extreme and defined those interests solely in terms of what the official leadership of AFL-CIO said they were — a tendency that was reinforced when some of his young associations like [David] Horowitz and [Tom] Kahn, found jobs working under Al Shanker on the staff of the United Federation of Teachers."

35. There is a vast literature on the intellectual immigration to the United States in the 1930s and the 1940s. See in particular Krohn (1993), Srubar (1988), Coser (1984); see also the introduction in Salvati (2000).

36. I borrow the expression from Packenham (1973: 197). For an overview of the structure of the social scientific field in the United States, see the superb study by Ross (1991).

37. On the place of formalization in the development of economics from the 1940s onwards, see Mirowski (2002).

38. Grémion writes this à propos French Trotskyists, but his analysis perfectly fits the situation of their American fellow militants.

39. In fact, it is possible to read her *On Revolution*, published in 1963, as a symptom of this passage, and as an important moment in the construction of this progressive image of the United States. Through a systematic comparison with the French revolution which, according to her, has been plagued by the "social question," Arendt shows that the American revolution was the only modern revolution which actually succeeded in "founding freedom" because it benefited from exceptional circumstances, and in particular from the egalitarian nature of colonial society and its capacity to solve the social question through territorial expansion and mobility.

40. On the theories of the New Class, see Szelenyi and King (2004).

41. Interview with author, Washington, March 27, 2000. Emphasis mine.

42. Leopold Labedz, editor of *Survey: A Journal of East and West Studies*, was a Russian born Polish émigré, who became one of the most influential cultural Cold Warriors in the Anglo-American world. Co-editor of *Soviet Survey* with Walter Laqueur — who would later become a major neoconservative thinker — Labedz became editor when Laqueur left and changed the journal's name to *Survey*. The publication quickly became a forum for the analysis of developments in Soviet politics, the publication of dissident writings, and systematic attacks on what Labedz called the Western "apologists," in fact meaning any intellectuals who dealt with the same issues without professing an intransigent anti-Communism or who were suspect of progressive views (from Edward H. Carr to Isaac Deutscher, to Noam Chomsky). While his personal networks in Eastern Europe allowed him to gather sometimes significant intelligence, Labedz also entertained continuous relations with Melvin Lasky, the editor of *Encounter*, the journal sponsored by the Congress for Cultural Freedom. (The Congress would finance Labedz from the 1960s onward according to Edward Shils). Labedz's activism would gain him the recognition of influential foreign policy circles in the United States, and in particular, through the mediation of Richard Perle, the attention of Senator Henry Jackson, the champion of the emerging neoconservative movement within the Democratic Party. His later affiliation with the National Endowment for Democracy somehow stands as the logical outcome of a political evolution characterized by a bottom-line anti-Communism, a strong intellectual commitment, and his status as prominent cold warrior. Labedz would thus be instrumental in providing the neoconservatives in general, and the NED in articular, with the appropriate *maîtres à penser*, such as Alexander Solzhenitsyn or Leszek Kolakowski. On Labedz, see Shils (1994), Brumberg (1993).

43. See the article by Massing (1987); Blumenthal (1987).

2. The Field of Democracy and Human Rights

1. There is a huge literature on human rights, which bears witness to the importance of this field in the contemporary world order. For an overview of the development of human rights, see Evans (1998).
2. Indeed, the break with Carter's human rights policy should not be overemphasized. It was emphasized by neoconservatives, who had an interest in sharply distinguishing their policy, and it thus tends to be an ideological construct rather than a real political discontinuity. It is significant that, in retrospect, many neoconservatives moderate their earlier criticisms of Carter and tend to positively reassess his foreign affairs record. Joshua Muravchik provides the perfect example: "I must say between parenthesis when I looked back later, I changed my opinion somewhat in the sense that I had seen the trees too much and not the forest. Even though these specific criticisms that I had made of Carter's conduct of foreign policy I still believed were accurate criticisms. But on second thoughts, after a few years, they seemed to me not so important. That the fact of emphasizing human rights was a much more important, in a positive sense, that any of the negative consequences of not doing it in what I thought was the best way." Muravchik, interview with author, March 21, 2000, American Enterprise Institute, Washington, D.C.
3. Thus, the perplexity of a Congressman who, during senate hearings, ingenuously expressed his confusion in the following manner: "various people have suggested to me that NED is a conservative program that I ought to be supporting. If that is so, why do I keep getting the post cards from South Carolina members of the conservative caucus urging me to stop funding of labor unions and activist groups — which I presume are the political party institutes as well as the one organized by the Chamber of Commerce — through NED?" U. S. Senate (1989: 605).
4. In the early 1990s, memoranda issued by conservative think tanks such as the libertarian Cato Institute (Conry 1993) or the neoconservative Heritage Foundation (Phillips and Holmes 1996) have taken up the issue and adopted divergent positions.
5. Reagan (1982). Earlier in his speech, the President presented, as elements of the ideological struggle against Communism, the emergence of neoliberal economics and the rightward drift of former leftists: "The hard evidence of totalitarian rule has caused in mankind an uprising of the intellect and will. Whether its is the growth of the new schools of economics in America or England or the appearance of the so-called new philosophers in France, there is one unifying thread running through the intellectual work of these groups — rejection of the arbitrary power of the state, the refusal to subordinate the rights of the individual to the superstate, the realization that collectivism stifles all the best human impulses."

6. The episode is narrated in Neier (2003), pp. 176–185.
7. Muravchik, interview.
8. Aryeh Neier correctly identifies this transformation when he writes that the Reagan administration "went from repudiating the human rights cause to embracing it, even while attempting to redefine it as the promotion of democracy" (2003, 187).
9. This transformation in the mode of political domination overlapped with a transformation of the mode of economic exploitation. As two sociologists have shown in a study of the changing forms of legitimation of capitalism, the new capitalism which has developed out the crisis of Fordism since the 1970s has systematically recycled to its own advantage the critique of capitalist exploitation of the 1960s and 1970s (Boltanski and Chiapello 1999).
10. Michael Hardt and Antonio Negri (2004) follow the same line of analysis and reach similar conclusions regarding the transformation of sovereign power.
11. See the interview with Lane Kirkland realized for the Cold War history project of George Washington University: http://www.gwu.edu/~nsarchiv/coldwar/interviews/episode-19/kirkland1.html
12. See ch. 1 n. 5.
13. In a political document written in 1973, Gershman thus writes that "the Cold War was not some scheme cooked up by imperialists in Washington but was and continues to be primarily the result of barriers erected by the East" (1973a: 3).
14. Labedz later became a member of the editorial board of the *Journal of Democracy*.
15. Freedom House was also a tax-exempt sponsor of the neoconservative journal *The Public Interest* (Steinfels 1979: 87). Freedom House was created in 1941 to provide "citizen support" for Roosevelt's efforts to engage the United States in the military conflict—in fact, at Roosevelt's request. After the war, the organization moved to Cold War anti-Communism and was instrumental in turning the concept of totalitarianism into a useful policy concept. The organization provided indeed legitimation: it acted as "a kind of moral compass for the government" (Korey 1998: 446). Freedom House maintained throughout the cold war an ideological line that was very close to that of the right-wing social democrats. In the 1980s, and especially after 1989, the institution espoused the neoconservative human rights doctrine and moved toward the promotion of democracy.
16. Gershman, interview, Washington, D.C., March 27, 2000.
17. Affiliated with the Hoover, Larry Diamond belongs to the younger generation of neoconservative scholars, while Seymour Martin Lipset belongs to the first (see chapter 3). The case of Juan Linz is more ambiguous, if only because this political scientist initially came from Spain to study in the U.S. Lipset, who was a young professor when Linz came to Columbia in 1950, recalls that "all

was not favorable in his background. He came . . . from Franco Spain, a nation and regime that was despised by . . . almost all the graduate students and faculty. Spaniards were wonderful if they had engaged in the civil war on the Loyalist side or if they were Loyalist émigrés. But Juan was neither and did not conceal his views. When he talked . . . about the conflict in Spain, it was one between the 'nationalists' and the 'reds'" (Lipset 1995: 3).

18. The NED maintains a database of experts which comprises all the members of the council.

19. The analyses that follow are based on the statistical treatment of the individual biographies of the Research Council members. I have collected data through a variety of sources — individual *vitae*, information available from personal web pages or rosters such as *Who's Who in America*, biographical notices, etc. For each member, I have also sought to measure with different indicators their "scientific capital": by making available number of times their work was quoted by others, the Social Science Citation Index provided a first rough indicator of scientific prestige. The number of publications has also been taken into account. I have also considered regular contributions to nonacademic journals or magazines, information which usually provides a clue as to political orientations. As most journals maintain an online archive of past issues mentioning authors, this information was readily available. I have also paid particular attention to the affiliation with think tanks or policy research centers, and to occasional advisory relations with state institutions or international organizations.

20. My analysis is the result of a more extensive statistical treatment known as homogeneity analysis. It makes it possible to represent under the form of a scatter-plot the spatial relations between different modalities of categorical variables. The closer two modalities, the more these properties tend to be associated, the further they are, the more the properties they represent tend to exclude each other. It is therefore possible to assess the social "proximity" between institutions, fields of research, etc. In order to avoid long developments, a presentation of the data and its step-by-step processing, I describe succinctly the major results of this analysis.

21. Packenham notes that between 1966 and 1989, "more than half of LASA's presidents . . . were forty-five or younger when they assumed office" (1992: 269–70).

22. Packenham, who stands as a conservative exception in the field of Latin American studies, recalls the "continuing, widespread barrage of hostile screams, shouts, and insults" that met James Cheek, Deputy Assistant Secretary of State for Inter-American Affairs, during a plenary session on Nicaragua held at the ninth LASA meeting, in 1980 (Packenham 1992: 278).

23. For instance, when the Association sent a delegation to observe the Nicaraguan elections of 1984, and released a report that denounced U.S. manipulation, the authors of the report, including then LASA president Wayne Cornelius,

hoped that such a publication "might have helped congressional opponents of President Reagan" (quoted in Packenham 1992: 286)

24. The NED, for instance, supported the "no" vote against Pinochet during the 1988 election in Chile. This episode constituted a turning-point in its relationship with a wider academic community. Its recruitment practices also became directed less by ideological considerations than by professional ones: in the early 1990s, it hired Michael Shifter, a former Ford foundation officer in Peru and Chile, as director of its Latin American and Caribbean program.

3. From the Development Engineers to the Democracy Doctors

1. I borrow the notion of "discourse coalition" from the work of Peter Wagner and Bjorn Wittrock (1987) on the relationships between the social sciences and the emergence of the modern state.

2. Along with area studies, this strategy included the support for, or creation of, more general centers of international affairs, such as: Harvard's Center for International Affairs, the Center for International Studies at MIT, Georgetown's Center for Strategic Studies, Berkeley's Institute of International Studies, and Princeton's Center for International Studies.

3. Packenham (1973: xvii). "Whereas I used to be moderately optimistic about the contributions that social science theories could make to policy and policymakers, I am now struck by the similarities between doctrines and theories and the relative poverty of the theories as guides to improvements in policy."

4. An example of these middle-men is Philip Mosely, head of Columbia's Russian Research Institute in the 1950s, member of several boards at the Ford Foundation, head of the Council of Foreign Relations (1952–1956), prominent leader of the American Political Science Association in the early 1950s, and top consultant of the CIA, where he had several clearances for agency work. See Cumings (1998).

5. "Wealth," for instance, includes among other things the number of radios, telephones and newspapers per thousand persons, or the number of persons to motor vehicles, thus denoting a middle-class pattern of consumption. (Lipset 1963: 33 ff).

6. Lazarsfeld (1969) retraces the making of the *Marienthal* study.

7. On the CDM, see Ehrman (1995).

8. Tilly (1975: 620), quoted in Cammack (1997: 168). Cammack also suggests that the failure to have produced a coherent theory of political development led, in this second period, to a relative retreat upon the study of European countries and Western developments, thus according less importance to the developing world at a theoretical level.

9. On Prebisch, see Lehmann (1990: 3–8); Sikkink (1991).

10. Among the most known *dependencistas,* one should mention Celso Furtado, Anibal Pinto, Osvaldo Sunkel.

11. David Dent writes that the criticisms emphasizing the provinciality of the discipline centered "on the need for political scientists [dealing with Latin America] to couch their analysis in terms of the fledgling concepts of political development and modernization while thriving toward greater methodological rigor and empirical quantification" (1990: 4).

12. According to Dent, "many political scientists, after spending time doing field work in Latin America, came to realize that their academic training in comparative politics or international relations was inadequate to understand fully the process of development and change in Latin America" (1990: 3).

13. On this topic see Martz (1966).

14. See Almond (1987: 455), who emphasizes the restrictions on research freedom.

15. This more liberal orientation appears even more clearly when one considers the domestic programs of the Ford, which sponsored neo-Marxist scholars as Bowles and Gintis, or became massively involved in civic rights activism by funding not only nonviolent, integrationist militants but also some 'Black power' groups (Berman: 1983). In Latin America, the involvement of the Ford Foundation with scholars of the left also served the purpose of extending social science research funding while overcoming the suspicions raised by the Ford's association with Cold War policies. It was eased by the difficult situation of left wing academics in Latin America, who needed to explore alliances that would have been difficult in the past, and by the intellectual and practical solidarity of their North American colleagues (Dezalay and Garth 2002; Valenzuela 1988)

16. After Vietnam, influential members of the Establishment such as executive officers of the Ford Foundation, or Henry Kissinger, openly questioned the conventional developmental wisdom (Berman 1983: 123).

17. Lehmann thus notes that O'Donnell in the early 1980s, "may not want to give too much rein to the ideas ... implied in his theoretical statements — that formal institutional democracy falls far short of guaranteeing a reasonable distribution of economic opportunities" (1989: 196). He also suggests that the abandoning of structuralism also entails the retrieval of support for the "shop-floor agitation of the early 1970s" which was its correlate political strategy (ibid.: 196–97).

18. Other major donors for social science research pursued objectives similar to those of the Ford Foundation. For the programs of the Swedish Agency for Research Cooperation with Developing Countries (SAREC) — also very active — see OECD (1992).

19. Quoted in Puryear (1983: 53). The retreat in private research centers also fostered among academics the development of managerial skills in terms of or-

ganization, administration, and fund-raising, as Puryear as recalled in his summary of his experience as a Ford Foundation officer (Puryear 1983).

20. "The collapse of popular regimes in much of Latin America made research
access much more difficult for both American and indigenous scholars."
(Almond 1987, 455).

21. Collier and Levitsky (1997) thus try to put some order in the proliferation of
"adjectives" surrounding the word democracy and to circumscribe a domain
of conceptual validity.

22. Some political scientists, not surprisingly affiliated with the NED's Research
Council, have suggested that 'getting the political institutions right' "may become the new mantra of political adjustment, and corollary of the mantra of
economic adjustment, i.e., 'getting the prices right.'" (Barkan 1997: 402).

4. Democratization Studies and the Construction of a New Orthodoxy

1. In the introduction to the volume on Latin America, O'Donnell writes indeed
that the arguments "may apply to all cases of nonrevolutionary regime transition
in countries that have a more than minimally activated popular sector and a
reasonably complex capitalist economy" (1986: 5). He adds that the choice of
studying only nonrevolutionary transitions stemmed from normative endorsement of political democracy.

2. Lowenthal, phone interview with author, May 2001.

3. Ibid.

4. Sol Linowitz served as ambassador at the Organization of American States
under President Johnson, and as chief negotiator of the Panama Canal Treaties
under President Carter. He was also Carter's envoy during the Middle East
peace talks. After graduating from Cornell Law School in 1938, Linowitz
worked as a lawyer in Rochester, New York, where he returned after serving in
Washington during the war. In 1948, acting in his capacity as a lawyer, he
assisted a friend in buying option rights under the patents for electrophotog-
raphy, a process that was then being developed, and that led to the creation of
the Xerox copy machine. Vice-president of Haloid-Xerox in 1953, Linowitz
became chairman of Xerox in 1959 and later chairman of the board.

5. For an overview of the project background, see the foreword by Lowenthal in
O'Donnell, Schmitter, and Whitehead (1986).

6. A decision all the more surprising, given that for many in this generation of
Latin American scholars, "the theme of development began to be accompanied
or replaced by the theme of revolution or fundamental structural change, and
in that context, transition meant the movement from capitalism to socialism"
(Garretón 1988: 358). On the notion of 'transition' within Marxism and, later,
democratization studies, see Guilhot (2001).

7. "If we are not in, they will manage to make the republic. If we want everything to remain the same, everything must change." Lampedusa (1995 [1957]: 41)
8. Przeworski suggests that "these conclusions [i.e. the necessity of trade-offs between political liberalization and economic stability] drew the accusation that they were unduly conservative. Such retrospective evaluations are easy to support, particularly for observers tucked safely away within the walls of North American academia. Indeed, for many protagonists, the central political issue at the time was whether their struggle should be simultaneously for political and economic transformation or only about political issues. Should it be for democracy and socialism simultaneously, or should democracy be striven for as a goal in itself? And the answer given in their political practice by most of the forces that turned out to be historically relevant was resolutely that democracy was an autonomous value, worth economic and social compromises that successful strategies to bring it about engendered" (Przeworski: 1991, 98).
9. The Coalition for a Democratic Majority comprised democrats "who espouse traditional liberalism on domestic issues but are hard line conservatives on foreign policy" (Finger 1988: 297). Blumenthal (1986: 128), defines it as the "neoconservative party shadow." Among the members of the Coalition were Daniel Bell, Nathan Glazer, Seymour Martin Lipset, Norman Podhoretz, Richard Pipes, Albert Shanker.
10. Richard Falk is probably the main exponent of this line of thinking within the "new foreign policy establishment."
11. Kirkpatrick thus writes in direct, if implicit, reference to Lipset: "Two or three decades ago, when Marxism enjoyed its greatest prestige among American intellectuals, it was the economic prerequisites of democracy that were emphasized by social scientists. Democracy, they argued, could function only in relatively rich societies with an advanced economy, a substantial middle class, and a literate population" (Kirkpatrick 1979: 37).
12. The same can be said of some of O'Donnell's analyses of the authoritarian state. To the extent that the BA coalitions are cemented by their fear of popular activation, the chances of liberalization (dependent on the fragmentation of the ruling coalition) are inversely proportional to the level of popular protest. The successful strategy toward democracy, therefore, would have to be based on the containment of popular demands and the moderation of the left. Such strategic considerations, as one can see, are easily compatible with the doctrine espoused by Kirkpatrick and followed by the Reagan administration.
13. Rostow had indeed subtitled his book *The Stages of Economic Growth* (1960) "A non-Communist Manifesto."
14. This is the "new left" interpretation of trilateralism (see for instance Sklar 1980) that would later inform the analyses seeing it as a redefinition of American power under the form of "hegemony", notably in the academic production of the so-called "Neo-Gramscian" school. See Gill (1990).

15. On the rise of technocratic expertise and the critique of technocracy, see Fischer (1990)
16. Once again, the short work of Lipset on "Economic Development and Democracy" (1963) provides the best example of such an approach.
17. The World Bank actually supported the project that resulted into Haggard and Kaufman's *The Politics of Economic Adjustment* (1992: xiii) and Haggard and Webb's *Voting for Reform* (1994: xiii). On the relations between economists and political scientists at the World Bank, see chapter 6.
18. Created in 1959 with funding from the Ford Foundation by Robert Maynard Hutchins, then chancellor of the University of Chicago, the Center for the Study of Democratic Institutions was a think-tank gathering academics and public figures of the West Coast.

5. International Relations Theory and the Emancipatory Narrative of Human Rights Networks

1. On the cosmopolitical tradition and its contemporary revival, see Zolo (1995) for a theoretical discussion. All the literature on "global governance" can be related to this tradition. Cassese refers human rights activism almost explicitly to the cosmopolitical tradition when he observes that "human rights are based on an expansive desire to unify the world by drawing up a list of guidelines for all governments" (1990: 158).
2. I here paraphrase Foucault, who suggested this definition of human rights as "rights opposed to every possible [form of] government" (1994: 349).
3. For an overview of this body of theory and a definition, see Wendt (1999: 94ff).
4. By the same token, this branch of international relations theory has also moved very closely to the history of ideas, as recent works suggest, such as Sikkink's (1991) on "developmentalism" or Hall's (1989) on Keynesianism. The problem — not yet solved — is to decide whether this leads to a neo-Kantian history of ideas or to a history of discursive practices (exemplified by J.G.A. Pocock and Q. Skinner).
5. The early debate on "epistemic communities" is a good illustration of this "technical" bias of the concern with the transnational: see Haas, Williams and Babai (1977).
6. Richard Falk has thus observed that human rights did not really fit the managerial agenda of trilateralism: "human rights diplomacy was at odds with the managerial imperatives of the soft approach to post-Vietnam adjustment, which aimed to improve the efficiency of the world economy and to diminish ideological rivalries" (Falk 1983: 134). This 'non-ideological' conception of transnational relations was challenged by the New Left (e.g. Sklar 1980).

7. See Nye and Keohane (1971:740). Huntington (1973) has made the same point, showing how the apparent "decline" of American power was based on a narrowly governmental view and compensated by a wider and more diffuse hegemony. That a CIA consultant (Nye) and a National Security Council adviser (Huntington) could emphasize the "usefulness" of transnational actors for governmental purposes is a very significant indicator of the constitutive ambiguity of this category.

8. "Moral/ideological incentives suffice to overcome the collective action problem." (Burgerman 1998:: 909).

9. I draw here on Quentin Skinner's discussion of the naturalist and anti-naturalist theses regarding the explanation of social action, and his distinction between causal and non-causal explanations, respectively related to motives as opposed to intentions. Skinner (1988: 79–96). For a broader overview of these debates, see Bohman (1991).

10. This anti-sociological bias is salient if one considers the evolution of this research program. Earlier works dealing with the political use of cognitive resources, such as those of Haas focusing on "epistemic communities,"(P. Haas 1992) were still dealing with a socially embedded agency, such as experts occupying specific positions and entrenching technical, scientific, and ethical discourses in this institutional environment. Potentially, this could have led to an interesting sociology of experts in which the "power of ideas" was not separate from the power of ideological agents. But subsequent theorizing ignored this and chose to isolate "ideas" as independent (in the strictest sense) "variables." As Yee argues, "the epistemic communities approach neglects these ideational qualities *that enable ideas themselves to affect policies.* Instead, the causal effects of ideas on policies are displaced onto the political effects of experts."

11. While borrowing from the notion of epistemic communities, more recent theories have indeed taken as their assumption the independent existence of ideas, and their capacity for self-realization, either by becoming "encased" or "embedded" within institutions or through the mediation of dedicated advocates who, as we have seen, coalesce under the impetus of cogent ideas.

12. See Kathryn Sikkink's (1991) study on the ideas that made up "developmentalism."

13. For a useful classification and analysis of these different labels, see Stone (1996).

6. *Financing the Construction of "Market Democracies"*

1. It is hard to overstate the efforts made by the higher echelons to turn the Bank into an activist, progressive, user-friendly organization. James Wolfensohn certainly made the boldest pronouncements: "we can say that we care, that we can cry about poverty, that we can laugh when people have a good time, that

we can embrace our clients, that we can feel part of them, where we can tell our kids we made a difference" (*Financial Times*, March 29, 1996, p. 4).

2. Woods himself had chaired the First Boston Corporation, while Eugene Black had been vice president of the Chase National Bank. These two banking institutions were the largest subscribers of the very safe World Bank bonds, rated "triple A."

3. In a calculation meant to stress the weight of economists within the Bank, Bank officer George Baldwin has shown that in 1982 the institution had between 50 and 60 tons of economists. But, he added, "if you shadow-price their weight, their 'social weight' . . . is a lot more than their nominal weight. Might even be more than 100 tons" (Baldwin 1986, 67).

4. Walter Salant (1989: 49) also observes that "economic ideas and practices in the 1960s represented a high point in the acceptance of Keynesian doctrines by government and private concerns in the United States."

5. Structural adjustment loans were, actually, an invention of McNamara. The first loan of this kind was extended to Turkey in 1979–1980. It was seen, however, as a form of "exceptional" loan. As a rule, the Bank set a limit of 10 percent of its lending volume for such operations. After the debt crisis and the "normalization" of structural adjustment, program lending would represent 25–30 percent of the Bank's operations. According to Shihata (1991), SAL represented 29 percent of Bank lending in 1989. This figure, however, does not include the abusive use of several simultaneous project loans to the same country meant to funnel more funds without falling into the category of "structural adjustment."

6. A point emphasized by all his biographers. See for instance Kraske (1996: 173). Senator Barry Goldwater nicknamed him an "IBM machine with legs." Cited in Caufield (1996: 96).

7. Wolfensohn has been extremely successful in turning this auto-critique into a proof that the Bank is an institution "prepared to listen, to learn, and to participate" (Wolfensohn 1998).

8. An NGO such as the International NGO Training Center (INTRAC), based in Oxford, has for instance specialized in the production of expertise for other NGOs. It organizes workshops which are a meeting place for nongovernmental activists and multilateral institutions, publishes books that even find their way onto academic library shelves (Clayton 1994) and 'sells' this useful expertise to organizations competing on this expanding market.

Bibliography

Aaron, Henry J. 1978. *Politics and the Professors: The Great Society in Perspective.* Washington, D.C.: The Brookings Institution.

Adler, J. H. 1972. "The World Bank's Concept of Development: An In-House *Dogmengeschichte.*" In Jagdish Bhagwati and Richard S. Eckaus, eds. *Development and Planning: Essays in Honour of Paul Rosenstein Rodan.* London: Allen & Unwin, pp. 30–50.

Ake, Claude. 1996. *Democracy and Development in Africa.* Washington, D.C.: The Brookings Institution.

Almond, Gabriel. 1960. "Introduction: A Functional Approach to Comparative Politics." In Gabriel A. Almond, and James S. Coleman, eds. *The Politics of the Developing Areas.* Princeton: Princeton University Press, pp. 3–64.

———. 1987. "The Development of Political Development." In Samuel P. Huntington, and Myron Weiner, eds. *Understanding Political Development.* Prospect Heights: Waveland Press.

Alston, Philip. 1981. "Prevention versus Cure as a Human Rights Strategy." In *Development, Human Rights, and the Rule of Law: Report of a Conference held in The Hague on 27 April – 1 May 1981.* International Commission of Jurists. Oxford: Pergamon Press.

Arendt, Hannah. 1961. *The Origins of Totalitarianism.* London: Allen and Unwin.

———. 1963. *On Revolution.* London: Penguin.

Arnove, Robert F. 1980. "Foundations and the Transfer of Knowledge." In Robert F. Arnove, ed. *Philanthropy and Cultural Imperialism: The Foundations at Home and Abroad.* Boston: G.. K. Hall & Co., pp. 305–30.

Ascher, William. 1996. "The Evolution of Postwar Doctrines in Development Economics." In A. W. Coats, ed. *The Post-1945 Internationalization of Economics.* Annual Supplement to Volume 28, *History of Political Economy.* Durham: Duke University Press.

Baldwin, George B. 1986. "Economics and Economists in the World Bank." In A. W. Coats, ed. *Economists in International Agencies: An Exploratory Study*. New York: Praeger, pp. 67–90.

Barkan, Joel D. 1994. "Resurrecting Modernization Theory and the Emergence of Civil Society in Kenya and Nigeria." In David Apter and Carl Rosberg, eds. *Political Development and the New Realism in Sub-Saharan Africa*. Charlottesville: University Press of Virginia, pp. 87–116.

———. 1997. "Can Established Democracies Nurture Democracy Abroad? Lessons from Africa." In Axel Hadenius, ed. *Democracy's Victory and Crisis*. Cambridge: Cambridge University Press, pp. 371–403.

Barrow, Clyde W. 1993. *Critical Theories of the State: Marxist, Neo-Marxist, Post-Marxist*. Madison: The University of Wisconsin Press.

Becker, Gary S. 1990. In Richard Swedberg, ed. *Economics and Sociology*. Princeton: Princeton University Press, pp. 27–46.

Becker, Howard S. 1963. *Outsiders: Studies in the Sociology of Deviance*. New York: The Free Press.

Bell, Daniel. 1960. *The End of Ideology*. Glencoe: The Free Press.

———. 1976. "Creating a Genuine National Society." *Current* (September): 18–19.

Berg, Elliot, and Allan Batchelder. 1985. *Structural Adjustment Lending: A Critical View*. CPD discussion paper n. 1985–21. The World Bank, Washington, D.C.

Berger, Peter L. 1981. "Human Rights and American Foreign Policy." *Commentary* 72, no. 5: 27–29.

Berghahn, Volker R. 2001. *America and the Intellectual Cold Wars in Europe*. Princeton: Princeton University Press.

Berman, Edward H. 1983. *The Ideology of Philanthropy: The Influence of the Carnegie, Ford, and Rockefeller Foundations on American Foreign Policy*. Albany: State University of New York Press.

Bermeo, Nancy. 1990. "Rethinking Regime Change." *Comparative Politics*: 359–77.

Bird, Kai. 1998. *The Color of Truth: McGeorge Bundy and William Bundy: Brothers in Arms*. New York: Simon and Schuster.

Bloom, Alexander. 1986. *Prodigal Sons: The New York Intellectuals and their World*. Oxford: Oxford University Press.

Blumenthal, Sidney. 1986. *The Rise of the Counter-Establishment: From Conservative Ideology to Political Power*. New York: Times Books.

Bohman, James. 1991. *New Philosophy of Social Science*. Cambridge: Polity Press.

Boltanski, Luc. 1973. "L'espace positionnel: Multiplicité des positions institutionnelles et habitus de classe." *Revue Française De Sociologie*, no. XIV: 3–26.

Boltanski, Luc, and Eve Chiapello. 1999. *Le nouvel esprit du capitalisme*. Paris: Gallimard.

Botero, Giovanni. 1997. *La ragion di stato*. Roma: Donzelli Editore.

Bourdieu, Pierre. 1990. *In Other Words: Essays Towards a Reflexive Sociology*. Cambridge: Polity Press.

———. 1997. *Méditations pascaliennes*. Paris: Editions du Seuil.

Bourdieu, Pierre, and Loïc Wacquant. 1992. *An Invitation to Reflexive Sociology*. Chicago: The University of Chicago Press.

Bovard, James. 1987. "The World Bank vs. the World's Poor." *Policy Analysis*, no. 92. September 28, 1987. Cato Institute, Washington, D.C.

Bratton, Michael, and Nicolas van de Walle. 1997. *Democratic Experiments in Africa: Regime Transitions in Comparative Perspective*. Cambridge: Cambridge University Press.

Bretton Woods Commission. 1994. *Bretton Woods: Looking to the Future. Conference Proceedings, Washington DC, July 20–22, 1994*. Washington D.C.: Bretton Woods Committee.

Brick, Howard. 1986. *Daniel Bell and the Decline of Intellectual Radicalism: Social Theory and Political Reconciliation in the 1940s*. Madison: University of Wisconsin Press.

———. 1998. *Age of Contradiction: American Thought and Culture in the 1960s*. New York: Twayne.

Bromley, Simon. 1995. "Making Sense of Structural Adjustment." *Review of African Political Economy* 65: 339-48.

Brumberg, Abraham. 1993. "Leo Labedz: An Appreciation of an Early Consultant to the *Journal of Contemporary History*." *Journal of Contemporary History* 28, no. 3: 553–55.

Brunner, Jose Joaquin, and Alicia Barrios. 1987. *Inquisición, Mercado y Filantropia: Ciencias Sociales y Autoritarismo en Argentina, Brasil, Chile, y Uruguay*. Santiago: FLACSO.

Brzezinski, Zbigniew. 1970. *Between Two Ages: America's Role in the Technetronic Era*. New York: Viking.

Burgerman, Susan D. 1998. "Mobilizing Principles: The Role of Transnational Activists in Promoting Human Rights Principles." *Human Rights Quarterly* 20, no. 4: 905–23.

Burnham, James. 1941. *The Managerial Revolution: What is Happening in the World*. New York: John Day.

Cammack, Paul. 1997. *Capitalism and Democracy in the Third World: The Doctrine for Political Development*. London and Washington: Leicester University Press.

Cardoso, Fernando Henrique. 1986. "Entrepreneurs and the Transition Process: The Brazilian Case." In Guillermo O'Donnell, Philippe C. Schmitter, and Laurence Whitehead, eds. *Transitions from Authoritarian Rule. Comparative Perspectives*. Vol. 4. Baltimore: The Johns Hopkins University Press, 137–53.

Carothers, Thomas. 2000. "Democracy Promotion: A Key Focus in a New World Order." *Issues of Democracy* 5, no. 1: 23–28.

Cassese, Antonio. 1990. *Human Rights in a Changing World*. Cambridge: Polity Press / Basil Blackwell.

Caufield, Catherine. 1996. *Masters of Illusion: The World Bank and the Poverty of Nations*. New York: Holt.

Cavell, Colin S. 2002. *Exporting 'Made in America' Democracy: The National Endowment for Democracy and U.S. Foreign Policy*. Lanham: University Press of America.

Centeno, Miguel A., and Patricio Silva, eds. 1998. *The Politics of Expertise in Latin America*. New York: St. Martin's Press.

Cernea, Michael M. 1991. *Using Knowledge from Social Science in Development Projects*, n. 114 World Bank Discussion Papers. The World Bank, Washington, D.C.

Chossudovsky, Michel. 1997. *Impacts of IMF and World Bank Reforms*. Penang: Third World Network.

Ciment, James, and Immanuel Ness. 1999. "NED and the Empire's New Clothes." *Covert Action Quarterly*, no. 67: 65–69.

Clayton, Andrew, ed. 1994. *Governance, Democracy and Conditionality: What Role for NGOs?* Oxford: Intrac.

Clough, Michael. 1994. "Grass-Roots Policymaking: Say Goodbye to the 'Wise Men'." *Foreign Affairs* (January–February): 2–7.

Coeurdray, Murielle. 2003. *Du dévoilement de la « corruption » à la gestion déontologique des affaires. Contribution à une sociologie des effets de l'internationalisation sur le champ du pouvoir économique*. Ph.D. thesis. Paris: Ecole des Hautes Etudes en Sciences Sociales.

Coleman, Peter. 1989. *The Liberal Conspiracy: The Congress for Cultural Freedom and the Struggle for the Mind in Postwar Europe*. New York: The Free Press.

Collier, David, and Steven Levitsky. 1997. "Democracy with Adjectives: Conceptual Innovation in Comparative Research." *World Politics* 49, no. 3: 430–452.

Collins, Randall. 1979. *The Credential Society: A Historical Sociology of Education and Stratification*. New York: Academic Press.

Connolly, William E. 1983. *The Terms of Political Discourse*. 2nd ed. Oxford: Martin Robertson.

Conry, Barbara. 1993. *Loose Cannon: The National Endowment for Democracy*. Foreign Policy Briefing No. 27. Cato Institute, Washington, DC.

Cooney, Terry A. 1986. *The Rise of the New York Intellectuals: Partisan Review and Its Circle*. Madison: University of Wisconsin Press.

Cooper, Frederick, and Randall Packard, eds. 1997. *International Development and the Social Sciences: Essays on the History and Politics of Knowledge*. Berkeley: University of California Press.

Corn, David. 1993. "Beltway Bandits." *The Nation* (July 12): 56.

Coser, Lewis. 1984. *Refugee Scholars in America: Their Impact and Their Experiences*. New Haven: Yale University Press.

Cox, Robert W. 1987. *Production, Power, and World Orders: Social Forces in the Making of History.* New York: Columbia University Press.

Craver, Earlene, and Axel Leijonhufvud. 1987. "Economics in America: The Continental Influence." *History of Political Economy* 19, no. 2: 173–82.

Crawford, Gordon. 1996. *Promoting Democracy, Human Rights, and Good Governance Through Development Aid: A Comparative Study of the Policies of Four Northern Donors.* Leeds: Center for Democratization Studies, University of Leeds.

Cumings, Bruce. 1998. "Boundary Displacement: Area Studies and International Studies During and After the Cold War." In Christopher Simpson, ed. *Universities and Empire.* New York: The New Press, pp. 159–88.

Cunningham, Susan M. 1999. "Made in Brazil: Cardoso's Critical Path from Dependency via Neoliberal Options and the Third Way in the 1990s." *European Review of Latin American and Caribbean Studies,* no. 67: 75–86.

Dahl, Robert A. 1961. "The Behavioral Approach in Political Science: Epitaph for a Monument to a Successful Protest." *The American Political Science Review* 55, no. 4: 763–72.

Dauvin, Pascal, and Johanna Siméant. 2002. *Le travail humanitaire: Les acteurs des ONG, du siège au terrain.* Paris: Presses de Sciences Po.

Delaunay, Jean-Claude. 1996. "Distinction hétérodoxe et champ économique." *Economies Et Sociétés* no. 2: 143–55.

Dent, David W. 1990. "Introduction: Political Science Research on Latin America." In David W. Dent, ed. *Handbook of Political Science Research on Latin America: Trends from the 1960s to the1990s.* New York: Greenwood Press, pp. 1–21.

de Soto, Hernando. 1989. *The Other Path: The Invisible Revolution in the Third World.* London: I. B. Tauris.

de Vries, Barend A. 1996. "The World Bank as an International Player in Economic Analysis." In A. W. Coats, ed. *The Post-1945 Internationalization of Economics.* Annual Supplement to Volume 28, *History of Political Economy.* Durham: Duke University Press.

Dewey, John. 1939. *Freedom and Culture.* New York: Putnam.

Dezalay, Yves, and Bryant Garth. 1998a. "Le 'Washington consensus': contribution à une sociologie de l'hégémonie du néolibéralisme." *Actes De La Recherche En Sciences Sociales,* no. 121–122: 3–22.

———. 1998b. "Droits de l'homme et philanthropie hégémonique." *Actes De La Recherche En Sciences Sociales,* no. 121–122: 23–42.

———. 2002. *The Internationalization of Palace Wars: Lawyers, Economists and the Contest to Transform Latin American States.* Chicago: University of Chicago Press.

Diamond, Larry. 1996. *Promoting Democracy in the 1990s: Actors and Instruments, Issues and Imperatives.* Washington, D.C.: Carnegie Corporation of New York.

Diamond, Larry and Gary Marks, eds. 1992. *Reexamining Democracy. Essays in Honor of Seymour Martin Lipset*. Newbury Park: Sage.

Diamond, Larry J., Juan J. Linz, and Seymour Martin Lipset, eds. 1988. *Democracy in Developing Countries*. Boulder: Lynne Rienner.

Dias, Clarence J. 1994. "Governance, Democracy and Conditionality: NGO Positions and Roles." In *Governance, Democracy and Conditionality: What Role for NGOs?* Oxford: INTRAC.

Diggins, John P. 1975. *Up from Communism: Conservative Odysseys in American Intellectual History*. New York: Harper & Row.

Di Lampedusa, Tomasi. 1995. *Il gattopardo*. 66 ed. Milano: Feltrinelli.

Di Palma, Giuseppe. 1990. *To Craft Democracies: An Essay on Democratic Transitions*. Berkeley and Los Angeles: University of California Press.

Dobkin Hall, Peter. 1992. *Inventing the Nonprofit Sector and Other Essays on Philanthropy, Voluntarism, and Nonprofit Organizations*. Baltimore: The Johns Hopkins University Press.

Domínguez, Jorge. 1982. "Consensus and Divergence: The State of the Literature on Inter-American Relations in the 1970s." *Latin American Research Review* 13, no. 2: 87–126.

———, ed. 1997. *Technopols: Freeing Politics and Markets in Latin America in the 1990s*. University Park: University of Pennsylvania Press.

———. 1998. *Democratic Politics in Latin America and the Caribbean*. Baltimore: The Johns Hopkins University Press.

dos Santos, Theotônio. 1998. "The Theoretical Foundations of the Cardoso Government: A New Stage of the Dependency-Theory Debate." *Latin American Perspectives* 25, no. 98: 53–70.

Drucker, Peter. 1994. *Max Shachtman: A Socialist's Odyssey Through the "American Century."* Amherst: Humanity Books.

Eastman, Max. 1945. "The Notion of Democratic Socialism: Can Planned Economy and Private Enterprise Co-Exist?" *The New Leader*, February 10.

Ehrman, John. 1995. *The Rise of Neo-conservatism: Intellectuals and Foreign Affairs 1945–1994*. New Haven: Yale University Press.

Eisenstadt, Schmuel N. 1985. "Macro-societal analysis: Background, Development and Indications." In S. N. Eisenstadt, and H. J. Helle, eds. *Macro-Sociological Theory: Perspectives on Sociological Theory*. Volume 1. London: Sage, pp. 7–24.

Evans, Peter. 2000. "Fighting Marginalization with Transnational Networks: Counter-Hegemonic Globalization." *Contemporary Sociology* 29, no. 1: 230–241.

Evans, Tony. 1996. *U.S. Hegemony and the Project of Universal Human Rights*. Basingstoke: Macmillan.

———, ed. 1998. *Human Rights Fifty Years On: A Reappraisal*. Manchester: Manchester University Press.

Fairbanks, Charles H. 1980a. "Designing a New Human Rights Policy for the Reagan Administration." The President-Elect's Transition Office.

———. 1980b. "Questions and Answers." Unpublished document written for the Reagan campaign.

———. 1989. "Human Rights." In Charles L. Heatherly, and Burton Yale Pines, eds. *Mandate for Leadership III: Policy Strategies for the 1990s*. Washington, D.C.: Heritage Foundation.

Falk, Richard. 1983. "Lifting the Curse of Bipartisanship." *World Policy Journal* 1, no. 1: 127–57.

Finger, Seymour Maxwell. 1988. *American Ambassadors at the UN: People, Politics, and Bureaucracy in Making Foreign Policy*. New York: Holmes and Meier.

Finnemore, Martha. 1997. "Redefining Development at the World Bank." In Frederick Cooper, and Randall Packard, eds. *International Development and the Social Sciences: Essays on the History and Politics of Knowledge*. Berkeley: University of California Press, pp. 203–207.

Fischer, Donald. 1993. *Fundamental Development of the Social Sciences: Rockefeller Philanthropy and the United States Social Science Research Council*. Ann Arbor: The University of Michigan Press.

Fischer, Frank. 1990. *Technocracy and the Politics of Expertise*. London: Sage Publications.

———, and John Forester, eds. 1993. *The Argumentative Turn in Policy Analysis and Planning*. Durham Duke University Press.

Fischer, Louis. 1947. "How to Prevent World War III." *The New Leader*, June 21.

Foot, Rosemary. 2000. *Rights Beyond Border: The Global Community and the Struggle over Human Rights in China*. Oxford: Oxford University Press.

Foucault, Michel. 1994. *Dits et Ecrits*, Vol. IV, 1980–1988. Paris: Gallimard.

Fox, Jonathan, and David L. Brown. 1998. *The Struggle for Accountability: The World Bank, NGOs, and Grassroots movements*. Cambridge: MIT Press.

Franck, Thomas M. 1992. "The Emerging Right to Democratic Governance." *The American Journal of International Law* 86, no. 1: 46–91.

Frischtak, Leila L. 1994. *Governance Capacity and Economic Reform in Developing Countries*. World Bank Technical Paper Number 254. The World Bank, Washington, D.C.

Fukuyama, Francis. 1992. *The End of History and the Last Man*. New York: Free Press.

Füredi, Frank. 1994. *The New Ideology of Imperialism*. London: Pluto Press.

Galtung, Johan. 1979. "After Camelot." In Johan Galtung, ed. *Papers on Methodology* Vol. II. Copenhagen: Christian Ejlers, pp. 161-79.

Garretón, Manuel Antonio. 1988. "Problems of Democracy in Latin America: On the Processes of Transition and Consolidation." *International Journal* 43: 357–77.

Gastil, Raymond D. 1988. "Aspects of a U.S. Campaign for Democracy." In Ralph

M. Goldman, and William A. Douglas, eds. *Promoting Democracy: Opportunities and Issues*. New York: Praeger, 25–50.

Geiger, Roger L. 1988. "American Foundations and Academic Social Science, 1945–1960." *Minerva* 26, no. 3: 315–41.

George, Susan, and Fabrizio Sabelli. 1994. *Crédits sans frontières: la religion séculaire de la Banque Mondiale*. Paris: La Découverte.

Gerbier, Bernard. 1996. "Orthodoxie et hétérodoxie économiques: le couple infernal." *Economies Et Sociétés* , no. 2: 193–201.

Gershman, Carl. 1969a. "Isolation of the New Left." *The Nation*, May 26: 666–68.

———. 1969b. "SDS, or the New Thermidor." *Pittsburgh Point*, June 5: 5.

———. 1972a. "Labor's Stand on McGovern." *The New Leader*, September 4: 10–12.

———. 1972b. "Why I'm for Scoop Jackson, Coalition Politics, Social Justice and Peace (and Against Know-Nothingism)." Carl Gershman Papers, [Box 3]. Hoover Institution Archives.

———. 1973a. "The New YPSL". Carl Gershman Papers, [Box 2]. Hoover Institution Archives.

———. 1973b. "Revising Orwell & Solzhenitsyn." *Social Democrat*, Fall: 3–6.

———. 1976. "What is a Liberal — Who is a Conservative?" *Commentary* 62, September: 69–61.

———. 1978. "Capitalism, Socialism, and Democracy." *Commentary* 65, April: 43–45.

———. 1980. "The Rise & Fall of the New Foreign-Policy Establishment." *Commentary* 70, July: 13–24.

Gerson, Allan. 1991. *The Kirkpatrick Mission: Diplomacy Without Apology: America at the United Nations 1981–1985*. New York: The Free Press.

Gil, Federico. 1985. "Latin American Studies and Political Science: A Historical Sketch." *LASA Forum* 16, no. 2: 8–12.

Gill, Stephen. 1990. *American Hegemony and the Trilateral Commission*. Cambridge: Cambridge University Press.

———, ed. 1993. *Gramsci, Historical Materialism, and International Relations*. Cambridge: Cambridge University Press.

Gills, B., J. Rocamora, and R. Wilson, eds. 1993. *Low Intensity Democracy: Political Power in the New World Order*. London: Pluto Press.

Gleason, Abbott. 1995. *Totalitarianism: The Inner History of the Cold War*. Oxford: Oxford University Press.

Goetz, Anne Marie, and David O'Brien. 1995. "Governing for the Common Wealth? The World Bank's Approach to Poverty and Governance." *IDS Bulletin* 26, no. 2: 17–26.

Goldman, Ralph M. 1988. "Transnational Parties as Multilateral Civic Educators." In R.M. Goldman and W.M. Douglas, eds. *Promoting Democracy: Opportunities and Issues*. New York: Praeger.

————, and William A. Douglas, eds. 1988. *Promoting Democracy: Opportunities and Issues*. New York: Praeger.

Goldstein, Judith, and Robert O. Keohane, eds. 1993. *Ideas and Foreign Policy: Beliefs, Institutions and Political Change*. Ithaca: Cornell University Press.

Gottlieb, Robert. 1993. *Forcing the Spring: The Transformation of the American Environmental Movement*. Washington, DC: Island Press.

Gramsci, Antonio. 1991. *Gli intellettuali e l'organizzazione della cultura*. Roma: Editori Riuniti.

Grémion, Pierre. 1995. *Intelligence de l'anticommunisme: Le Congrès pour la liberté de la culture à Paris 1950–1975*. Paris: Fayard.

Grew, Raymond, ed. 1978. *Crisis of Political Development in Europe and the United States*. Princeton: Princeton University Press.

Guilhot, Nicolas. 2002. "'The Transition to the Human World of Democracy.' Notes for a history of the concept of transition, from early Marxism to 1989." *European Journal of Social Theory*. 5, no. 2: 219–243.

Gunnell, John G. 1988. "American Political Science, Liberalism, and the Invention of Political Theory." *The American Political Science Review* 82, no. 1: 71–87.

Haas, Ernst B., Mary Pat Williams, and Don Babai. 1977. *Scientists and World Order: The Uses of Technical Knowledge in International Organizations*. Berkeley and Los Angeles: University of California Press.

Haas, Peter. 1992. "Introduction: Epistemic Comunities and International Policy Coordination." *International Organization* 46, no. 1: 1–36.

————, and Robert R. Kaufman. 1992. "Economic Adjustment and the Prospects for Democracy." In Stephan Haggard, and Robert R. Kaufman, eds. *The Politics of Economic Adjustment. International Constraints, Distributive Conflicts, and the State*. Princeton: Princeton University Press, pp. 319–50.

Haggard, Stephan, and Robert R. Kaufman, eds. 1992. *The Politics of Economic Adjustment: International Constraints, Distributive Conflicts, and the State*. Princeton: Princeton University Press.

————, and Steven B. Webb, eds. 1994. *Voting for Reform: Democracy, Political Liberalization, and Economic Adjustment*. New York: Oxford University Press / The World Bank.

Hagopian, Frances. 1993. "After Regime Change: Authoritarian Legacies, Political Representation, and the Democratic Future of South America." *World Politics* 45, no. 3: 464–500.

Halberstam, David. 1972. *The Best and the Brightest*. London: Barrie & Jenkins.

Hall, Peter A., ed. 1989. *The Political Power of Economic Ideas: Keynesianism Across Nations*. Princeton: Princeton University Press.

Halpern, Manfred. 1963. *The Politics of Social Change in the Middle East and North Africa*. Princeton: Princeton University Press.

Hardt, Michael, and Antonio Negri. 2000. *Empire*. Cambridge: Harvard University Press.

————. 2004. *Multitude*. New York: Penguin.

Heclo, Hugh. 1978. "Issue Networks and the Executive Establishment." In Anthony King, ed. *The New American Political System*. Washington, D.C.: American Enterprise Institute for Public Policy Research, pp. 87–124.

Held, David, and Daniele Archibugi, eds. 1995. *Cosmopolitan Democracy: An Agenda for a New World Order*. Cambridge, MA: Polity Press.

Heper, Metin. 1991. "Transitions to Democracy Reconsidered: A Historical Perspective." In Dankwart A. Rustow, and Kenneth Paul Erickson, eds. *Comparative Political Dynamics: Global Research Perspectives*. New York: Harper-Collins, pp. 192–210.

Hirschman, Albert O. 1989. "How the Keynesian Revolution Was Exported from the United States and Other Comments." In Peter A. Hall, ed. *The Political Power of Economic Ideas: Keynesianism across Nations*. Princeton: Princeton University Press, pp. 347–59.

Hodge, Merle, and Eloise Magenheim. 1994. "Women, Structural Adjustment and Empowerment." In Kevin Danaher, ed. *50 years is enough: the case against the World Bank and the International Monetary Fund*. Boston: South End Press.

Hodson, Roland. 1997. "Elephant Loose in the Jungle: The World Bank and NGOs in Sri Lanka." In David Hulme, and Michael Edwards, eds. *NGOs, States and Donors. Too Close for Comfort?* New York: St. Martin's Press / Save the Children, pp. 168–187.

Hook, Sidney. 1947. "The Future of Socialism." *Partisan Review*, January–February.

Hours, Bernard. 1998. *L'idéologie humanitaire ou le spectacle de l'altérité perdue*. Paris: L'Harmattan.

Huntington, Samuel P. 1965. "Political Development and Political Decay." *World Politics* 7, no. 3: 386–411.

————. 1973. "Transnational Organizations in World Politics." *World Politics* 25, no. 3: 333–68.

————. 1981. "Human Rights and American Power." *Commentary* 72, no. 3: 37–43.

————, and Joan M. Nelson. 1976. *No Easy Choice: Political Participation in Developing Countries*. Cambridge: Harvard University Press.

————, and Myron Weiner. 1987. *Understanding Political Development*. Prospect Heights: Waveland Press.

Hürni, Bettina S. 1980. *The Lending Policy of the World Bank in the 1970s: Analysis and Evaluation*. Boulder: Westview Press.

Hyden, Goran. 1992. "Governance and the Study of Politics." In David Hulme and Michael Edwards, eds. *Governance and Politics in Africa*. Boulder: Lynne Rienner, pp. 1–26.

————, and Michael Bratton, eds. 1992. *Governance and Politics in Africa*. Boulder: Lynne Rienner.

Hyman, Herbert Hiram. 1969 [1959]. *Political Socialization; A Study In The Psychology of Political Behavior*. New York: Free Press.

Isserman, Maurice. 1993. *If I Had a Hammer: The Death of the Old Left and the Birth of the New Left*. Urbana: University of Illinois Press.

Jacoby, Russell. 1987. *The Last Intellectuals: American Culture in the Age of Academe*. New York: Basic Books.

Kagan, Robert. 1998. "Democracy Promotion as an Objective of Foreign Policy." In *International Relation and Democracy*.

Kaldor, Mary. 2003. *Global Civil Society: An Answer to War*. Cambridge, MA: Polity Press.

Kapur, Devesh, John P. Lewis, and Richard Webb, eds. 1997. *The World Bank: Its First Half Century*. Washington, D.C.: Brookings Institution Press.

Katsiaficas, George. 1987. *The Imagination of the New Left: A Global Analysis of 1968*. Boston: South End Press.

Kaufman, Robert R. 1986. "Liberalization and Democratization in South America: Perspectives from the 1970s." In Guillermo O'Donnell, Philippe C. Schmitter, and Laurence Whitehead, eds. *Transitions from Authoritarian Rule: Comparative Perspectives*. Vol. 4. Baltimore: The Johns Hopkins University Press, pp. 85–107.

Keane, John. 2003. *Global Civil Society?* Cambridge: Cambridge University Press.

Keck, Margaret E., and Kathryn Sikkink. 1998. *Activists Beyond Borders: Advocacy Networks in International Politics*. Ithaca: Cornell University Press.

———. 1998b. "Transnational Advocacy Networks in International and Regional Politics." *International Social Science Journal* 51, no. 1: 89–101.

Kelsen, Hans. 1960. *Das Problem der Souveraenitaet und die Theorie des Voelkerrechts Beitrag zu einer reinen Rechtslehre*. Aalen: Scientia.

King, Anthony. 1978. *The New American Political System*. Washington, D.C.: American Enterprise Institute for Public Policy Research.

Kirkpatrick, Jeane. 1979. "Dictatorships and Double Standards." *Commentary*: 34–45.

———. 1979b. "Politics and the New Class." *Society*, January–February.

———. 1981. "Human Rights and American Foreign Policy." *Commentary* 72, no. 5: 42–45.

Koh, Harold Hongju. 1997. "Why Do Nations Obey International Law?" *Yale Law Journal*, no. 106: 2599–659.

Korey, William. 1999. *NGOs and the Universal Declaration of Human Rights*. London: Macmillan.

Kornhauser, William. 1960. *The Politics of Mass Society*. London: Routledge and Kegan Paul.

Kraske, Jochen. 1996. *Bankers with a Mission: The Presidents of the World Bank, 1946–91*. Oxford: Oxford University Press.

Kreindler, Charles. 1946. "A Foreign Policy for Organized Labor: Democracy in Asia as in Europe Depends on Labor." *The New Leader*, March 23.

Krohn, Claus-Dieter. 1993. *Intellectuals in Exile: Refugee Scholars and the New School for Social Research*. Amherst: University of Massachusetts Press.

Krugman, Paul. 1994. "The Fall and Rise of Development Economics." In Lloyd Rodwin, and Donald A. Schön, eds. *Rethinking the Development Experience: Essays Provoked by the Work of Albert O. Hirschman*. Washington, D.C.: The Brookings Institution and The Lincoln Institute of Land Policy.

Lal, Deepak. 1987. "The Political Economy of Economic Liberalization." *World Bank Economic Review*, no. 2.

Lancaster, Carol. 1993. "Governance and Development: The Views from Washington." *IDS Bulletin* 24, no. 1: 9–15.

Landell-Mills, Pierre. 1992. "Governance, Cultural Change, and Empowerment." *The Journal of African Studies* 30, no. 4: 543–67.

Lane, Robert E. 1966. "The Decline of Politics and Ideology in a Knowledgeable Society." *American Sociological Review* 32, no. 5: 649–62.

Lasch, Christopher. 1969. "The Cultural Cold War: A Short History of the Congress for Cultural Freedom." In Barton J. Bernstein, ed. *Towards a New Past: Dissenting Essays in American History*. New York: Vintage Books, pp. 322–59.

Lasky, Melvin. 1947. "Inside the Soviet Cultural Front." *The New Leader*, October 25.

Latham, Michael E. 1998. "Ideology, Social Science, and Destiny: Modernization and the Kennedy-Era Alliance for Progress." *Diplomatic History* 22, no. 2: 199–229.

Lazarsfeld, Paul. "An Episode in the History of Social Research: A Memoir." In Donald Fleming and Bernard Bailyn, eds. *The Intellectual Migration: Europe and America 1930–1960*. Cambridge: Harvard University Press, pp. 270–337.

Lehmann, David. 1989. "A Latin America Political Scientist: Guillermo O'Donnell." *Latin American Research Review*, no. 24: 187–200.

———. 1990. *Democracy and Development in Latin America: Economics, Politics and Religion in the Postwar Period*. Cambridge: Polity Press.

Leijonhufvud, Axel. 1973. "Life among the Econ." *Western Economic Journal*, no. 9: 327–37.

Lerner, Daniel, and Harold D. Lasswell. 1951. *The Policy Sciences*. Stanford: Stanford University Press.

Levine, D. 1988. "Paradigm Lost: Dependence on Democracy. *World Politics* 40, no. 3.

Levitt, Cyril. 1984. *Children of Privilege: Student Revolt in the Sixties*. Toronto: University of Toronto Press.

Liebowitz, Nathan. 1985. *Daniel Bell and the Agony of Modern Liberalism*. Westport: Greenwood Press.

Linz, Juan J., and Alfred Stepan. 1996. *Problems of Democratic Transition and Con-*

solidation: Southern Europe, South America and Post-Communist Europe. Baltimore: The Johns Hopkins University Press.

Lipset, Seymour Martin. 1960. *Political Man: The Social Bases of Politics.* London: Heinemann.

———. 1963. *Political Man: The Social Bases of Politics.* 2nd ed. New York: Anchor Books.

———. 1996a. *American Exceptionalism: a Double-Edged Sword.* New York: Norton.

———. 1995. "Juan Linz: Student, Colleague, Friend." In H. Chehabi, and Alfred Stepan, eds. *Politics, Culture, and Society: Essays in Honor of Juan Linz.* Boulder: Westview Press, pp. 1–9.

———. 1996b. "Transcript of Interview by Brian Lamb." *American Exceptionalism: A Double-Edged Sword.* C-SPAN, June 23, 1996.

Lowe, David. 2000. Idea to Reality: The National Endowment for Democracy at 15. Washington, D.C.

Lowenthal, Abraham. 1986. "Foreword." In Guillermo O'Donnell, Philippe C. Schmitter, and Laurence Whitehead, eds. *Transitions from Authoritarian Rule.* Baltimore: The Johns Hopkins University Press, pp. vii–x.

Luhmann, Niklas. 1981. "Die Organisationsmittel des Wohlfahrtsstaates und ihre Grenzen." *Zum Thema: Bürger und Bürokratie,* Inneminister des Landes Nordrhein-Westfalen.

MacGaffey, Janet. 1990. "The Endogenous Economy. In *The Long-Term Perspective Study of Sub-Saharan Africa.* World Bank vol. 3. Washington, D.C.: The World Bank.

Markwick, Roger D. 1996. A Discipline in Transition? From Sovietology to 'Transitology'. *Journal of Communist Studies and Transition Politics* 12, no. 3: 255–76.

Martz, John D. 1966. "The Place of Latin America in the Study of Comparative Politics." *The Journal of Politics* 28, no. 1: 57–80.

Mason, Edward, and Robert Asher. 1973. *The World Bank Since Bretton Woods.* Washington, D.C.: Brookings Institution.

Massing, Michael. 1987. "Trotsky's Orphans: From Bolshevism to Reaganism." *The New Republic,* June 22, pp. 18–22.

Mills, Charles Wright. 1959. *The Sociological Imagination.* London: Oxford University Press.

Mirowski, Philip. 2002. *Machine Dreams: Economics Becomes a Cyborg Science.* Cambridge: Cambridge University Press.

Moore, Mick. 1993a. "Declining to Learn from the East? The World Bank on 'Governance and Development'." *IDS Bulletin* 24, no. 1: 39–50.

———. 1993b. "The emergence of the 'Good Government' Agenda: Some Milestones." *IDS Bulletin* 24, no. 1: 1–8.

Morgan, Ted. 1999. *A Covert Life: Jay Lovestone: Communist, Anti-Communist, and Spymaster.* New York: Random House.

Mosley, P., J. Harrigan, and J. Toye. 1991. *Aid and Power: The World Bank and Policy-based Lending*. London: Routledge.

Muravchik, Joshua. 1986. *The Uncertain Crusade. Jimmy Carter and the Dilemmas of Human Rights Policy*. Washington, D.C.: American Enterprise Institute for Public Policy Research.

———. 1992. *Exporting Democracy: Fulfilling America's Destiny*. Washington, D.C.: AEI Press (American Enterprise Institute for Public Policy Research).

———. 2002. *Heaven on Earth: The Rise and Fall of Socialism*. San Francisco: Encounter Books.

National Endowment for Democracy. 1997. *Promoting Democracy in a Time of Austerity: NED's Strategy for 1997 and Beyond*, Washington, D.C.: NED.

———. 1998. *Annual Report 1998*. National Endowment for Democracy. Washington, D.C.: NED.

Neier, Aryeh. 2003. *Taking Liberties: Four Decades in the Struggle for Human Rights*. New York: Public Affairs.

Nelson, Joan M. 1995. *Is the Era of Conditionality Past? The Evolving Role of the World Bank in the 1990s*. Madrid: Instituto Juan March de Estudios e Investigaciones.

Ninkovich, Frank A. 1981. *The Diplomacy of Ideas: U.S. Foreign Policy and Cultural Relations, 1938–1950*. Cambridge: Cambridge University Press.

Nye, Joseph S., and Robert O. Keohane. 1971. "Transnational Relations and World Politics." *International Organization* 25, no. 3: 721–48.

O'Donnell, Guillermo. 1973. *Modernization and Bureaucratic-Authoritarianism: Studies in South American Politics*. Berkeley: Institute of International Studies, University of California.

———. 1979. "Tensions in the Bureaucratic-Authoritarian State and the Question of Democracy." In David Collier, ed. *The New Authoritarianism in Latin America*. Princeton: Princeton University Press, pp. 285–318.

———. 1986. "Introduction to the Latin American Cases." In Guillermo O'Donnell, Philippe C. Schmitter, and Laurence Whitehead, eds. *Transitions from Authoritarian Rule: Latin America*. Vol. 3. Baltimore: The Johns Hopkins University Press, pp. 3–18.

———. 1988. "Bureaucratic Authoritarianism: Argentina, 1966–1973." In *Comparative Perspective*. Berkeley: University of California Press.

———. 1995. "Do Economists Know Best?" *Journal of Democracy* 6, no. 1: 23–28.

———. 1999. *Counterpoints: Selected Essays on Authoritarianism and Democratization*. Notre Dame: University of Notre Dame Press.

———. 2003. "Ciencias sociales en América Latina: Mirando hacia el pasado y atisbando el futuro." Paper given at the Congress of the Latin American Studies Association, Dallas, April 2003.

O'Donnell, Guillermo, and Philippe C. Schmitter. 1986. *Transitions from Authori-*

tarian Rule: Tentative Conclusions about Uncertain Democracies. Vol. 4. Baltimore: The Johns Hopkins University Press.

————, Philippe C. Schmitter, and Laurence Whitehead. 1986. *Transitions from Authoritarian Rule*. Baltimore: The Johns Hopkins University Press.

Packenham, Robert A. 1973. *Liberal America and the Third World: Political Development Ideas in Foreign Aid and Social Science*. Princeton: Princeton University Press.

————. 1992. *The Dependency Movement: Scholarship and Politics in Development Studies*. Cambridge: Harvard University Press.

Page, Charles H. 1982. *Fifty Years in the Sociological Enterprise*. Amherst: The University of Masschusetts Press.

Paggi, Leonardo. 1989. *Americanismo e riformismo*. Torino: Einaudi.

Parmar, Inderjeet. 1999. "The Carnegie Corporation and the Mobilisation of Opinion in the United States' Rise to Globalism, 1939–1945." *Minerva* 37: 355–378.

————. 2002. " 'To Relate Knowledge and Action': The Impact of the Rockefeller Foundation on Foreign Policy Thinking During America's Rise to Globalism 1939–1945." *Minerva* 40: 235–263.

Paulston, Rolland G. 1976. *Conflicting Theories of Social and Educational Change: A Typological Review*. Pittsburgh: University Center for International Studies.

Petiteville, Franck. 1998. "Three Mythical Representations of the State in Development Theory." *International Social Science Journal*, no. 115: 115–24.

Phillips, James, and Kim R. Holmes. 1996. *The National Endowment for Democracy: A Prudent Investment in the Future*. Executive Memorandum 9/13/96 — 461. The Heritage Foundation, Washington, D.C.

Picciotto, Robert. 1995. *Putting Institutional Economics to Work: From Participation to Governance*, n. 304 World Bank Discussion Papers. The World Bank, Washington, D.C.

Pocock, John G. A. 1985. *Virtue, Commerce, and History*. Cambridge: Cambridge University Press.

Pollak, Michael. 1979. "Paul F Lazarsfeld: fondateur d'une multinationale scientifique." *Actes de la recherche en sciences sociales*, no. 25: 45–59.

Pollard, Robert A. 1985. *Economic Security and the Origins of the Cold War, 1945–1950*. New York: Columbia University Press.

Pouligny, Béatrice. 2003. "UN Peace Operations, INGOs, NGOs, and Promoting the Rule of Law: Exploring the Intersection of International and Local Norms in Different Post-War Contexts." *Journal of Human Rights* 2, no. 3: 359–377.

Przeworski, Adam. 1980. "Material Interest, Class Compromise, and the Transition to Socialism." *Politics and Society* 10, no. 2: 125–53.

————. 1986. "Some Problems in the Study of the Transition to Democracy." In Guillermo O'Donnell, Philippe C. Schmitter, and Laurence Whitehead, eds.

Transitions from Authoritarian Rule. Comparative Perspectives. Vol. 4. Baltimore: The Johns Hopkins University Press, pp. 47–63.

———. 1991. *Democracy and the Market*. Cambridge: Cambridge University Press.

Puryear, Jeffrey M. 1983. *Higher Education, Development Assistance, and Repressive Regimes*. Ford Foundation, New York.

———. 1994. *Thinking Politics: Intellectuals and Democracy in Chile, 1973–1988*. Baltimore: The Johns Hopkins University Press.

Pye, Lucian W. 1966. *Aspects of Political Development*. Boston: Little, Brown & Co.

———. 1990. "Political Science and the Crisis of Authoritarianism." *The American Political Science Review*, no. 84: 3–19.

Quigley, Kevin F. 1997. "Political Scientists and Assisting Democracy: Too Tenuous Links." *PS: Political Science & Politics* 30, no. 3: 564–67.

Ravenhill, John. 1993. "A Second Decade of Adjustment: Greater Complexity, Greater Uncertainty." In Thomas M. Callaghy and John Ravenhill, eds. *Hemmed In: Responses to Africa's Economic Decline*. New York: Columbia University Press, pp. 18–53.

Reagan, Ronald. 1982. "Address to the British Parliament." University of Texas: Ronald Reagan Presidential Library.

Remmer, Karen L. 1991. "New Wine or Old Bottlenecks? The Study of Latin American Democracy." *Comparative Politics* 23, no. 4: 479–95.

Ricci, David. 1984. *The Tragedy of Political Science: Politics, Scholarship and Democracy*. New Haven: Yale University Press.

Risse-Kappen, Thomas, ed. 1995. *Bringing Transnational Relations Back In: Non-State Actors, Domestic Structures, and International Institutions*. Cambridge: Cambridge University Press.

Risse, Thomas, Stephen C. Ropp, and Kathryn Sikkink. 1999. *The Power of Human Rights: International Norms and Domestic Change*. Cambridge: Cambridge University Press.

Robinson, William I. 1996. *Promoting Polyarchy: Globalization, US Intervention, and Hegemony*. Cambridge: Cambridge University Press.

Rodgers, Daniel T. 1998. *Atlantic Crossings: Social Politics in a Progressive Age*. Cambridge: The Belknap Press.

Roelofs, Joan. 2003. *Foundations and Public Policy: The Mask of Pluralism*. Albany: SUNY Press.

Ross, Dorothy. 1991. *The Origins of American Social Science*. Cambridge: Cambridge University Press.

Rostow, Walt Whitman. 1960. *The Stages of Economic Growth: A Non-Communist Manifesto*. Cambridge: Cambridge University Press.

Salant, Walter S. 1989. "The Spread of Keynesian Doctrines and Practices in the United States." In Peter A. Hall, ed. *The Political Power of Economic Ideas: Keynesianism Across Nations*. Princeton: Princeton University Press.

Salvadori, Massimo L. 1981. "La critica marxista allo stalinismo." In *Il marxismo nell'età della terza internazionale — Dalla crisi del '29 al XX congresso.*, 83–128. Storia del Marxismo, Vol. 3**. Torino: Einaudi.

Salvati, Mariuccia. 2000. *Da Berlino a New York: Crisi della classe media e futuro della democrazia nelle scienze sociali degli anni trenta.* Torino & Milano: Bruno Mondadori.

Santiso, Javier. 1996. De la condition historique des transitologues en Amérique Latine et Europe Centrale et Orientale. *Revue Internationale De Politique Comparée* 3, no. 1.

Saunders, Frances Stonor. 1999. *Who Paid the Piper? The CIA and the Cultural Cold War.* London: Granta.

Schechter, Michael G. 1988. "The Political Role of Recent World Bank Presidents." In Lawrence S. Finkelstein, ed. *Politics in the United Nations System.* Durham: Duke University Press.

Schlesinger, Arthur M. 1970 [1950]. *The Vital Center: The Politics of Freedom.* London: Deutsch.

Schmitter, Philippe C. 1974. "Still the Century of Corporatism?" In F. B. Pike, and T. Stritch, eds. *The New Corporatism: Social-Political Structures in the Iberian World.* Notre Dame: University of Notre Dame Press, pp. 85–131.

———. 1994. "Transitology and Consolidology: Proto-Sciences of Democratization?" Latin American Program Woodrow Wilson International Center. Washington, D.C.

Seybold, Peter J. 1980. "The Ford Foundation and the Triumph of Behavioralism in American Political Science." In Robert F. Arnove, ed. *Philanthropy and Cultural Imperialism: The Foundations at Home and Abroad.* Boston: G. K. Hall, pp. 269–303.

Shachtman, Max. 1962. "Reflections on a Decade Past [1950]." In *The Bureaucratic Revolution: The Rise of the Stalinist State.* New York: The Donald Press.

Sharpe, L. J. 1978. "Government as Client for Social Science Research." In Martin Bulmer, ed. *Social Policy Research.* London: Macmillan, pp. 67–82.

Shihata, Ibrahim F. I. 1991. *The World Bank in a Changing World: Selected Essays.* Dordrecht: Martinus Nijhoff Publishers.

Shils, Edward. 1955. "The End of Ideology?" *Encounter*, no. 5: 52–58.

———. 1994. "Leopold Labedz." *The American Scholar* 63, no. 2: 239–57.

Shore, Samuel. 1945. "Totalitarian or Democratic World? Democracy Endangered at Home and Abroad." *The New Leader*, June 8.

Sikkink, Kathryn. 1991. *Ideas and Institutions: Developmentalism in Brazil and Argentina.* Ithaca: Cornell University Press.

———. 1993. "The Power of Principled Ideas: Human Rights Policies in the United States and Western Europe." In Judith Goldstein and Robert O. Keohane, eds. *Ideas and Foreign Policy: Beliefs, Institutions, and Political Change.* Ithaca: Cornell University Press, pp. 139-72.

———. 1999. "The Socialization of International Human Rights Norm into Domestic Practices: Introduction." In Thomas Risse, Stephen C. Ropp, and Kathryn Sikkink, eds. *The Power of Human Rights: International Norms and Domestic Change*. Cambridge: Cambridge University Press, pp. 1–38.

Silvert, Kalman H. 1975. "Politics and the Study of Latin America." In Harry Eckstein and Lucian W. Pye, eds. *Political Science and Area Studies: Rivals of Partners?* Bloomington: Indiana University Press.

Simon, Rita J., ed. 1967. *As We Saw the Thirties: Essays on the Social and Political Movements of a Decade*. Urbana: University of Illinois Press.

Simpson, Christopher, ed. 1998. *Universities and Empire: Money and Politics in the Social Sciences During the Cold War*. New York: The New Press.

Skinner, Quentin. 1988. " 'Social Meaning' and the Explanation of Social Action." In James Tully, ed. *Meaning and Context: Quentin Skinner and his Critics*. Princeton: Princeton University Press, pp. 79–96.

Sklar, Holly, ed. 1980. *Trilateralism: The Trilateral Commission and Elite Planning for World Management*. Boston: South End Press.

———, and Chip Berlet. 1991–1992. "NED, CIA and the Orwellian Democracy Project." *Covert Action Information Bulletin*, no. 39: 10–13, 59–62.

Smith, James A. 1991. *The Idea Brokers: Think Tanks and the Rise of the New Political Elite*. New York: The Free Press.

Smith, Peter H. 1991. "Crisis and Democracy in Latin America." *World Politics* 43: 608–34.

———. 1995. "The Changing Agenda for Social Science Research on Latin America." In Peter H. Smith, ed. *Latin America in Comparative Perspective: New Approaches to Methods and Analysis*. . Boulder: Westview Press, pp. 1–29.

———. 2000. *Talons of the Eagle: Dynamics of U.S.-Latin American Relations*. 2nd ed. Oxford: Oxford University Press.

Smith, Tony. 1994. *America's Mission: The United States and the Worldwide Struggle for Democracy in the Twentieth Century*. Princeton: Princeton University Press. A Twentieth Century Fund Book.

Srubar, Ilja. 1988. *Exil, Wissenschaft, Identität: Die Emigration deutscher Sozialwissenschaftler 1933–1945*. Frankfurt am Main: Suhrkamp.

Steinfels, Peter. 1979. *The Neoconservatives: Changing America's Politics*. New York: Simon and Schuster.

Stern, Nicholas, and Francisco Ferreira. 1997. "The World Bank as an 'Intellectual Actor.' " In Devesh Kapur, John P. Lewis, and Richard Webb, eds. *The World Bank: Its First Half Century*. Washington, D.C.: The Brookings Institution, pp. 523–610.

———, and Joseph Stiglitz. 1997. "New Role for Government: The Market Revolution has Created Different Obligations for the State." *Financial Times*, July 8.

Stiglitz, Joseph E. 1998. "More Instruments and Broader Goals: Moving Toward the Post-Washington Consensus." Washington, D.C.: The World Bank.

Stone, Diane. 1996. *Capturing the Political Imagination: Think Tanks and the Policy Process*. London: Frank Cass.

Streeten, Paul. 1993. "Markets and States: Against Minimalism." *World Development* 21, no. 8: 1281–98.

Szelenyi, Istvan, and Lawrence Peter King. 2004. *Theories of the New Class: Intellectuals and Power*. Minneapolis: University of Minnesota Press.

Tilly, Charles. 1975. "Western State-Making and Theories of Political Transformation." In Charles Tilly, ed. *The Formation of National States in Western Europe*. Princeton: Princeton University Press, pp. 601–38.

———. 1995. *Popular Contention in Great Britain, 1758–1834*. Cambridge: Harvard University Press

Tiryakian, Edward A. 1991. "Modernisation: Exhumetur in Pace (Rethinking Macrosociology in the 1990s)." *International Sociology* 6, no. 2: 165–80.

Toye, John. 1987. *Dilemmas of Development*. Oxford: Blackwell.

Traverso, Enzo. 2002. *Il totalitarismo*. Milano: Bruno Mondadori.

Treillet, Stéphanie. 1996. "Des conditions de la reconstitution d'une économie du développement hétérodoxe." *Economies et Sociétés*, no. 2: 157–64.

U.S. Department of State. 1981. Human Rights Report, Bulletin Reprint. U.S. Department of State, Bureau of Public Affairs, Washington, D.C.

———. 2000. "The Third Globalization: Transnational Human Rights Networks." *1999 Country Reports on Human Rights Practices*, Department of State, Washington, D.C.

U.S. House of Representatives. 1983. *Report [to accompany H.R. 2915]*, 98th Cong. 1st sess. Report No. 98–130.

U.S. Senate. 1983. Hearings before the Committee on Foreign Relations. 98th Cong., 1st sess. March 2, 9, and April 27.

———. 1989. Hearings before a Subcommittee of the Committee on Appropriations, 101 Cong., 1st sess. April 11, 1989.

Valenzuela, Arturo. 1988. "Political Science and the Study of Latin America." In Christopher Mitchell, ed. *Changing Perspectives in Latin American Studies: Insights from Six Disciplines*. Stanford: Stanford University Press, pp. 63–86.

Virno, Paolo. "Do You Remember Counterrevolution?" In Nanni Balestrini, and Primo Moroni, eds. *L'orda d'oro, 1968–1977: La grande ondata rivoluzionaria e creativa, politica ed esistenziale*. Milano: Feltrinelli, pp. 639–69.

Wade, Robert. 2001. "Showdown at the World Bank." *New Left Review* 7, no. January-February: 124–37.

Wagner, Peter, and Björn Wittrock. 1987. *Social Sciences and Societal Developments: The Missing Perspective*. WZB Papers, 1987. Berlin: WZB.

———, and Hellmut Wollmann. 1986. *Patterns of the Engagement of Social Scientists in Policy Research and Policy-Consulting: Some Cross-National Considerations*. WZB Papers, 1986. Berlin: WZB.

Wald, Alan M. 1987. *The New York Intellectuals: The Rise and Decline of the Anti-*

Stalinist Left from the 1930s to the 1980s. Chapel Hill: The University of North Carolina Press.

Wallerstein, Immanuel. 1995. *After Liberalism*. New York: The New Press.

Wapner, Paul. 1995. "Politics beyond the State: Environmental Activism and World Civic Politics." *World Politics*, no. 47: 311–40.

Weaver, Richard M. 1948. *Ideas have Consequences*. Chicago: University of Chicago Press.

Weber, Max. 1978. *Economy and Society*. eds. Guenther Roth, and Claus Wittich. Berkeley: University of California Press.

Weinstein, Michael. 1992. "Economists and the Media." *Journal of Economic Perspectives* 6, no. 3: 73–77.

Wendt, Alexander. 1999. *Social Theory of International Politics*. Cambridge: Cambridge University Press.

Whitehead, Laurence, ed. 1996. *The International Dimensions of Democratization: Europe and the Americas*. Oxford: Oxford U P.

Wiarda, Howard J. 1990. *The Democratic Revolution in Latin America*. Holmes and Meier.

Williams, David, and Tom Young. 1994. "Governance, the World Bank, and Liberal Theory." *Political Studies* 42: 84–100.

Williamson, John. 1993. "Democracy and the 'Washington Consensus.' " *World Development* 21, no. 8: 1329–36.

———, ed. 1994. *The Political Economy of Policy Reform*. Washington, D.C.: Institute for International Economics.

Wolfensohn, James D. 1998. Remarks at the World Bank: NGO Conference on Participatory Development, Washington, D.C., November 19.

Wolhforth, Tim. 1994. *The Prophet's Children: On the American Left*. Atlantic Highlands: Humanities Press.

Wood, Robert E. 1986. *From Marshall Plan to Debt Crisis: Foreign Aid and Development Choices in the World Economy*. Berkeley: University of California Press.

Wooster, Martin Morse. 1991. "This Is No Way to Promote Democracy." *Wall Street Journal* July 17: A8.

World Bank. 1989. *Sub-Saharan Africa: From Crisis to Sustainable Growth: A Long-Term Perspective Study*. The World Bank, Washington, D.C.

———. 1992. *Governance and Development*. Washington, D.C.: The World Bank.

———. 1994. *Governance: The World Bank's Experience*. Washington, D.C.: The World Bank.

———. 1996. *The World Bank's Partnership with Nongovernmental Organizations*. Participation and NGO Group, Poverty and Social Policy Department. The World Bank, Washington, D.C.

———. 1997. *The State in a Changing World*, World Development Report 1997. The World Bank, Washington, D.C.

———. 1997. *Cooperation between the World Bank and NGOs: FY96 Progress Re-*

port. NGO Group, Social Development Department. The World Bank, Washington, D.C.

Yee, Albert S. 1996. "The Causal Effects of Ideas on Policies." *International Organization* 50, no. 1: 69–108.

Zolo, Danilo. 1995. *Cosmopolis: La prospettiva del governo mondiale*. Milano: Feltrinelli.

Index of Names

Abrams, Elliot, 228n8
Alfonsin, Raúl, 141
Almond, Gabriel, 104, 106, 109, 116, 123, 125, 157
Alston, Philip, 76
Ardito Barletta, Nicola, 141
Arendt, Hannah, 61
Arias, Oscar, 141
Aron, Raymond, 47

Baker, James, 216
Barkan, Joel, 220
Bauer, Otto, 55
Becker, Gary, 203
Bell, Daniel, 45, 47, 48, 53–54, 61, 241n9; on the liberal establishment, 65; on totalitarianism, 34
Bell, Peter, 141
Berger, Peter, 79, 96
Black, Eugene, 194
Botero, Giovanni, 8, 222–223
Bourdieu, Pierre, 23
Bratton, Michael, 220
Bukharin, Nikolai, 38
Bundy, McGeorge, 64

Burnham, James, 35, 45, 55, 229n10
Bush, George H. W., 140

Cannon, James, 54
Cardoso, Fernando Henrique, 124, 125, 130, 138–142, 161; career, 163–164
Carmichael, William, 139
Carter, Jimmy, 29, 71, 75–76, 141, 178–179, 181, 191, 235n2, 240n4; administration, 64–65, 70, 76, 97, 155–156, 158
Cavarozzi, Marcelo, 142
Chamorro, Violeta, 141
Cheek, James, 237n22
Chenery, Hollis, 202
Clark, James, 12, 217
Clausen, A.W. "Tom," 191, 198, 201–202
Coleman, James, 116
Coleman, Peter, 38
Conable, Barber, 191, 194, 216
Cornelius, Wayne, 97, 237n23

Dahl, Robert, 96, 124, 133, 151
Dallin, David, 34

De Brody, Pelecer, 139
Decter, Midge, 115
Derian, Patricia, 181
Dewey, John, 34, 35, 45
Diamond, Larry, 91, 236n17
Dominguez, Jorge, 120
Dos Santos, Theotônio, 163

Eastman, Max, 55, 230n18
Eigen, Peter, 6

Fairbanks, Charles, 78, 96
Falk, Richard, 241n10
Fascell, Dante, 83
Ffrench-Davis, Ricardo, 139
Foxley, Alejandro, 141
Friedman, Irving, 194, 200
Friedman, Milton, 203
Fukuyama, Francis, 96, 166, 232n28
Furtado, Celso, 239n10

Garretón, Manuel, 137, 142
Gastil, Raymond, 165
Gershman, Carl, 63, 66, 78, 84, 181,
    236n13; career, 87–91; on the lib-
    eral establishment, 65
Glazer, Nathan, 54, 66, 241n9
Gouldner, Alvin, 61
Gramsci, Antonio, 15–16, 142
Gunder Frank, Andre, 152, 163

Haber, Al, 73
Haggard, Stephan, 161
Harrington, Michael, 65, 89
Hayden, Tom, 73
Hayek, Friedrich, 47
Hesberg, Theodore, 139
Hirschman, Albert, 138, 142
Hook, Sydney, 34, 35, 39, 45, 47, 54,
    55, 230n17

Horowitz, Rachelle, 63
Howe, Irving, 54
Huntington, Samuel, 96, 113, 117,
    228n3
Hutchins, Robert Maynard, 242n18
Hyden, Goran, 219

Jackson, Henry "Scoop," 64, 85, 89,
    234n42
Joseph, Richard, 220

Kahler, Miles, 161
Kahn, Tom, 63, 84, 88
Karatnycky, Adrian, 96
Karl, Terry, 97
Katzenbach, Nicholas, 83
Kaufman, Robert, 146–147, 151,
    161–162
Kazin, Alfred, 54
Kelsen, Hans, 1–2
Kemble, Eugenia, 84
Kemble, Penn, 88, 89
Keynes, John Maynard, 193
Kirkland, Lane, 85
Kirkpatrick, Jeane, 11, 65–66, 96, 132,
    140, 153, 163, 241n12; on democra-
    tization, 154–158, 241n11; at the
    UN, 78, 90; and US interests, 79
Kissinger, Henry, 239n16
Koestler, Arthur, 47, 73
Koh, Harold Hongju, 172
Kristol, Irving, 54, 114
Krueger, Anne, 202, 205

Labedz, Leopold, 66, 90, 234n42,
    236n14
Laqueur, Walter, 234n42
Lasky, Melvin, 42–43, 53–54, 90,
    234n42
Lazarsfeld, Paul, 57–58, 113–114
Lederer, Emil, 57

Lefever, Ernest, 75
Linowitz, Sol, 140–141, 240n4
Linz, Juan, 90–91, 96, 124, 236n17
Lippmann, Walter, 113
Lipset, Seymour Martin, 45, 47, 53–54, 57, 84, 96, 157, 236n17, 241n9; on democracy, 48, 91, 112–115, 232n27, 242n16; on working class politics, 61
Lovestone, Jay, 34, 38, 54
Lowenthal, Abraham, 98, 138–141, 143
Lynd, Robert, 114

McCarthy, Mary, 34
McClintock, Cynthia, 97
McDonald, Dwight, 34
McGovern, George, 64, 89, 154
McNamara, Robert, 141, 190–191, 194–195, 197–199, 204, 207, 244n5
Mainwaring, Scott, 97
Manatt, Charles, 84
Manigot, Leslie, 139
Mannheim, Karl, 57
Marini, Mauro Ruy, 163
Marx, Karl, 17, 142
Meany, George, 34, 38, 85
Merton, Robert, 114
Mosely, Philip, 238n4
Muravchik, Joshua, 63, 66, 78–79, 84, 88–89, 96, 228n3, 235n2

Neier, Aryeh, 6, 19, 72–73, 228n8, 233n33, 236n8
Nelson, Joan, 161
Neuman, Franz, 57
Nicolaevski, Boris, 34
Niebuhr, Reinhold, 157
Nitze, Paul, 154

O'Donnell, Guillermo, 97, 130, 137, 139, 153, 239n17; academic career, 123–128; and economists, 132; on transitions, 142–150, 240n1, 241n12
Orwell, George, 73

Pérez de Cuellar, Javier, 141
Picciotto, Robert, 212
Pinto, Anibal, 239n10
Pipes, Richard, 241n9
Plattner, Marc, 78, 90
Plaza, Gabriel, 140
Podhoretz, Norman, 241n9
Prebisch, Raúl, 118–119
Przeworski, Adam, 96, 112, 128, 142, 144, 147–148, 151
Putnam, Robert, 96
Pye, Lucian, 104, 106, 109, 110, 116, 135

Rahv, Philip, 34
Raymond, Walter, 229n5
Reagan, Ronald, 19, 52, 65, 67, 69, 74–75, 78, 81, 84, 91, 97–98, 139, 155, 179, 181, 191, 197–198, 224, 235n5; administration, 10–11, 18, 26–27, 32, 51, 69–72, 75, 82–83, 97, 133, 140, 154, 178–180, 191, 198, 200, 202
Richardson, John, 229n5
Robinson, Pearl, 220
Robinson, William, 15–17
Rotberge, Eugene, 197
Rustin, Bayard, 88, 90, 181

Schlesinger, Arthur, 39, 43, 47
Schmitter, Philippe, 97, 137, 139, 142–150, 153
Schultz, George, 140
Selznik, Philip, 114

Shachtman, Max, 53–54, 84, 88, 114;
    on democracy, 39, 42–43; political
    agenda, 56, 61–63; and Stalinism,
    35–36, 45, 55, 65, 230n12; and
    trade unions, 233n34
Shanker, Al, 84, 89
Sheahan, John, 161
Shifter, Michael, 238n24
Silone, Ignazio, 73
Silvert, Kalman, 120
Skidmore, Thomas, 139
Solow, Herbert, 35
Soros, George, 6, 233n33
Spalding, Karen, 139
Sprinkel, Beryl, 198
Stallings, Barbara, 161
Stepan, Alfred, 124
Stiglitz, Joseph, 189
Sunkel, Osvaldo, 239n10

Thomas, Norman, 54, 73
Tilly, Charles, 118
Trotsky, Leon, 35–36, 55

Vance, Cyrus, 141
Vargas Llosa, Mario, 141
Verba, Sidney, 157

Wattenberg, Ben, 115
Weber, Max, 149
Weinstein, Allen, 165
White, Dexter, 193
Whitehead, Laurence, 137
Williamson, John, 161
Wolfensohn, James, 243n1, 244n7
Woods, George, 194–195, 199, 244n2
Wriston, Walter, 199

Young, Andrew, 181

Index of Subjects

AFL-CIO, and civil rights, 181; and democracy promotion, 81; fight
against Communism, 38, 41, 56;
and the National Endowment for
Democracy, 66, 83–84; relations
with Max Shachtman, 62, 88,
233n34
Alliance for Progress, 118–119, 134,
155
American exceptionalism, 30, 61, 114
Anti-Stalinist left, see Non-Communist
Left
Area studies, 25, academic status,
108–110; origins, 105–106; transformation of, 131, 135

Brookings Institution, 66

Carnegie Corporation, 45, 106
Centro Brasileiro de Análise e Planeja-
mento (CEBRAP), 121, 125, 164
Centro de Estudios de Estado y Sociedad (CEDES), 121, 125
CEPAL (UN Economic Commission
for Latin America), 117–118, 124

CIA, 9, 38, 43, 49, 64, 69, 83, 105,
238n4
City College of New York (CCNY), 54,
60, 114
Civic virtue, 5–6
Coalition for a Democratic Majority,
115, 154, 241n9
Commentary, 65, 67, 78, 88, 155
Committee on the Present Danger,
115, 154
Congress for Cultural Freedom (CCF),
9–10, 38, 46, 223, 234n42; bibliography on, 231n20; revelation of CIA
funding, 49, 64, 69; mission of, 43;
and National Endowment for Democracy, 83, 85

Debt crisis, 198–201, 206
Democracy, and the bureaucratic-
authoritarian state, 128, 145–146;
crusade in defence of, 40–44,
51–52, 84; and the economy,
146–148, 163, 241n8, 241n11; as an
idea, 19–20, 31, 33, 44, 166; and
international law, 1–2; meaning of,

Democracy *(continued)*
19–20; political democracy, 143,
150–152; in political science, 132.
See also democracy promotion, human rights
Democracy experts, 11, 21, 92–100
Democracy promotion, as academic
field, 24–26; as sequel to the Cold
War, 31, 33, 67; institutionalization
in the 1980s, 70–74, 80–83; as
moral crusade, 91; as policy tool, 8;
as research topic, 93, 100; as vested
interests, 18. *See also* democracy,
human rights
Democratization studies, 161, 223,
228n11; international context,
26–27, 100–102; and modernization theory, 135–136; political
agenda, 136–137, 151–152. *See
also* transition to democracy
Dependency theory, 118–119, 123,
135, 137–138, 143, 152
Development assistance, 104–105,
190, 197, 206; and social reform,
107

Economic liberalization, 14, 153,
191–192
Economics, 58, 102; in Latin America,
132; neoclassical, 196, 208–209; as
an orthodoxy, 203; at the World
Bank, 202, 205
End of ideology, 46–48, 115, 232n26,
232n28

Ford Foundation, 9, 66, 239n16,
242n18; and the Congress for Cultural Freedom, 49, 64; in Latin
America, 117, 121–122, 125–127,
130, 138–139, 142, 238n24,
239n15, 239n18, 239n19; and the
social sciences, 45, 105–106; and

the World Bank Economic Devel-
opment Institute, 194
Free Trade Union Committee
(FTUC), 38, 40, 85
Freedom House, 4, 90, 165, 223,
236n15

Governance, in Africa, 219–220;
global, 5, 7, 13, 242n1; good, 3–4,
11, 17, 28, 189; intellectual promotion of, 162, 191–192; endorsement
by the World Bank, 210–215

Hegemony, 15–16, 228n7, 241n14
Human rights, and communism, 9; and
democracy promotion, 74–76,
78–82; diplomacy, 242n6; in international relations theory, 167,
171–174; meaning of, 13, 19–21,
69, 242n2; human rights movement,
70–71; as natural rights, 76; and
neoconservatives, 70, 77–79, 82; as
a principled idea, 178–180; as a
professional field, 72–73; and the
Reagan administration, 18–19, 69,
71, 75, 78, 81–83, 180, 236n8; and
socioeconomic rights, 76–77,
82–83; and the state, 222–223. *See
also* democracy, democracy promotion
Human Rights Watch, 6, 19, 71–73,
94, 233n33

Inter-American Dialogue, 97–98,
140–142, 153, 164
International Monetary Fund (IMF),
129, 164, 197, 200–202
International relations theory, 166–170
Issue networks, 4, 5, 18, 22, 170, 185,
192; academic approach to,
174–176; and human rights, 18–19,
171–174, 177–181; in the 1970s, 182

Journal of Democracy, 92

Keynesianism, 138, 147, 196–197, 204, 244n4

Latin American Studies Association (LASA), 97–98, 137, 237n21, 237n22, 237n23
Latin American Studies, 93–94; as academic discipline, 97; and democratization, 96, 137–140; evolution of, 118–121, 130–131, 150; political role of, 11, 25
Liberal anticommunism, see Non-Communist Left

Middle classes, 59–61, 112, 114, 115
Modernization theory, 101, 103, 118, 134, 137, 185, 207, 223; and academic disciplines, 108–111; authoritarian modernization, 117, 124–125, 144; and decolonization, 104–105, 111–112; and democracy, 111–112; crisis of, 116–123; and Marxism, 156–157; neoconservative critique of, 155–156, 159–160; revival of, 135

National Endowment for Democracy (NED), 3, 10, 27, 69, 78, 90, 115, 136, 180–181, 223, 238n24; and the CIA, 229n5; and dissidents, 66; history of, 32, 74, 83–87, 164–165; political status, 235n3; and professionalization of human rights struggles, 71, 73, 80, 117; research council, 91–100, 220, 237n18
Neoconservatives, 28, 53, 56; as counter-establishment, 67; and the liberal establishment, 141, 150; and human rights, 13, 20, 69, 75, 102;

and the National Endowment for Democracy, 10; style of policy advocacy, 159–160
New Class, 65–67, 160
New Leader, The, 34, 38, 40–42, 88
New left, 62–64, 88, 98
NGOs, and democracy promotion, 80, 82; actors of globalization, 4, 7, 29–30; and human rights, 171–174; and participation, 5–6; professionalization of, 8–9, 192–193, 227n3; transnational, 168, 170
Non-Communist Left, and Communism, 33–35, 39–40, 223; and defence of democracy, 41–44; in the field of democracy and human rights, 31–32, 83–84; as intellectual milieu, 45, 49, 60–62, 112; move to the right, 51–53, 55, 57, 64, 66

Partisan Review, 34–35, 39
Policy research, 67, 185–186, 207; exportation of, 86–87; and issue networks, 182–184
Political Economy, 17, 21, 94–95; of the state, 11, 28, 99, 137, 192
Political Science, 94–96, 122; and democratization, 32, 50, 101, 118, 129, 136, 138, 151, 163–164; as expertise, 24–25, 102, 132–133, 192, 214, 219; and Latin American Studies, 97, 119–121, 124–125; transformed by modernization theory, 104, 108–111, 115, 135; politicization of, 103, 122, 150, 158; and refugee scholars, 58–59; and transnational networks, 12, 19, 21, 172–174, 176, 182, 186; analysis of the World Bank, 188
Popular Front, 36
Public Interest, The, 67, 90

Refugee scholars, 57–61
Rockefeller Foundation, 45, 121, 139,
    141, 194

Social constructivism, 28, 169–174,
    181, 192; epistemology of, 19,
    174–176, 242n4
Social Democrats, U.S., 65, 66, 67,
    89–90
State Department, U.S., 4, 38–39, 81,
    83, 94, 95, 96, 117, 126, 140, 141,
    166, 172, 182; "State Department
    socialism," 39, 46, 69, 70, 85, 91,
    165, 230n16
Structural adjustment, 162, 189–191,
    198, 201–202, 205; and condition-
    ality, 206, 211–213; failure of,
    212–213; political implications,
    211, 220; first SA loan, 244n5
Students for a Democratic Society
    (SDS), 73, 88

Technopols, 129, 162
Totalitarianism, 33–36, 40–41, 78,
    229n7
Transition to democracy, 2, 30, 33, 86,
    92, 100, 103, 112, 123, 126; as aca-
    demic topic, 25, 101, 118, 130, 133,
    135–136; as type of regime change,
    128; to socialism, 63; *Transitions
    from Authoritarian Rule*, 96,
    138–153, 158, 161–163. *See also*
    democratization studies
Transparency International, 4, 6–7
Truman doctrine, 33, 41, 223

United States Agency for International
    Development (USAID), 3, 94, 95,
    107

US delegation at the UN, 78, 90, 96,
    155
US foreign policy, critique of, 15–17;
    and democracy, 30, 31, 41, 42, 43,
    50, 67, 68; and human rights, 21,
    78–80, 155, 170; and Latin Amer-
    ica, 25, 97–98, 102, 117, 126, 134,
    139, 140, 141

Washington consensus, 158, 190, 210,
    218; as context of democratization,
    129, 132, 133, 137, 142, 162–164;
    end of, 189, 212; and good gover-
    nance, 190–191, 214, 232n28; intel-
    lectual promoters of, 196–197,
    205–206
Woodrow Wilson Center for Scholars,
    97, 98, 115, 149, 152, 154, 158,
    162–163; Latin American program,
    138–140, 153; political agenda,
    142–143
World Bank, 4, 11, 17, 28, 99, 107,
    129, 137, 141, 162, 182, 223,
    242n17; as a development agency,
    190; early years, 192–194; and
    economists, 195–196, 202,
    204–205, 244n3; and environment,
    191; and human rights, 191, 211; fi-
    nancial growth of, 197, 199; and
    non-economists, 218–221; and
    NGOs, 12, 188–189, 191, 211,
    214–218; and Reagan administra-
    tion, 191, 197–198, 200, 202; and
    Transparency International, 6; as a
    trustee of commercial banks, 201;
    view of the state, 189, 210, 212
World Business Council for Sustainable
    Development, 4

Young People's Socialist League
    (YPSL), 56, 62–63, 88, 89, 114